STRATER:
S
ST

ONE WEEK LOAN

STRATIFICATION AND POWER: STRUCTURES OF CLASS, STATUS AND COMMAND

John Scott

Polity Press

First published in 1996 by Polity Press in association with Blackwell Publishers Ltd.

2 4 6 7 8 9 10 7 5 3 1

Editorial office:
Polity Press
65 Bridge Street
Cambridge CB2 1UR, UK

Marketing and production:
Blackwell Publishers Ltd
108 Cowley Road
Oxford OX4 1JF, UK

Blackwell Publishers Inc.
238 Main Street
Cambridge, MA 02142, USA

ISBN 0–7456–10412
ISBN 0–7456–10420 (pbk)

A CIP catalogue record for this book is available from the British Library and the Library of Congress.

Typeset in 10.5 on 12pt Palatino
by Graphicraft Typesetters Ltd, Hong Kong
Printed in Great Britain by TJ Press Ltd, Padstow, Cornwall

This book is printed on acid-free paper.

Contents

Figures

Preface

The framework presented in this book has been developing, in one form or another, for a number of years. Indeed, my use of the contrast between 'class' and 'status' dates back to an undergraduate essay and to my PhD thesis, completed in 1976. Thanks to a suggestion from David Held that I should write the book, I gradually came to clarify the central idea of a three-dimensional approach to social stratification. In particular, work on the book helped to remove the lingering reservations that I had about the value of the concept of 'elite'. This had always seemed to me to be a confused and unnecessary idea, and it was not until the nature of the third dimension of stratification was clarified that I was able to see how it fitted into a comprehensive framework. Many confusions do, indeed, surround the use of the word 'elite', but I do now believe that the concept must play a central part in the analysis of social stratification. The key to this rehabilitation of the idea of 'elite' was to recognise authority and command relations as an autonomous dimension of stratification alongside the more familiar recognition of 'class' and 'status' relations.

Some of the arguments of the book can be seen as extended, and rather belated, responses to questions that I was asked at job interviews. When I was interviewed for a lectureship at Leicester in 1975, the economic historian the late Ralph Davis asked me – as he did all the candidates – what I understood by the phrase 'working class'. I cannot now recall my answer, but I discovered later that Davis felt that none of the candidates had given a satisfactory answer and that this was fairly typical of sociologists. I hope that my discussion of the working class in chapters 1 and 8 goes some way towards answering Davis's question and vindicating sociologists. When I was interviewed for a chair at Essex in 1993, Tony Giddens asked me how I would justify my emphasis on 'class' to the person in the street who claims that we live in a classless society. Again, my answer was inadequate – though I blame the inadequacy, in part, on the brevity of the time allowed to answer. The whole of my discussion in chapter 1 is a preamble to the more systematic argument of the rest of the book that, I hope, answers Giddens's question more adequately.

The emerging ideas of the book have benefited from discussions at a number of institutions. They have been used in courses at Leicester and at Essex, and the preparation and delivery of these courses has helped me to refine the framework and to explore its applications. Informal discussions with colleagues at both institutions have helped to shape the ideas and the book, as have seminar and workshop discussions at a number of institutions. Most recently, colleagues at Plymouth and Reading Universities have provided helpful comments on the developed version of the framework. Numerous individuals have contributed to the development of the ideas over the years, both in conversation and in writing. A number of these have kindly commented on drafts of various parts of the book, and I would particularly like to thank Barry Barnes, Fiona Devine, David Lee, Nirmal Puwar, Garry Runciman and Malcolm Waters. Anonymous readers for Polity Press provided very useful comments.

The final version of the manuscript was produced while I was still 'in limbo' after moving to Essex University, spending weekdays away from home for over a year. The long quiet evenings at West Lodge, on the Essex campus, provided the opportunity to get on with the work, while the depression of living away from home and trying to negotiate a way through a collapsing housing market made it all but impossible to make best use of this opportunity. I hope to have completed my long period of transition by the time that this book appears.

John Scott
West Lodge, University of Essex

1

Images of Stratification

The social stratification of a society can be most straightforwardly defined as its internal division into a hierarchy of distinct social groups, each having specific life chances and a distinctive style of life. In contemporary societies, social stratification has most typically been described in the language of 'class' and, in Britain in particular, 'class' divisions and 'class' distinctions have been a perennial topic of both popular and political discussion. The concept of 'class' has also been central to sociological discourse. Indeed, it has often been seen by critics of sociology as a defining characteristic of the discipline: sociologists, they hold, reduce everything to class. While this criticism is overstated, there is an element of truth in it. The sociological emphasis on class can be traced back to the ideas of Karl Marx, who saw the history of all societies as grounded in the revolutionary struggles of social classes. Weber and Durkheim were no less convinced of the centrality of class conflict to the struggles of their times, and it was the ideas of these 'founding fathers' that shaped contemporary sociological concerns (Dahrendorf 1957; Aron 1964; Bottomore 1965; Giddens 1973a).

American sociologists have tended to put less emphasis on class than have their European counterparts, reflecting a popular view that American society is more 'open' and less divided by class. England, it is often claimed, is a peculiarly 'class-ridden' society, its members being obsessed with the minutiae of accent, schooling, dress and behaviour. America, by contrast, has invariably been depicted in popular commentary as being a particularly 'open' society: even a 'classless' society. In such a society – a society of 'opportunity' – people can move up and down the social hierarchy with great ease, and there are no marked differences of culture or life style. This image of 'classlessness' has served as a foil for critics of the snobbery and 'class distinction' that are alleged to deform British society and to disadvantage many of its members.

This image of 'openness' can be found behind the claims of many American commentators that class is a factor of declining salience in *all* contemporary societies. 'Class', such commentators hold, is an outmoded nineteenth-century idea that has little relevance for understanding an advanced industrial or post-industrial society (see Nisbet 1959). The drive towards full modernity, it is argued, eliminates outmoded class distinctions and leads to a society in which merit and ability count for more than social background. 'Class' is ceasing to have any relevance for individual and social identity, having been supplanted by the more salient divisions of gender, ethnicity and sexuality. 'Class' is dead, and new identities have arisen (see the debate in Lee and Turner 1996).

The increasing acceptance of this view has produced something of a crisis for class analysis. Once this was the mainstream of the discipline, but now its practitioners seem to be stuck in a backwater. Paradoxically, this has been associated with the appearance of numerous texts on class and stratification (Scase 1992; Edgell 1993; Crompton 1993; Breen and Rottman 1995; Devine 1996) and a continuing stream of monographs (Erikson and Goldthorpe 1993; Westergaard 1995). What is striking, however, is the great diversity in this output, perhaps reflecting the crisis in class analysis. My intention in this book is, in the words of a group of American sociologists, that of 'bringing class back in' (McNall et al. 1991). I seek to return the analysis of social stratification to the mainstream of the discipline by providing a revamped set of conceptual tools that can make sense of popular views on 'class' and can show how the contemporary malaise in the sociological analysis of stratification can be seen as a misreading of contemporary trends. While people in their everyday lives may, indeed, now be less likely to identify themselves in 'class' terms, this does not mean that class relations, as objective realities, have disappeared.

I will argue, however, that the apparently simple word 'class' has been overloaded with meaning and has been stretched beyond its defensible, core meaning. I will also show the relationship between class *structure* and the *consciousness* of class to be empirically quite variable. Much popular and academic discussion of class ignores this distinction between 'structure' and 'consciousness'. Indeed, most discussions of 'class distinctions' and 'classlessness' are not concerned with 'class' at all, but with what Max Weber termed 'status'. They focus on issues of prestige and social honour rather than those of differences in economic power. The distinction between class and status is, I hold, fundamental to any viable investigation of social stratification, and a return to Max Weber's ideas is the means through which the current crisis can be resolved.

The distinction between class and status has a long history. Medieval writers had generally described their social worlds using an imagery and vocabulary of *estates*, legal or quasi-legal categories of people that were defined by their social functions and responsibilities and that occupied distinct positions in a social hierarchy of status. In modern thought, by contrast, it was the imagery and vocabulary of *classes* that seemed to offer a more plausible basis for social understanding. Classes were seen as economic categories that were defined by their position in the system of production and that formed themselves into groups that entered into political struggle with one another. Classes were seen as rooted in inequalities of property and income that cross-cut 'traditional' status distinctions and created new forms of social division. The transition from medieval to modern societies, then, was seen as a process of social change in which stratification by 'status' was giving way to stratification by 'class'.

The concept of 'class' first emerged as a central theoretical concept in the socialist tradition of political thought, where it was used to describe economically founded social divisions. It was particularly through Marx and Marxism that this view had a major impact on sociological ideas and on popular and official discourse. Very early on, however, the concept was stretched from a purely economic idea to one that grasped political and ideological divisions as well, 'classes' coming to be seen as collective historical actors. Weber sought to reappropriate the concept's core meaning, restricting its reference to the role of economic power and resources in the generation of advantages and disadvantages. This conceptualisation of 'class' was contrasted with that of 'status', which Weber saw as referring to moral judgements of relative social standing and differences of life style. Taken together, he believed, the concepts of class and status provided powerful analytical tools that had a greater purchase on the social realities that political and popular discourse had attempted to understand through the single word 'class'.

This theoretical distinction between class and status was not original to Weber, being found in many of the leading German sociologists, though it was Weber who gave it a particularly clear expression. Sombart (1902), for example, used the distinction in his contrast between the 'organic' societies of the medieval past and the 'mechanistic' societies of the modern era. In organic societies, distinctions of status separated groups that each had a common way of life and a specific legal and political identity. In a mechanical society, on the other hand, class divisions were rooted in individualised differences of economic interest. Tönnies (1931) drew a similar contrast as one feature of his distinction between *gemeinschaftlich* and *gesellschaftlich* societies. Weber's particular contribution was to have allied this historical perspective to his methodology of the ideal type and, in so doing, to convert the concepts into analytical distinctions that could be used in the analysis of *all* societies. While there may, indeed, be 'status societies' and 'class societies', status and class coexist, in varying combinations, as features of all societies.

Not all sociological discourse has followed Weber's usage. Marxist writers have generally continued to rely on an 'economic' concept of class alone and to see 'status' – to the extent that it is considered at all – as an aspect of the ideological mystification of class relations. The mainstream of American sociology, on the other hand, has tended to follow popular discourse and has conflated the two ideas into a single concept that emphasises social standing and relative 'prestige' and that minimises economic divisions. Thus, in much American social thought the word 'class' is used to designate the social rankings and judgements of relative social standing that Weber had termed 'status'. This confusion reflects the reluctance of American commentators to see 'classes' as collectively organised social groups. Instead, the 'open' character of American society has been emphasised, and its stratification system has been depicted as a social hierarchy with numerous grades and no sharp boundaries. Vance Packard's enormously popular book on *The Status Seekers* (1959), for example, thoroughly mixed class and status ideas, arguing that stratification in American society was defined by patterns of education and consumption that underpinned social mobility and status attainment.

This conceptual confusion in academic and popular discourse on social stratification has given credence to the views of those commentators who have suggested that the idea of 'class' should be abandoned. The concept is, they argue, purely rhetorical and has no scientific value for the study of social reality. Furbank, for example, has argued that

> the terms 'middle class', 'upper class', 'working class' work most unproblematically not as nouns but as *epithets* – impressionistic epithets . . . For their power and attraction seem to lie, partly, precisely in the scope that they offer for prevarication, deviousness and the playing of social and political games. They are, essentially, rhetorical concepts. (1986: 5)

The solution to the crisis in stratification research does not, however, consist in abandoning the concept of class. My argument is that the crisis can be overcome if researchers return to the analytical distinctions that were made by Weber.

A coherent and systematic conceptual framework can be built from Weber's distinction between 'class' and 'status' and from his related analysis of 'authority'. Relations of authority establish powers of command among the members of a society, and they are a frequent accompaniment to class and status relations. They must, however, be distinguished from them for analytical purposes. The discussion of command has, in fact, proceeded in virtual isolation from the discussion of class, though not a few writers – most notably Mosca – have attempted to redefine 'class' in terms of the holding of powers of political command. The framework that I derive from Weber's work provides a basis for integrating the arguments of those writers who have tended to concentrate their attention on one or other of the concepts in the Weberian framework. Marxist theories of 'class', American functionalist theories of 'status', and the more diverse writings of those concerned with the powers of 'command' can all find their place in the sociological toolbox. They provide essential and complementary analytical points of view on social stratification, and they allow us to understand *why* popular discourse has, from a sociological point of view, appeared confused. Popular discourse grasps the concrete interdependence of these elements of stratification in particular societies, but academic discourse must also attempt to isolate them in order to assess their relative salience in those societies.

This was the concern that lay behind the work of Weber. He developed his own ideas in order to clarify what he saw as the central developmental trend in Western societies, the development from medieval 'status societies' to modern 'class societies', each of which also involved distinctive patterns of authority. Indeed, the founding and pioneer sociologists of the nineteenth and early twentieth centuries were all concerned, in various ways, with this same transition. Those who lived through the transition began to develop a new language of analysis that could properly grasp the novel and distinctive features of modern patterns of social stratification. This contrast between 'traditional' and 'modern' systems of stratification lay at the core of both the academic and the popular discourses aimed at understanding the transition to modernity.

The language of 'class' has persisted for most of the twentieth century, though the recent sociological debates over the apparent 'death of class' have occurred because some have claimed that the language of 'class' – understood in Weber's sense – may have lost its purchase on contemporary forms of stratification. The increasing reluctance of many people to employ the language and imagery of class to describe their own social situation, it has been held, may signal a fundamental social transformation. The very conditions that gave rise to modern forms of class stratification may, themselves, have given way to new and fundamentally different social circumstances. Some have described this as a transition from the conditions of modernity to those of post-modernity, a transition that matches in scale and significance that from medievalism to modernity (Bauman 1992). This suggestion raises critical questions about the direction of social change, and answers to these questions go well beyond my immediate concerns. I will suggest, however, that while claims concerning the death of class have been much exaggerated, there have, indeed, been important shifts in patterns of social stratification during the last fifty years.

Pre-modern hierarchies: the language of status

Beginning at least as early as the eleventh century, official and intellectual social thought depicted European societies as being strongly hierarchical. This social hierarchy was most typically described as comprising three estates: a religious estate of priests, a military and political estate of knights or lords and the 'common' estate of the ordinary people. With minor variations in terminology, this image of a tripartite hierarchy prevailed throughout the whole of medieval Europe (Mohl 1933; Duby 1978). Actual patterns of social stratification were, of course, more complex than this simple imagery suggested, and there was a general awareness that each of the estates was internally sub-divided. The clergy, for example, were differentiated by their position in the Church hierarchy into cardinals, abbots, priests, and so on. Similarly, the knightly estate was differentiated into various grades of peerage (duke, earl, viscount and baron) that were all distinguished from the 'mere' knights by their various roles in systems of royal administration. In some respects, these divisions cross-cut the official categories. The commons, for example, were widely seen as divided along the lines of wealth and status into a hierarchy that ran from the 'rich' through the mass of the commons to the 'poor'. Peers and church leaders, by virtue of their wealth, would often be assimilated to the category of the rich. A subsidiary imagery, then, introduced fine distinctions within the overall social hierarchy. This imagery further defined common people by their agricultural function or their type of residence, and it allowed more nuanced identifications to be made in the everyday face-to-face contexts in which most people lived their lives. The official tripartite imagery was generally employed in public contexts and in legal documents, such as wills and leases, while the subsidiary imagery provided the terminology of day-to-day popular discourse. Whatever specific designations might be used, however, the social strata were seen in status terms as 'estates' characterised by specific privileges and life styles.

In England it was in the early modern period that this imagery and vocabulary began to alter (Wrightson 1991; see also Burke 1992). Agriculture had become more commercial and 'capitalistic' in orientation, and the growing importance of urban market centres had generated new social divisions that were more difficult to assimilate to the established tripartite model of society. While official and intellectual discourse continued to employ the language of 'estates', these came to be seen in a more complex and more differentiated way than before. In part, this involved an incorporation of the kinds of distinctions that had been made in the subsidiary popular imagery, but it also went beyond this. In addition to the clergy, the knights and the commons there were estates of merchants, lawyers, physicians, yeomen, schoolmasters and numerous other professional and occupational groups. Alongside these specialised groups were other recognised social categories, such as those of labourers, cottagers, servants and paupers. Behind this growing complexity of status distinctions was the growing significance of commercial activity, the growing visibility of new sources of economic division and inequality, and consequent shifts in collective identities. The early modern period, then, was characterised by a proliferation of categories that did not always fit into the traditional social hierarchy.

In the face of this growing social complexity, the language of 'estates' began to give way to a looser vocabulary of 'orders', 'degrees' or 'ranks' to reflect the more differentiated pattern of stratification that was emerging. This complexity was particularly marked at the upper levels of the social hierarchy, where these distinctions had become so complex that an official scale of status precedence for public occasions was codified by law in the mid sixteenth century. This was subsequently revised and updated on a number of occasions and, in its developed form, this official scale of 'nobility' and 'gentry' indicates clearly the many modifications that had been made to the traditional hierarchy of estates. Headed by the monarch and the royal family, the scale listed the varying 'degrees' of the peerage, the peerage itself being defined as a specific 'rank' of nobility. It showed the relative standing of those with official positions at Court and in the church, and of the sons of peers of various types. After these in the official scale of precedence came knights and, later on, baronets, followed by the commanders, members and officers of the various orders of knighthood. At the lowest level of the highest order were the 'esquires', a rank that possessed a 'name of dignity' that set them apart from mere 'gentlemen'. Esquires were entitled to heraldic arms by virtue of the prestige of their occupations (as, for example, barristers or army officers) or their holding of public office. They were entitled to be addressed in writing as 'Esq.' rather than using the 'Mr' with which the ordinary gentlemen had to make do. These 'gentlemen' were a particularly important sign of social change. They were, in terms of the traditional classification, merely 'commoners', but their importance as landowners, farmers and merchants led them to be recognised by the Court and the nobility as a rather superior type of commoner. Indeed, many of them obtained official positions, leading to much confusion between 'gentlemen' and 'esquires' and to the awarding of titles of knighthood to many of them.

Outside the public and official sphere of the state and its concern for precedence, these new inequalities began to be grasped in a new vocabulary. This was particularly noticeable from the middle of the sixteenth century, and centred on the idea of a society divided into distinct 'sorts' of people. Economic inequalities associated with the expansion of capitalist agriculture and trade created social differences that ran counter to the traditional status distinctions. Market relations had not, of course, been absent from medieval society, but they had been relatively insignificant as sources of social stratification. With the growth of capitalism this was no longer the case, and the market achieved a much expanded role in the generation of propertied wealth. Conflicts and divisions rooted in economic differences of resources and market power were initially expressed in terms of an opposition between the 'better sort' and the 'poorer sort' of person (Wrightson 1991: 48). The better sort comprised the wealthy gentry and farmers who were dominant in the towns and parishes, while the poorer sort – alternatively described as the vulgar, common, meaner or ruder sort – were those who owned little or nothing in the way of resources and who had to support themselves through their own labour.

From the middle of the seventeenth century, a 'middling sort' of person was often identified. This middling sort consisted mainly of urban merchants, tradesmen and artisans, who were growing in numbers and wealth, though yeomen, tradesmen and freeholders in rural areas also came to be seen in the same way as a middling sort of people. The phrase was, most significantly, used to describe the manufacturers that were appearing in ever larger numbers during the seventeenth and eighteenth centuries. Thus, a popular social imagery of 'better', 'poorer' and 'middling' sorts was established, with the nobility, the gentry and paupers coming to be seen as mere elements or fractions of these larger categories. This popular imagery of 'sorts' led eventually to a recasting of the dominant imagery of stratification. This same terminology was taken to North America by English settlers and adapted to new circumstances. 'Negro slaves', for example, were added as an additional category at the bottom of the hierarchy (Main 1965).

By the eighteenth century, then, medieval status certainties had given way to a confusion of terminology in which competing discourses made themselves felt. The discourse of status was apparent in the widespread use of such terms as 'estates', 'orders', 'degrees' and 'ranks', while the language of 'sorts' reflected the growing significance of a more modern discourse of economic division. It was from this confusion that a new language of stratification was to emerge. This language of 'class' first appeared in the seventeenth and eighteenth centuries. It was taken up in the works of the political economists, and was eventually to prevail in intellectual and popular usage and to make itself felt in official discourse. This was not, however, a simple change in language. The new discourse of class emerged as an attempt to describe the very forces that had brought it into being. 'Class' was not a new term for old structures, but a term that identified the appearance of radically new forms of social division and collective action (Bauman 1982: 38). Thus, in the United States, class terminology developed first and most rapidly in the north. In the southern states, permeated by the experience of slavery, older styles of thought persisted for much longer. The language of class was a response to the new conditions of modernity that had been unleashed by capitalist development.

Modernity and the language of class

The Latin word *classis* first appeared in English during the sixteenth century, when it was used in historical writings to describe the economic and political differentiation of Roman citizens. It was not until the eighteenth century, however, that it was used to describe the contemporary social divisions of English society. This change in usage seems to have been inspired, in great part, by the successful scientific 'classifications' that had been produced in biology and in geology. The Latin word had been adapted by natural scientists and philosophers to refer to categories within theoretical schemes, and advances in the natural sciences had involved the development of highly refined classifications of, for example, animal species. Corresponding advances in social understanding seemed possible if human populations could also be 'classified' according to their social types. A social classification appeared, to the political economists, to be the essential requirement for the social investigation of the new economic forms of modern society (Calvert 1982: chapter 1). Classical political economy was underpinned by the individualistic social imagery of Hobbes and Locke (Macpherson 1962), but it began to employ such terms as rank, order and class to refer to categories of individuals with similar economic characteristics in the modern agrarian and industrial society. In the work of Adam Smith (1766), classes were seen as integral and interdependent elements in the economic structure of modern society, while Adam Ferguson (1767) was the first of these writers to employ the word 'class' within a systematic framework of historical analysis. A similar move occurred in France, where Quesnay and Turgot began to distinguish productive from unproductive classes. Unlike the words 'rank' and 'order', 'class' was unencumbered with connotations of feudal hierarchy and set an appropriately modern and scientific tone for economic analysis.

According to the classical economists, the three fundamental classes of capitalist society were landlords, capitalists and labourers, rooted respectively in landed rent, industrial capital and wage labour. Each class was seen as having a distinct position in the system of production. This theoretical position helped to popularise the ideas of class and class division. The term 'class' was taken up in liberal and socialist political discourse, where it was used to designate groups with a distinct social consciousness and involvement in political struggle: classes were seen as *collective agents*. A popular social imagery of 'higher', 'middling' and 'lower' classes replaced the earlier language of 'sorts', and this paved the way for the classic nineteenth-century imagery of the 'upper', 'middle' and 'working' classes (Corfield 1991: 123–6).

It was from the 1760s that the poorer, subordinate strata of the capitalist social order came to be described as the 'industrious' or 'labouring' classes and then, from around 1789, as the 'working class'. This new terminology marked a shift from 'lowliness' in a status hierarchy to economic role in a system of production as the principal criterion of their social position. By the 1820s the term 'working class' was very widely used to describe an economic category defined by its dependence on manual work. Liberals and those who were opposed to socialist politics tended to see this working class merely as an aggregate of individuals who shared a similar economic position, while socialists saw the working class as a progressive political force and emphasised its unity and consciousness as a collective actor. These political differences were reflected in the language used, socialists preferring the singular term 'working class' and liberals preferring the plural term 'working classes'. Collective class unity was emphasised more forcefully in France, where the singular *classe ouvrière* was far more widely used than was the plural *classes ouvrières* (Dubois 1962). The great strength of liberal individualism in Britain made many reluctant to use a language that suggested the idea of collective agency. This reluctance was manifest in a tendency to restrict the concept of class to the classification of individuals: 'class' was treated as an *aggregate* term rather than a *group* term. For this reason, British usage showed a greater preference for the plural term 'working classes' (Crossick 1991: 151, 156).

It is somewhat unclear when the phrase 'middle class' first came into use in written English. The term 'middling classes' seems to have appeared around 1748, and Mary Wollstonecraft (1792) was using the phrase 'middle class' just over 40 years later. It was

certainly a widely recognised term by 1812, and the plural variant
of 'middle classes' developed slightly later. The term was used to
describe those property owners who could not rely simply on rentals
and other propertied income but had to put their property to use
and to work at producing an income from it. Capitalist entrepreneurs, for example, owned workshops and machinery, and they
were actively occupied in 'managing' their capital and their employees. The middle classes, then, were distinguished from both
the 'leisured' aristocracy and the working class (Seed 1992).

The language of 'class' spread across the whole of Europe. In
France, for example, the transition to capitalist modernity was seen
as a change from a society of *états* to a society of *classes* (Sewell
1981), while in Germany it was seen as a transition from one of
Stände to one of *Klassen*. Capitalist development in Germany was
much slower than in Britain, and the language of *Stand* persisted
until late in the eighteenth century, when the particular privileges
and occupations of the *Adelsstand* (nobility), *Bauernstand* (peasantry)
and *Handwerkstand* (artisans) were recognised (Melton 1991: 134).
Klasse began to appear in German usage in the 1830s as a way of
contrasting a pauperised lower class (*niedere Klasse*) with the higher
or educated classes. In Britain, however, a 'class' vocabulary was
well established by the 1840s and, though it had not become the
dominant language of stratification, it had begun to make inroads
in official discourse.

The great diversity of occupations in the new industrial system
meant that occupational designations acquired an importance as a
means of social placement. Though occupations were now less likely
to be defined as 'estates', differences in social standing were apparent in the usage of such terms as 'profession' to describe particularly privileged occupations. This lay behind the attempt of the
Census Office to devise a classification of occupations that would
reconcile occupational distinctions and class divisions. The 1841
Census made little attempt to classify occupations, but from 1851
the Census Office did attempt to bring some order to the analysis
of occupations. It was not until the 1880s, however, that the language of class became a central characteristic of official discourse.
An important factor behind this was the concentration of economic
activity into larger financial and technical units and a corresponding centralisation of the whole national economy. As capital
became more 'organised' economically, so labour took a more organised form in large national trade unions. The growing political
assertiveness of organised labour was a major factor responsible

for the wider recognition of the need to see social differences as divisions of class. This acceptance of class terminology is clear in the official occupational schema that was devised by the Registrar General for use in the 1911 Census. Reflecting the advances that had been made in the great social surveys undertaken by Booth and Rowntree, who had developed relatively sophisticated class schemata (Scott 1994a), the official class schema – the Registrar General's Classification – grouped occupations together into larger social classes. This schema assumed that specific economic and housing resources were associated with each occupational category and that the relative social standing of each class was also reflected in its members' incomes and culture (Marwick 1980: 62; Scott 1990a).

Official acceptance of the language of class is apparent in its increasing usage in parliamentary discussion and legislation. Acts of Parliament concerned with housing and welfare made reference to the 'working class', the 'working classes' or, on occasion still, the 'labouring classes'. Legislation on welfare and housing rights, for example, treated the working classes as a group in need of specific legal status entitlements that need not be extended to those in the middle classes, who were presumed to be able to look after themselves. Most typically, the working classes were seen as those who were working in manual trades for a wage and were not employing others. Those on a weekly *wage*, rather than an annual *salary*, were seen as being in less secure employment, and perhaps as being subject to periods of unemployment and casual labour. The precise meaning of 'working class' was rarely spelled out, as it was assumed that the words were so widely used that their meaning could be taken for granted.

This combination of economic divisions with legal and social standing was central to the discourse of 'class'. While this involved a valuable recognition that 'class' and 'status' were closely related in the modern social order, use of the single term 'class' to describe patterns of social stratification contained the seeds of later confusion. Crossick (1991: 154), for example, has shown that the equating of the landlords, capitalists and labourers of political economy with the upper, middle and lower classes of public discourse involved a conflation of distinct ideas that was to 'bedevil conceptions of social order' throughout the nineteenth century. Specifically, he sees it as conflating an economic conception of classes as positions in the system of production and the more traditional conception of estates as positions in a vertical hierarchy of superiority and inferiority. Nineteenth-century social thought, he argues, failed to clarify the relationship between these differing views of stratification. The confusion could only be resolved when writers such as Weber provided the appropriate analytical tools for recognising the interplay of class and status elements, along with their associated powers of command, in *all* systems of social stratification.

Usage of the word 'class', then, combined the two elements that Weber was to distinguish as 'class' and 'status'. On the one hand, its root meaning had come to refer to the differences of economic power and resources that arose in modern, capitalist society and to the differences in life chances (health, mortality, income, and so on) that were associated with them. On the other hand, it also included the moral judgements that were attached to these differences and that clothed them in conceptions of social prestige. This is apparent not only in the official 'class' schema that was used in the Census, but also in the wider public discourse of stratification. Through the latter part of the nineteenth century and into the twentieth century, popular thought separated the 'respectable' from the 'rough' working class, the 'deserving' from the 'undeserving' poor, and the 'respectable poor' from the 'residuum' (Crossick 1991: 161–2; Joyce 1991: 57). Unskilled workers who were subject to casual employment or to protracted periods of unemployment became the objects of a moralising derogation of their life style and of their supposed unwillingness to adopt the 'respectable' life style of skilled workers. Those whose circumstances forced them into poverty were held, by middle class and respectable working class opinion, to be capable of helping themselves to rise above their circumstances, and those who did so were regarded as 'deserving' of help to attain proper respectability. Economic differences, then, were fused with moral judgements of status, and the language of 'class', as a result, became infused with moral connotations. 'Class' became a particularly sensitive matter for many in the upper and middle classes, for whom it was, like sex and religion, almost a taboo subject in polite conversation.

For those who were committed to a greater degree of equality, the moral dimension to the language of class made this language itself an obstacle to social change. The 'class-ridden' character of British society came to be seen as a matter of attitudes alone. 'Snobbish' moralising about the life styles of those regarded as social 'inferiors', and 'envious' criticism of those regarded as putting on airs of 'superiority', were increasingly seen as central to 'class'. Only in the labour movement, and in the working class communities that sustained it, did a conception of class as rooted in economic power persist. For most others in British society, class was seen simply as a matter of accent, dress, education and manners.

The conflation of class and status in the popular discourse of 'class', then, is the reason why contemporary discussions of class have been so confused. Instead of using Weber's concept to dissect the language of everyday life, many sociologists and commentators have simply taken over that language and have incorporated the same confusions into their own work. Mainstream American sociology, for example, equated class with status and simply lost sight of any real concern for structured social inequalities rooted in economic divisions. Equally, it lost sight of the linkages that exist between these divisions and the powers of command. 'Stratification' came to be seen as an exclusively normative matter of invidious status distinctions. The claim that America is an 'open' or 'classless' society rests as much on this conceptual blindspot as it does on any empirical evidence. This is not, however, to prejudge the issue of whether class – as defined by Weber – is still the most salient characteristic of social stratification in contemporary societies. Beginning with Nisbet (1959), the view has taken firm root that class is, indeed, dead.

A post-modern discourse of stratification?

The economic trends of the post-war period have given a particular thrust to the argument that 'class' as a source of economic division is no longer relevant. The growth of mass consumerism and a prolonged period of economic growth and relative affluence during the 1950s and 1960s have been seen as betokening the demise of the very economic conditions that gave birth to class relations in the rise of modernity. Most recently, this has been interpreted as a shift from a modern society of production to a 'post-modern' society of consumption (Bauman 1992). Where modern societies are, indeed, class societies, their successor societies, it is claimed, are societies of a fundamentally new kind. While they are not status societies in the sense of the traditional 'estate' societies of the feudal past, they *do* distinguish people on the basis of their life styles. In a post-modern society, social distinctions are based on consumer life styles and, as these are highly differentiated, they produce a fragmentary, kaleidoscopic differentiation of life styles rather than rigid and bounded social strata (Baudrillard

1981). The conception of post-modern society envisages, in a very real sense, not only the end of class but the end of stratification itself.

This has been stated in a particularly clear and radical way by Beck (1986: chapter 3), who argues that the conditions that some have described as 'post-modern' are, in fact, radicalised expressions of modernity that appear when the final vestiges of traditionalism have disappeared. The solidarities of social class, he argues, resulted from the fusion of economic differentiation with cultural conceptions of status. These status conceptions are no mere 'traditional' survivals, but are essential cultural supports of capitalist economic forms. As a result of rising living standards with the continued expansion of modernity, the communal bonds of communities of producers are dissolved and their subcultural distinctiveness disappears. The labour market is finally emancipated from status restrictions and exclusions, and occupational attainment becomes a matter simply of individual competition. People are motivated to acquire the educational credentials that will help them to achieve upward mobility (or to avoid downward mobility) in a competitive system that is completely individualised. As a result, orientations towards social inequalities involve an attitude of privatism that undermines collective identities of a class kind. Problems of attainment in a competitive market are regarded as individual failings that have to be explained in psychological terms. Class and class politics are dissolved, and individualised life styles are diversified. The society of late modernity is an inegalitarian society without social stratification. It is 'a capitalism *without* classes, but with individualized social inequality and all the related social and political problems' (1986: 88).

In these circumstances, the experience and the language of class no longer seem relevant to people, and Beck holds that they are more likely to acquire their identities from 'ascribed' differences and personal relations than they are from the sphere of work and employment. Differences of ethnicity, gender and age become important sources of social identity, as do such matters as sex and disability. New social movements arise around these identities and around the growing perception of environmental 'risk', and these social movements replace those based around class. Concerns over 'risk' indicate, for Beck, the fact that the era of late modernity is one in transition towards a 'risk society' in which inequalities will be rooted in 'risk positions' rather than class or status positions. His wider speculation goes beyond my immediate concerns, but

Beck's central claims about the demise of class are at the heart of current debates (see also Eder 1993).

Beck's argument draws together themes that have appeared, in less radical forms, in a number of guises in the post-war period. The theory of 'embourgeoisement' and the ensuing debate over the working class is, perhaps, its most familiar form. In this theory, affluence, improved working conditions and new forms of housing and residence are seen as having destroyed the solidarities of community and collective action that characterised the classic working class of the late nineteenth century and early twentieth century. Its members become committed to individualistic attainment within an occupational hierarchy that is organised around education and expertise rather than manual skills. When all members of society are committed to this 'middle class', or 'bourgeois' frame of reference, the society has become – to all intents and purposes – 'classless'. Class is dead.

Such arguments raise important issues of sociological analysis that are impossible to resolve without appropriate conceptual tools. The question 'Is class dead?' is not one that can be resolved through the mere accumulation of empirical data, as an answer to the question depends on what is meant by 'class'. My aim in this book is to try to provide these conceptual tools. In chapter 2 I return to Max Weber to uncover the core ideas, setting out his understanding of class and status, and suggesting that these concepts must be related to structures of command. I argue that Weber is the only writer to offer a firm basis for understanding the interplay of class, status and command in systems of social stratification, and in chapters 3, 4 and 5 I pursue these ideas through a consideration of the theoretical perspectives that have explored these three dimensions of social stratification.

These three perspectives are those of Marxism, normative functionalism and the 'elite' theories of Mosca and Pareto. In Marx and the mainstream of orthodox Marxism is found a rigorous and systematic exploration of the economic foundations of class relations, and this conceptualisation has a value for sociological analysis that is quite independent of the specific empirical claims that Marxists have made. Similarly, Durkheim, Parsons and normative functionalism have provided a coherent and fruitful conceptualisation of status and its location in the communal structures of cultural values and norms. Finally, Mosca and Pareto provide the tools for understanding the ways in which authority relations establish divisions between rulers and ruled that may underpin class and status relations or may run counter to them and, under certain circumstances, create distinct patterns of social stratification. I will show that adherents to this latter position have seen the communist societies of Russia and Eastern Europe as societies that stood outside the transition to modernity that has structured mainstream debates on social stratification. In these societies, modern class relations were only partially developed from pre-modern forms of stratification. They were swept aside by the establishment of societies in which political command had a predominant position and, therefore, in which 'elites' were central to social stratification.

In chapter 6 I look in more detail at the changing relations of property and authority in contemporary capitalism as these have been examined by Dahrendorf and Wright. Both of these writers have, in their different ways, attempted to modify the Marxian model of class by incorporating elements of authority or command into the economic level. Where Dahrendorf argues that command has superseded class in contemporary capitalism, Wright argues that command has become an essential adjunct to property and market relations in the very definition of class.

Chapter 7 draws together the threads of my argument and sets out a systematisation of the Weberian framework. In that chapter I consider, in particular, the work of Goldthorpe and the debates that have surrounded his ideas. In considering Goldthorpe's work, I show how class, status and command can, indeed, be combined into what is, I believe, a novel and powerful perspective on social stratification. I argue that class, status and command, as aspects of the distribution of power in any society, enter into the constitution of power situations from which social strata of various kinds are formed. Following Weber, I see the formation of social strata as a demographic process. Demographic relations, in the sense that I use that term here, are the relations that result from the movement or circulation of people through intermarriage, household formation, social mobility and migration, and from the interaction of people in contexts of intimacy and informality. It is through such demographic relations that the occupants of social positions are formed into the collectivities that I call social strata.

At a number of points, I raise the question of how gender and ethnic divisions are involved in social stratification. The view of social stratification that I develop is one that recognises the 'gendered' and 'racialised' aspects of social stratification but does not reduce gender and ethnicity to stratification. Gender and ethnicity, like stratification, permeate all levels of social structure in contemporary societies, but gender categories and ethnic groups are not, in general, social strata. Social stratification, like other social processes, is gendered and racialised, but it does not, and ought not to, subsume these other forms of division. Inequalities and divisions rooted in conceptions of gender and ethnicity have a significance independent of the particular kinds of structured social inequalities that constitute stratification, making it essential to consider them as phenomena in their own right as well as in relation to social stratification (see Bradley 1996 for a recent and contrasting view).

Finally, chapter 8 concludes with a reconsideration of the social stratum that has figured centrally in this introductory discussion, the working class. I seek to use my conceptual tools to provide a coherent reinterpretation of data and debates that might allow us to begin to see how the question of the 'death of class' and the end of the working class might be more fruitfully pursued in the future.

2

From Max Weber: a Framework

Max Weber's work on social stratification has proved immensely influential for sociological studies of social stratification. Despite this lasting influence, however, his ideas have still more to offer to sociological research than is commonly assumed. His work has, in fact, been interpreted in remarkably simplistic terms, and the significance of his conceptual distinctions has not been properly appreciated. This situation reflects the fact that his explicit work on the subject was both sketchy and superficial. Weber's major work – *Economy and Society* – is incomplete, and it was not published during his own lifetime.[1] Like Marx, whose manuscript for the third volume of *Capital* breaks off in the midst of a brief discussion of classes, Weber's work breaks off in the midst of each of his two separate discussions of stratification. Despite their incomplete character, however, Weber's discussions remain extremely rewarding to read, and a close examination of his work reveals it to be both more complex and more profound than the conventional use of his ideas would suggest.

In this chapter, I will discuss Weber's conceptualisation of 'class' and 'status' as the basic dimensions of social stratification. Weber has often been seen as arguing that 'party' constitutes a third dimension of stratification, but I will argue that this interpretation is fundamentally misguided. I will suggest that Weber can more accurately be seen as moving towards an awareness that 'command' could be seen as a third aspect of stratification, alongside class and status. His analysis of command was central to his discussion of authority in state and bureaucratic administration, and it is in these parts of his work that we must look for the ideas that could have completed his conceptual discussions of stratification.

Weber's initial views on stratification were set out in the draft of a much wider historical and comparative text. This draft, written between 1910 and 1914, was posthumously published as the second section of *Economy and Society* (Weber 1914), though Weber had left it incomplete, internally contradictory, and replete with personal notes for subjects that were in need of further elaboration. Weber did, however, return to the text of his manuscript some years after first drafting it, and he began to draw out the elements of a conceptual framework that might serve as an introduction to a published version of the comparative and historical material. This introductory framework was written between 1918 and 1920 (Weber 1920) and drew on new ideas and new data. The conceptual introduction, too, was left incomplete, and while it succeeded in resolving some of the ambiguities in the original text, it created others. The very brief section on social stratification is, perhaps, the most unsatisfactory part of the whole text. The new conceptual framework was never reconciled with the earlier work, and the text that is known to us today as *Economy and Society* (Roth and Wittich 1968) is an edited amalgam of these two draft manuscripts.

The two separate discussions of social stratification in *Economy and Society* have to be understood in the light of Weber's discussions of law, the economy and religion in the same text, as these sections contain numerous comments on class and status relations and on the political organisation of power.[2] Further elucidation of his ideas involves reference to other sections of *Economy and Society* and to certain other texts, most especially those on the sociology of religion that he produced while working on the various drafts for *Economy and Society* (Weber 1915; 1916; 1917a). In this chapter, I will try to uncover a Weberian account of social stratification. My aim is not, however, to produce a textual exegesis. Rather, I aim to *reconstruct* the Weberian framework in as systematic a form as possible, using extensions to his own arguments wherever necessary. At a number of points I will suggest what Weber *might* have said if he had completed *Economy and Society* in its finally intended form. This is, of course, highly speculative, and it should, perhaps, be said that I am using Weber's fragments for my own purposes rather than simply 'reconstructing' his own views. Wherever I go beyond what Weber actually wrote, I have indicated this in the text or in the notes.

Stratification and domination

Weber held that 'class' and 'status', along with 'parties', were to be seen as aspects of the distribution of power within politically organised communities. To understand Weber's argument, it is necessary to begin with his distinction between the general phenomenon of 'power' (*Macht*) and the more specific phenomenon of 'domination' (*Herrschaft*).[3] The concept of power in Weber's work has generated a great deal of discussion and a considerable secondary literature (see Scott 1994b). Paradoxically, however, these extensive discussions have resulted in obscurity rather than clarity, and Weber's ideas have been widely misunderstood. At heart, however, his basic ideas are quite simple.

Power, Weber held, comprises the chance that an actor's will can be imposed on the other participants in a social relationship, even against their resistance (1914: 926, 942; 1920: 53). The power of an actor, whether individual or collective, is measured simply by the *chance* that they have of realising their will; it makes no difference what the basis of that chance might be. Power is a potential that is realised through the actions in which an actor engages, and this potential is determined not only by accidental or fortuitous circumstances but also by the structurally defined opportunities and capacities that are available to an actor. The particular circumstances of actors may give one individual power over another because of a superior physique, because he or she has information that is unavailable to the other, or for a number of other contingent factors. An individual's power is shaped by structural factors, on the other hand, wherever the determinants of power are systemic rather than merely contingent. This occurs, for example, where the social distribution of resources improves or worsens the chances of realising his or her will. In its most general sense, then, power is an integral element in human action that combines both contingent and structured determinants.

Weber gave particular attention to those forms of power that involve stable and enduring social relationships, and when power is structured in this way he termed it 'domination'. Power is structured into distinctive forms of domination through processes of rationalisation: power relations that were formerly matters of unreflective custom and habit become more conscious and deliberate social practices. The rationalisation of action involves replacing the unreflective patterns of customary and habitual action by actions that are oriented towards calculations of self-interest and commitments to ultimate values. Weber seems to imply two forms of rationalisation, which may be called, respectively, 'instrumental rationalisation' and 'value rationalisation'. Customary or habitual forms of social order evolve through instrumental rationalisation into forms of social order that are sustained by calculations of expediency. Through value rationalisation they become forms of social order that are sustained by a conception of legitimacy (Weber 1920: 30).

This contrast between expediency and legitimacy seems to echo Weber's earlier delineation of a typology of 'two diametrically contrasting types of domination' (1914: 943). The first type of domination that he identified was that which involves a rational, calculative alignment of interests, such as that which occurs in competitive exchange relationships. The participants in the relationship act rationally in accordance with their interests, and the 'subordinate' actors perceive it as being in their interest to allow the 'dominant' actors to realise their competing interests. Small companies producing textile goods that are sold to a monopoly retail outlet, for example, are subject to the power of the retailer on whose continued goodwill they have to rely for their livelihood. There is a structure of domination between retailer and producer in these circumstances, the structure arising from a rational adjustment of economic interests. Although these relations need not be purely 'economic', this domination 'by virtue of a constellation of interests' has its clearest form in the monopolistic control of goods and skills in the market (1914: 943).[4]

The second type of domination that Weber recognised was termed domination 'by virtue of authority'. In this kind of relationship, dominant groups are able to issue commands and orders that the subordinate actors accept as the basis for their own behaviour. The power inherent in an authority relationship, then, is the chance that 'a command with a given specific content will be obeyed by a given group of persons' (1920: 53). Domination takes this form of authority when it is based on a claim to the *legitimacy* of the commands. Dominant actors draw upon a normative framework to ensure that their commands can be presented as valid.[5]

While his principal attempt to define domination highlighted these two forms – domination by virtue of a constellation of interests and domination by virtue of authority – Weber did not see these as being the only ways in which power relations are structured in complex societies. No additional forms of domination are given such explicit definition as these two, but his work implies that at least one further type of domination plays a major role in social development. Where interaction is rooted in more diffused social relations, commitment to ultimate values can endow people with a power that falls short of the ability to 'command', but, nevertheless, is an important source of 'influence' over the actions of others. This power rests on the 'prestige' that ultimate values accord, and in its rationalised form it may be termed 'domination by virtue of prestige'. This form of rationalisation might be described as 'expressive rationalisation'. It involves neither a calculative alignment of interests nor a formal structure of command, but is, instead, rooted in communal beliefs of a 'charismatic' kind that allow people to shape the actions of others through influence, persuasion and example.

Underpinning domination in all its forms, in all historical societies, are structures of coercion. The exercise or threat of violence is not, of course, a routine feature of domination, but it is the ultimate guarantor of a social order and the last resort for its maintenance. Weber recognised that states had increasingly claimed – and achieved – a monopoly of the legitimate use of violence and that the interplay of interests in the economy, as much as the exercise of authority, depended upon a framework of legal coercion that could be called into play whenever required (1914: 312ff).

I am suggesting, then, that Weber's work can be interpreted as pointing towards a threefold typology of domination: domination by virtue of a constellation of interests, by virtue of authority, and by virtue of prestige. As ideal types, these rarely occur in their pure forms, and actual patterns of power in particular societies are likely to involve all three forms of domination in combination. Those who hold authority, for example, are often likely to possess great prestige and to have an array of sanctions that can serve as inducements to conform. The mandarins of traditional China, for example, combined high prestige with ultimate authority in the state (Weber 1915). Indeed, 'traditional' forms of domination typically involve a close relationship between prestige and authority. At the same time, control over the means of violence entered into the ways in which prestige and authority were related to one another.

Weber's analysis of stratification can be understood in terms of this threefold typology of domination. Stratification, he had argued, concerned the social distribution of power, and this distribution of power involves the formation of social strata into structures of domination. I have suggested that Weber's three dimensions of stratification were 'class', 'status' and 'command', and my argument is that each of these dimensions arises from specific forms of domination. Class relations are relations of domination by virtue of a constellation of interests; status relations are relations of domination by virtue of prestige; and command relations are relations of domination by virtue of authority. I will discuss each of these in turn.

Class situations and social classes

Weber started out from a claim that 'property and lack of property' were the basis of class divisions. These property relations were, however, seen as having their greatest significance when they were expressed through those market relations that Weber equated closely with the 'economic' sphere of modern society. The class situation of a person, then, was seen by Weber as being their 'market situation': 'the kind of chance in the *market* is the decisive moment which presents a common condition for the individual's fate' (1914: 928). The power that people are able to exercise in the labour, commodity and capital markets rests upon the kind of goods and labour services that they possess and that they are able to bring to the market and use in order to generate an income (1914: 927).[6] Property and the lack of property, then, generate specific power situations – 'class situations' – that comprise opportunities for the exercise of power in the market. These class situations constitute 'causal components' in the life chances of those who live in a political community. Power in the market generates specific kinds of opportunities, conditions of living and life experiences. People occupy similar class situations when they can be regarded as having a similar ability to secure market-mediated life chances. In these circumstances, they have equivalent power in the market as a result of the resources that they are able to mobilise in pursuit of their economic goals.

A strict equation of class situation with market situation would, however, be too simple, and Weber relaxed this view in his second formulation of the problem. It is, indeed, striking that his final discussion of class refers only to the economic sphere and not specifically to the market or to market situation (1920: 302–5). His final position was that class relations exist wherever property relations create divisions that exercise a significant influence on people's life chances, and that these divisions have their greatest impact when they are expressed through market relations. Thus, class divisions are found in both Antiquity and the Middle Ages, but it is only with modern capitalism – where market relations reach their fullest extent – that it is possible to speak of a true 'class society'. In a modern capitalist society, property relations are expressed through market relations: 'a modern market economy essentially consists in a complex network of exchange contracts' that are concerned with the 'deliberate planned acquisition of powers of control and disposal' (1920: 67). In such a society, it is through the market mechanism that economic power is distributed.

Weber's analysis of market relations formed part of a broader discussion of rational economic action that derived from his critical engagement with the work of Menger (1883), von Mises (1912) and Schumpeter (1914), who shared an emphasis on rational choice and an orientation to market maximisation as the defining characteristics of economic action (Holton 1989a; Osterhammel 1986). This form of action, Weber argued, involves the 'peaceful use of an actor's control over resources', and is intended to satisfy a desire for 'utilities' (1920: 63). Economic action involves the pursuit of those opportunities that can enhance an individual's present or future achievement of utilities, and 'economic interests' are the subjective desires of people to preserve or to enhance their utilities. Actors seek to realise these economic interests by acting in such a way as to influence the distribution of utilities (Burger 1985). This typically involves entering into exchange relationships, where exchange is understood as 'a compromise of interests on the part of the parties in the course of which goods or other advantages are passed as reciprocal compensation' (Weber 1920: 72). Weber held that exchange relations are necessarily relations of conflict (*Kampf*), as the scarcity of resources means that it is not possible to satisfy the interests of all participants equally. Rationally oriented exchange relations, then, rest upon the resolution of a conflict of economic interests, and this is achieved through the use of power to establish a 'rational adjustment' or 'constellation' of interests – a compromise – among the individuals involved. In a conflict relation, individuals must draw upon the resources that are the basis of their power; and power itself is understood as the chance of realising one's will or of achieving one's interests.

Weber held that a 'market' exists wherever there is competition for opportunities to engage in monetary-mediated exchange relations. The market situation of an object, then, comprises all the opportunities that participants in the exchange relationship have of exchanging it for monetary gain.[7] Economic action in the market involves an exclusively rational and purposeful pursuit of interests, and so is 'the most impersonal relationship of practical life into which humans can enter with one another' (1914: 636). The market – seen as an ideal type – 'knows no personal distinctions . . . It knows nothing of honor': it concerns 'mere economic acquisition and naked economic power' (1914: 936).

Relations of possession (*Besitz*) were identified by Weber as the fundamental and original sources of class division. Those who possess or acquire property (*Eigentum*) are positively advantaged in their transactions, and Weber saw classes as receiving their fullest expression when possession is linked with market-based opportunities for acquisition (*Erwerb*). Weber was very clear that possession was a *de facto* relation and not simply a *de jure* legal entitlement. Possession, he claimed, refers to the 'control' or 'effective disposition' over resources (1920: 67).[8] Legal relations of ownership are normally, in a modern society, an important element in this control, but control itself may not be directly reduced to legal ownership (1920: 72; 1914: 311–12, 333–4). What Weber recognised was that control relations may alter while legal relations remain unchanged, and vice versa: it is always necessary to identify control relations by taking account of what Renner (1904) called the 'social function' of the law.[9]

The class situations that generate these opportunities can arise from a myriad of different forms of property – Weber lists property in land, in men, in ships, in minerals, in financial securities, and so on.[10] Each form of property has its own distinctive characteristics, and each is able to yield certain specific advantages. These various class situations can also be differentiated according to the social meanings that are given to property and that shape the orientation of the individual to its uses. Weber concentrated his attention on two broad patterns of meaning: the possessive orientation of the *rentier* and the acquisitive orientation of the *entrepreneur*. Whereas a rentier is interested in the benefits that arise from the sheer fact of the possession of an object, an entrepreneur seeks to employ commercial skills in order to put the object to work (1914: 928; 1920: 303). While concentrating on the advantages of property ownership, Weber gave a certain amount of attention to the distinction between advantaged and disadvantaged class situations. Those who lack property have neither the opportunity to derive an income from its possession, nor the opportunity to advantage themselves through its acquisitive use on the market. Where the propertied are 'positively privileged', the propertyless are 'negatively privileged' in the market.

Using these ideas, Weber contrasted 'possession classes' and 'acquisition classes' – the former were seen as having interests that derived from their control over 'consumer goods, means of production, assets, resources and skills', while the latter were seen as involved in the marketing of goods and services (1920: 302).[11] Rentiers and entrepreneurs occupy, respectively, possession and acquisition class situations of a positively privileged type. Negatively privileged and less privileged class situations, on the other hand, are those that arise where people have no property except for their own labour power or particular kinds of marketable skills. Weber claimed, for example, that business executives and legal professionals are advantaged by the specific competencies that help them in acquisitive contexts; that artisans are advantaged by their craft skills; and that manual labourers are disadvantaged by their lack of skills. A person's position in the occupational division of labour, then, reflects the particular capacities that can be brought to the labour market; it is the outcome of those market processes.

These considerations make it possible to distinguish not only the advantaged and disadvantaged class situations, but also various 'middle' or intermediate class situations. Weber's discussion of these complex issues was far from complete, but he did give some examples. He recognised, for example, a number of 'middle class' situations[12] that combine elements of both advantage and disadvantage. Small-scale property holders, he held, make acquisitive use of their own property, but they must also engage in labour; they cannot live from property alone. This is, Weber held, the class situation of peasant farmers.

Weber's discussion of these issues was merely illustrative and suggestive; it is far from being definitive. His aim seemed to be that of highlighting the extraordinary diversity and plurality of class situations that can be found in human history, and that can be observed within any particular society. A political community, Weber argued, is likely to comprise a bewildering kaleidoscope of economically constituted class situations. While this was, indeed, the case analytically, and the identification of class situations was a fundamental step in social analysis, Weber recognised that the concrete social strata that existed in particular societies were not so diverse. The social strata that form the basis of communal social action and that may enter into struggle with one another are real social groups, not mere economic categories.

Weber made this leap from the conceptual to the historical through his fundamental distinction between *class situations* and *social classes*. Whereas economic class situations comprise the specific causal components in individuals' life chances that are determined by property and lack of property, social classes are the actual social groups that are formed on the basis of these class situations. Social classes are the actual strata that are formed within concrete systems of stratification. A social class, Weber argued, comprises 'the totality of those class situations within which individual and generational mobility is easy and typical' (1920: 302). Weber is, as usual, difficult to translate on this point, though his meaning is clear. He holds that social classes comprise clusters of class situations among which a personal and generational 'circulation' (*Wechsel*) of individuals is feasible and typically does occur.[13] That is, circulation is readily possible *in principle* and does actually occur *in fact* – any barriers between class situations are not so sharp that they cannot be crossed by significant numbers of people. 'Individual' or personal mobility involves both intra-generational 'career' mobility and any tendency for the occupancy of class situations to overlap. An individual may, for example, move from an executive to an entrepreneurial class situation, or may be simultaneously both a rentier property holder and an active entrepreneur. 'Generational mobility', on the other hand, is the mobility that occurs between the class situations of parents and those of their children. Thus, the son or daughter of an entrepreneur may have entered an executive career. It is through such mobility processes that the boundaries of social classes are determined.

There may, for example, be easy mobility between the two distinct class situations that are defined by the possession of land and its acquisitive use. This might occur wherever a landowner has many opportunities to put land to commercial use and when this kind of commercial use of land does, in fact, frequently occur. In these circumstances, it may be appropriate to regard the two class situations as constituting elements in a single social class. In the same way, professional and executive class situations might be grouped into a single social class wherever there is easy and frequent inter- or intra-generational mobility between them. If owners of mines, owners of land, and owners of factories overlap to any considerable extent, then the occupants of these locations can be considered as members of a single social class. Similarly, the movement between generations from manual labourer to skilled worker, if easy and typical, will combine these class situations into a single social class.

Weber stressed the role of inter- and intra-generational social mobility in the constitution of social classes, but his argument clearly pointed more widely than this to other demographic processes. Intermarriage and restrictions on marriage, informal interaction, shared participation in social activities, and the overlapping occupancy of distinct class situations are all relevant to the formation of social classes, as they are all elements in the demographic circulation of people among class situations. Social classes, then, are clusters of interlinked economic class situations, and their boundaries can be identified from evidence on the demographic circulation of individuals.[14]

Weber did not himself undertake any first-hand empirical research into social mobility or into other aspects of demographic circulation, but he did attempt to sketch out the principal social classes that he believed would be shown to exist in a modern capitalist society by any such studies. While his listing of these social classes is confused and incomplete, it is, nevertheless, instructive to look at the social classes that he depicted in his class map for modern capitalist society. He identified just four social classes: the working class, the petty bourgeoisie, the propertyless intelligentsia, and the propertied class. The working class he defined by their dependence upon labour power having varying degrees of skill, while the petty bourgeoisie was seen as a 'middle class' that depends upon the individual's use of small-scale property. The propertyless intelligentsia are the propertyless officials, professionals and intellectuals that Karl Renner (1953) was later to call the 'service class'. The propertied class, finally, was identified simply as comprising the 'classes privileged through property and education', and Weber gave no further account of them.[15]

Status situations and social estates

The explicit parallels that Weber drew between class situation and status situation make it very clear that he intended the latter concept to designate a specific causal component in life chances that is distinct from the economic component involved in the possession and acquisition of property. While class divisions arise in the economic sphere of instrumental action, status divisions are phenomena of the 'social sphere', understood as a sphere of non-instrumental, communicative action that establishes communal relations.[16] Thus, Weber asserts that

In contrast to the purely economically determined 'class situation', we wish to designate as *status situation* every typical component of the life chances of men [*sic*] that is determined by a specific, positive or negative, social estimation of *honor*. (1914: 932)[17]

Where class situations comprise the economic relations through which control over marketable resources is organised for the attainment of income, status situations are the more narrowly 'social' or communal relations through which the social honour that is attributed to a style of life becomes the basis of life chances. Where economic action involves an interest in the preservation or enhancement of utilities, status-oriented actions involve interests in the preservation or enhancement of social honour.[18]

The concept of social honour is not given a specific definition by Weber, but Burger (1985: 31) has suggested that it can be seen as involving the communal conception of prestige that Durkheim (1912) saw as defining the 'sacred' aspects of social life (see also Milner 1994). It is the religious organisation of communities that must be looked to for the sources of status divisions. It is through such sacred conceptions that judgements of moral superiority and inferiority are made and that status situations arise. Status relations revolve around the identification with a specific 'reference group' and its distinctive style of life.[19] Identification as a 'member' of a particular reference group is the basis of exclusive networks of interaction within which social actions are geared to stressing the distinctiveness of its style of life. These actions involve attitudes of acceptance and rejection, recognition and denial, or approval and disapproval of others in terms of their conformity to the preferred style of life. In its purest form, this social estimation of honour expresses a conception of the prestige that is associated with a particular style of life. Status, then, 'is a quality of social honor or a lack of it, and is in the main conditioned as well as expressed through a specific style of life' (Weber 1916: 39; 1914: 932ff). Traditional religious world views and ideologies, along with the hereditary charisma of patrimonial kinship groups, are the most frequent sources of those social meanings that define one particular style of life as highly valued and that derogates others.

The claims to honour that individuals make are made effective whenever they are able to establish the degree of social 'closure' that allows them to monopolise access to specific occupations, forms of property and types of education. Social closure involves the identification of certain specific attributes of life style as the basis for excluding those without these attributes from access to particular resources. In this way, the limited circle of those deemed 'eligible' for access can achieve a monopoly in the resource. This closure is expressed, Weber argued, in connubium (restrictions on inter-marriage) and commensality (shared eating and living arrangements). It is reinforced by preferred consumption patterns and by leisure activities; and the symbolic degradation of 'outsiders' may involve residential segregation and physical expulsion. In all these ways, groups are able to establish the distance and exclusiveness from others that allows them to assert and to defend their claims to social honour.

Any attribute of individuals may be picked out as a marker of status honour, and so status situations will be highly diverse: 'Differences in the styles of beard and hairdo, clothes, food and eating habits, division of labor between the sexes, and all kinds of other visible differences can . . . give rise to repulsion and contempt' (Weber 1914: 387, 932). The use of a particular attribute as a status marker is often quite arbitrary, and Weber holds that there is little point in searching for the ultimate 'origin' of status distinctions. The crucial issue in the analysis of status is the *continuing* relevance of particular life style markers to status divisions: 'The original motives or reasons for the inception of different habits of life are forgotten and the contrasts are then perpetuated as conventions' (1914: 387).

Central to these valued and derogated styles of life are the particular occupational pursuits, forms of property or patterns of education with which specific cultural assumptions and outlooks are associated. Status divisions may sometimes, therefore, relate to the very same factors that are responsible for class relations. Property, for example, is recognised as a status qualification 'with extraordinary regularity' (1914: 932). Where this occurs, property holding will generate both class advantages and social honour. More typically, however, status 'normally stands in sharp opposition to the pretensions of sheer property' (1914: 932). Distinctions may be made, for example, between 'old' and 'new' wealth, between landed and industrial property, and so on, with higher status being accorded to one form of property holding than to the other. In modern America, for example, Weber saw the emergence of purely 'conventional' status distinctions that identify certain 'old' families as 'Society' families. The crucial consequence of this autonomy of status judgements from considerations of class is that status divisions tend to result in 'the hindrance of the free development of the market' (1914: 937). Particular goods and services may be withheld from the sphere of market exchange and may be distributed according to non-market principles. To the extent that status relations restrict the operation of the market 'the power of naked property *per se* which gives its stamp to class formation, is pushed into the background' (1914: 937).

Each specialised occupational, educational or property category may be expected to claim a specific social honour, resulting in a plurality of status situations in a society. In this respect, the inherent diversity and plurality of status situations in a society parallels that which is found in class situations. In his analysis of class, Weber had claimed that class situations must be seen as being clustered through processes of social mobility and of informal and intimate interaction into the social strata that he termed 'social classes'. His analysis of status implies that a parallel idea is required, though this is far less well developed in his work and it is necessary to try to enlarge upon his argument. In the communal sphere, it may be said, status situations are clustered through demographic relations of mobility and interaction into 'social estates'.[20]

Processes of approval and disapproval, and of inclusion and exclusion, form people into specific status situations. As there can be numerous networks of social action based around alternative conceptions of social honour, there may be a myriad of status situations within a society. Where these networks intersect with one another, particular individuals may find themselves occupying a number of different status situations. A white, male, professional worker, for example, may have identities – perhaps competing – as a 'white', a 'male', a 'professional' and a 'worker'. Wherever these networks of social action intersect in such a way that their fundamental social relationships coincide, distinct clusters of status situations will be formed into social estates. Thus, mobility from one occupation to another, whether intra- or inter-generational, will cluster these status situations into a single social estate. Separate status situations may also be clustered together as a result of the leisure-time interactions, residential patterns, and other forms of intimate and informal interaction that result from the exercise of social closure. The 'circulation' of individuals, then, defines a totality of status situations among which mobility is easy and typical, and this may be reinforced by informal and intimate interaction. This totality of status situations comprises a social estate. By virtue of their demographic formation – their formation through processes of circulation and interaction – social estates have a communal

Social spheres	Power situations	Social strata
Economic	Class situations	Social classes
Communal	Status situations	Social estates

Figure 1   Social classes and social estates

character. They are 'communal groups which, through various means, enjoy certain forms of privileged access to scarce resources, especially where those scarce resources are of a cultural, moral or symbolic character' (Turner 1989: 139–40).

The typology of class and status that I have constructed is summarised in figure 1. The concepts of 'social class' and 'social estate' are ideal types that are rarely – if ever – found in their pure form. They can, nevertheless, be used to highlight broad contrasts between types of society and their patterns of stratification. Where the market mechanism predominates in a society, social stratification will tend to take the form of a system of social classes. Where, on the other hand, status principles predominate, social stratification will tend to take the form of a system of social estates. In the former case we may speak of a 'class society', and in the latter case of a 'status society' (Weber 1920: 306). Class and status can be seen, in Lockwood's words, as defining 'variable configurations of total societies' (1986: 12). Each is able to shape the character of a whole society, though societies vary in the extent to which one or other mechanism predominates. Even in class societies, some will owe their life chances principally to their status situations and may even be formed into social estates. Weber held, for example, that 'There is no doubt that educational difference is nowadays the most important difference giving rise to true social "*estates*", in contrast to the stratifying effect of possessions and economic function (which create differences of *class*)' and that it is on this basis that state administrators are formed into 'an exclusive estate of university-educated officials with professional training' (1917b: 83, 104; 1918b: 277).

Weber's initial suggestion was that status divisions are likely to predominate when the economic order is stable, while class relations come to the fore whenever economic transformations are taking place (1914: 938). This was, however, a great over-simplification and it did not accord with the conclusions of his own historical and comparative investigations. Weber's work demonstrated that pre-capitalist societies tended to be stratified by status, while class relations made themselves more strongly felt wherever market relations were able to develop. In pre-capitalist societies, then, status relations predominate over class relations and define the overall character of stratification, despite the existence of specific class-related advantages and disadvantages. In status societies, class is a secondary factor in social stratification. Such societies become increasingly class divided whenever market relations are strengthened, but this does not, in itself, make them into 'class societies'. Class relations are especially fostered by *capitalist* relations: capitalism, class, and the market are interlinked phenomena; capitalist societies are 'class societies'.[21]

Weber approached the conceptual discussion of class and status in an analytical way, seeking to construct ideal types that could be combined in various ways to describe particular concrete situations. For this reason, it must be recognised that class and status relations always coexist. As Holton has remarked, 'The analytical distinction between class and status does not require their empirical separation as distinct entities. They may be intertwined in a most complex manner in the empirical world' (1989b: 184). The task of the sociologist is to disentangle their interrelations in particular situations and to identify which of the two predominates in the circumstances under investigation. Wherever 'traditional' factors persist and continue to restrict the operation of the market, status divisions may harden and cross-cut class divisions. In these circumstances, specific status situations, such as those defined as 'women', 'blacks', 'peers', 'pensioners', and so on, may generate cultural identities that mask or suppress the recognition of class identities. This was often the case, Weber believed, for ethnic divisions in modern societies.[22] In a capitalist society, where the structures of the market reach their fullest development, class relations, nevertheless, tend to predominate in social stratification, and status relations tend to become of secondary importance. The decline of religion and of other forms of traditionalism undermine the premodern forms of status division that imposed customary and legal restrictions on the operation of the market and, as traditional status withers away, so class relations are able to achieve their fullest realisation.

Weber holds that class situations 'will become most clearly efficacious when all other determinants of reciprocal relations are . . . eliminated in their significance' (1914: 930). It is difficult to imagine the complete elimination of all status differentiation, and it seems likely that Weber actually had in mind situations where status divisions are, themselves, rooted in modern 'rational' considerations, rather than in traditional religious meanings. In these circumstances, status is secondary to class and reinforces its effects (Wenger 1980: 363–4). As a result, large-scale social estates are unlikely to form, and there will be, at most, the formation of loose 'status groups'. Class situations would be fundamental to the distribution of power, and stratification would take the form of a hierarchy of social classes within which the various status groups are located.

The social classes that form in modern capitalist society, then, are likely to have certain status characteristics, even where traditional status ideas have disappeared. In modern societies, that is to say, new – specifically modern – forms of status may develop. These forms of status are especially likely to reflect the strengthened class relations.[23] These class relations, expressed in an occupational division of labour, may become the basis of social valuations of 'occupational prestige' and so may come to be associated with relatively distinct styles of life that express the educational or training requirements of the various occupations. They may, for example, be defined as 'professions' and accorded a higher status than other occupations. In this way, aspects of class situation become visible as status markers (Weber 1914: 937). In modern societies, then, there may be loosely defined 'occupational status groups' within the principal social classes, and social class boundaries may themselves be reinforced by boundaries of a status kind.

Weber paid greatest attention, however, to status situations and social estates in traditional 'status societies'. Social estates, he held, are typically closed through conventional or legal means, and Weber instances such cases as the knights of feudal Europe, the mandarin scholar-officials of traditional China, the priestly brahmins of India, the *samurai* military courtiers of Japan, the *noblesse de robe* of pre-revolutionary France, and the county 'gentlemen' of sixteenth- and seventeenth-century England. In traditional China, for example, literary education, as accredited in formal, competitive examinations, was the basis of social honour, and the pervasiveness of this status criterion allowed the Confucian-trained literati to establish an unchallenged position for themselves as the principal social estate of their society. Their education was the basis of their monopolisation of access to the civil service, which gave them considerable power within the state. It was this fusion of status and political dominance that made them the leading social estate of traditional China (1915: 107).[24]

Where the imputation of honour and dishonour involves the recognition of supposed 'ethnic' characteristics and a reinforcement of social closure through the use of religious sanctions that create tightly closed boundaries, Weber spoke of the formation of 'castes' rather than mere estates. Weber attached particular importance to the ethnic basis of caste differences. Ethnic groups, he held, are those groups

> that entertain a subjective belief in their common descent because of similarities of physical type or of customs or both, or because of memories of colonization and migration. (1914: 389)

This ethnic basis of caste divisions led Weber to see parallels with the relations that existed between whites and 'Negroes' in the United States, but he argued that true caste relations involve more than simply ethnic division. Caste, Weber held, 'intensifies "status" principles in an extreme manner' by employing a combination of legal and religious or magical rules of closure (1916: 42; 1914: 933). In a system of castes, status principles reach their fullest extent, and the relations between castes are governed by ideas of ritual purity and stigma. The gulf between strata is so great that individual castes often develop their own particular cults and gods. These particularly tight and rigidly defined social estates are found in traditional India and in those societies where particular ethnic communities have lived as 'pariah' or outcaste groups. Pariah groups, for example, form distinct communities and follow specific occupations. While they are economically indispensable and may be advantaged in certain respects, they live under legal restrictions that are imposed by virtue of their ethnic identity and its link with their specific occupational life style. Weber cites the Jews in medieval Europe as being a particularly striking example.

Ethnicity is generally associated with the linguistic or religious differences that carry the culture of a group and may be rooted in tribal or political divisions, especially when these result from migration or imperial expansion. Such ethnic identity, not infrequently expressed in the idea of the nationhood of a 'people',[25] may be expressed in 'aesthetically conspicuous' differences of physical appearance and differences in patterns of everyday life – differences in clothing, housing, food and eating patterns, occupational specialisation, and so on. Ethnic identity may or may not have an objective basis in real biological differences, and Weber regarded the question of the scientific reality of 'race' as being irrelevant to the attribution of ethnicity in social life. What is important is the subjective belief in ethnic membership (*ethnische Gemeinsamkeit*), which may involve ethnic fictions or myths of common descent and which can become the basis of social circles organised around the presumed 'honour' of their members.

Weber is at pains to point out, however, that ethnic identity and status identity are not one and the same thing. While ethnicity and status are both rooted in solidarities of social honour, ethnicity implies a solidarity of the whole 'people', regardless of any internal differences of class or status.[26] Thus, multi-ethnic political communities may be seen as being what later writers have called 'plural societies' rather than simply 'status societies' (see Smith 1965; Rex 1970). In a plural society, each ethnic community considers its own honour to be the highest. Ethnic groups in such plural societies are transformed into social estates only when there is an acknowledgement by some ethnic groups of the superiority of others (Weber 1914: 934). In such circumstances, a status ranking of ethnic identities is created, and this comes to override the internal status divisions of the separate ethnic groups.

Class, status and party

So far, I have concentrated on Weber's view of stratification as a *structure* of social relations, but he also considered the forms of *action* that social strata may be involved in. His point of reference here, of course, was the Marxist view of 'class struggle', which Weber sought to clarify and to restrict to its appropriate place in sociological analysis.

Weber rejected any idea that it is possible to infer action directly from the occupancy of a class situation. Those who are similarly situated in the class relations of a society may come to see their interests in many different ways, and it is quite possible for people to be unaware of their class situation. For this reason, the actions of those who occupy similar class situations may be quite diverse. Nevertheless, there are likely to be many circumstances when those in a similar class situation will engage in objectively similar actions, and Weber described this as a pattern of *mass action* (1914: 929). The occupants of the class situation simply act, in the aggregate, in a homogeneous way, without any mutual awareness of this or any intent to do so. For occupants of a class situation to engage in truly *social action*[27] of a cohesive and purposive kind, however, there must exist a particular state of consciousness. These conditions are most likely to occur – though not inevitably so – when social classes have been formed from the various class situations. Members of a solidaristic social class are more likely than are isolated individuals to perceive a link between the causes and the consequences of their class situations and to be willing to engage in collective action that is oriented towards the alteration and enhancement of their circumstances. Even this is not, in itself, sufficient. Social action in common by the members of a social class occurs where their cultural and intellectual circumstances have provided fertile conditions for the growth of class consciousness:

> For however different life chances may be, this fact in itself . . . by no means gives birth to 'class action' (social action by the members of a class). For that, the real conditions and the results of the class situation must be distinctly recognizable. For only then the contrast of life chances can be felt not as an absolutely given fact to be accepted, but as the resultant from either (1) the given distribution of property, or (2) the structure of the concrete economic order. It is only then that people may react against the class structure not only through acts of intermittent and irrational protest, but in the form of rational association. (1914: 929)

The social class *per se* does not act. A social class is not itself a 'communal group' (*Gemeinschaft*) that is collectively capable of action. The communal solidarity that its members are able to achieve can only be expressed through the formation of groups and associations, such as trade unions and political parties. Similar considerations apply to social estates. Although social estates may always have the degree of communal solidarity that is necessary to achieve and to defend their social closure, they are groups only 'of an amorphous kind' (1914: 932). Social estates, like social classes, can become historically effective only through the formation of specific groups and associations that express their interests. In the absence of such organisations, the members of social classes and social estates will be involved only in 'mass action'. It is to understand these linkages of class and status to organised action that Weber introduced the concept of 'party'.

Social classes, Weber held, are rooted in the economic sphere, while social estates are rooted in the social sphere of communal relations. Parties, on the other hand, find their specific home in the sphere of power.[28] This statement appears somewhat paradoxical, as Weber had already claimed that class, status and party were *all* to be seen as 'phenomena of the distribution of power within a [political] community' (1914: 927). The point that Weber was making, however, is that parties are concerned with power *per se*: they are organised groups that can arise in relation to class or to status power, to the connections between these forms of power, or to any other feature of social life (such as, for example, ethnic or religious differences). A party is a body of persons that are united in a cause or interest. It is a body that engages in associated action (*Vergesellschaftung*) and that 'takes sides' in public disputes. Parties, then, are rationally oriented towards the acquisition of power – whatever its basis – in order to affect social actions in any sphere of social life. They are associations that are based on free recruitment and that seek to secure power within a larger organisation in order to promote the goals and interests of their own members. Parties are specifically, but not exclusively, engaged in 'political action' in pursuit of interests and values within that sphere of power that constitutes the state. The interests of social classes and social estates, for example, may be expressed in a struggle for political power when they become the basis for collective action on the part of the political parties that compete for electoral power within the state. Thus, Weber argued that

> In any individual case, parties may represent interests determined through class situation or status situation, and they may recruit their following respectively from one or the other. But they need be neither purely class nor purely status parties; in fact, they are more likely to be mixed types, and sometimes they are neither. (1914: 938)

Parties may, then, have considerable autonomy from the class or status interests of their members, and they may pursue enduring or transient purposes quite unconnected with social stratification.

Command situations and social blocs

I have followed through and enlarged upon Weber's discussions of class and the economic sphere, status and the social sphere, and the relations of class and status to party organisation and action. It might be anticipated that Weber would have analysed parties and the political sphere in precisely analogous terms to class and status, and this has, indeed, been claimed by some commentators (Runciman 1968). That Weber did *not* do this is apparent from his view of parties as interest or conflict groups that may give voice to class or status interests. Parties are not themselves seen as social strata within systems of stratification. I wish to argue, nevertheless, that there is, implicit within Weber's work, a conception of a sphere of action that *does* parallel the economic and social spheres. Recovering this implicit conception will not only allow a proper understanding of the significance of Weber's own work, but also demonstrate very clearly his intellectual connection with the works of those of his contemporaries, such as Michels, Mosca and Pareto, who were also concerned with this sphere of action. This sphere of action is that of 'authority', seen most clearly, though not exclusively, as the sphere of the state.

Weber's 'missing' analysis of a third dimension of stratification can, I believe, be uncovered through introducing the concept of 'command situations' to designate those causal components in individual life chances that result from the differentials of power that are inherent in structures of authority.[29] Command situations are defined by the distribution of the powers of command within the state and other authoritarian organisations, such as business enterprises or churches. In these organisations, there are those who command, those who are on the receiving end of commands, those who have delegated powers of command, and so on. Any structure of authority involves a distribution of its powers of command in more or less concentrated or dispersed forms, and the distribution of these powers of command generates structured differentials of power that exert an independent influence on the life chances of those in particular command situations.

The overall framework of stratification in a society may, then, be summarised as involving three kinds of power situation: class situations derived from differentials of power in the economic sphere of *property* and the *market*, status situations derived from differentials of power in the social sphere of *communal prestige*, and 'command situations' derived from differentials of power in the sphere of *authority*. Just as class situations are rooted in possession, but achieve their fullest expression with the development of the market, so command situations are rooted in authority, but achieve their fullest expression with the establishment of systems of bureaucratic administration. This argument suggests that the typology set out in figure 1 can be extended to that shown in figure 2.[30]

What I call 'social blocs' can be defined as those clusters of command situations among which mobility is 'easy and typical'. These ideas have been more widely discussed, though not by Weber himself, in the context of 'elites' and 'masses', seen as specific kinds

Social spheres	Power situations	Social strata
Economic	Class situations	Social classes
Communal	Status situations	Social estates
Authoritarian	Command situations	Social blocs

Figure 2   Social classes, social estates and social blocs

of social bloc. An elite is a social grouping of individuals who occupy similar advantaged command situations in the social distribution of authority and are linked to one another through demographic processes of circulation and interaction. Occupants of leading positions in the state, in an established church, or in capitalist enterprises and associations of capital, for example, may form a single 'elite' if there is an easy and frequent circulation among these various positions of command and if they are linked through inter- and intra-generational mobility, informal and intimate interaction, and household formation. In ideal typical terms, it is possible to envisage 'command societies' alongside status societies and class societies.[31]

Weber did not himself set out these ideas in his discussions of authority, nor did he pursue the question of the demographic processes of circulation and interaction that can form the occupants of command situations into social blocs such as 'elites'. For all the rigour and sophistication of his analysis of authority, and despite the fact that he wrote of 'rulers' (*Herren*) and 'ruled' (*Beherrschte*), Weber failed to make the crucial theoretical breakthrough that can be found in the contemporary work of Mosca and other 'elite' theorists. As a result, Weber provided an account of class, status and party, rather than one of class, status and bloc. Had Weber made this crucial theoretical breakthrough, he might have seen that 'parties' – conflict or interest groups – may arise on the basis of economic, communal, *or* authoritarian interests and so may claim to represent social classes, social estates, or social blocs. Such speculation, however, points beyond Weber's own argument, and I wish merely to highlight the fact that such a viewpoint is, at least, compatible with Weber's work and is, in many respects, implicit in much of what he has written. This can be seen by returning to Weber's own discussion of authority.

The most important structure of authority that Weber discussed was the state, which he set out to define in sociological terms. He began his definition with the general concept of organised territorial authority, which takes a 'political' form whenever it operates through ultimate reliance on physical force and violence and its commands are enacted and enforced by an administrative staff. A political authority that is both compulsory and enduring is termed a 'state' in so far as it claims, within its territory, the monopoly of the legitimate use of force (1920: 54; 1914: 901ff). A state must assert its sole right to exercise physical coercion, or it will cease to be a state and will become merely one of a number of competing political authorities within a territory. To the extent that actors act rationally, an established state will exhibit a momentum towards expansion. Those who hold high office within the state – bureaucrats, politicians and military officers, for example – have individual interests in the income, honour and authority that they enjoy, and they can maximise their interests by expanding the power of the state (1914: 911; 1895: 277).

In a fully established system of state authority, the use of force and violence is always a final resort. Weber held that 'Violence is, of course, not the normal or sole means used by the state . . . But it is the means specific to the state' (1919: 310). To the extent that domination is legitimate, the subjects or citizens of the state will regard the commands of its officials as binding upon them. They may not like the commands and they may run counter to their particular interests, but they are, nevertheless, treated as 'authoritative'. Obedience, then, is normal in a system based on legitimate domination. Force will be required only where the legitimacy of the state is challenged or denied. This may arise, for example, when separatist political movements pose a 'principled' challenge to state authority, or when organised criminal groups pursue their interests with systematic disregard for state authority. In these circumstances, the state will seek to enforce its power by force and coercion – for example, through military and police action and through incarceration – and if such challenges become at all widespread, then the authority of the state will crumble and it will be able to secure a degree of stability only through establishing a regime of force or a *de facto* alignment of interests.

It is important to note, however, that Weber's concept of legitimacy does not rest upon the idea of a complete consensus among subjects or citizens. It is not necessary that subordinate actors be morally committed to the specific claims that are made by the dominant actors or to the contents of their commands. All that is necessary is that there be actual consent and that claims to legitimacy are grounded in a broad framework of shared understandings (Weber 1914: 946; Beetham 1991; Parkin 1982: 75–6). A king, for example, may claim the divine right to rule, but his subjects may not actually believe him to be a holy or sacred personage. Indeed, the mass of the population may be completely unaware of the intellectual doctrines on which the claim to legitimacy is based. The existence of authority, then, is based upon a successful *claim* to legitimacy and not on the actual motives for obedience. For this reason, Weber's classification of types of authority is essentially a classification of the types of claims that dominant groups may make for obedience to their commands. It refers to what Parkin (1982: 77) has called the 'moral vocabularies' of discourse through which dominant groups seek to justify their dominance.

Weber recognised three bases for claims to legitimacy – 'traditional', 'legal-rational' and 'charismatic'. There have been many discussions of the utility and exhaustiveness of Weber's ideal types, and it is unnecessary to go into these here.[32] For present purposes, only the broad contrast between traditional and legal-rational legitimation is important. In a system of traditional authority, the rules governing the exercise of command are grounded in beliefs in the sanctity of the past. These rules, then, take the form of custom and established practice. Traditional authority has its origins in the patriarchal authority relations of households. When the power of male heads of households is enlarged into wider structures of domination through the establishment of a framework of custom and convention, it takes the form of 'patrimonial' authority. Patrimonial authority, as it expands, acquires a distinctively political form with the delegation of customary powers to administrative officials. Despite this, however, patrimonial authority does not involve a truly 'public' form of authority, as there is no clear separation between the private sphere of the household and the official sphere of the administrator. Powers of administration are an adjunct to the property of the official and may be bought, sold, or inherited like any other form of property. Where the relationships among those who exercise traditional authority are contractual, Weber spoke of 'feudalism' – the characteristic form of traditional authority in pre-modern Europe.

When traditional legitimation is replaced by purely rational claims to the legitimacy of authority as grounded in a framework of law that has been established through due procedures, Weber spoke of legal-rational authority.[33] Patrimonial states were headed by rulers who claimed personal powers within a framework of custom whose origins were lost in the mists of time. In a legal-rational structure of authority, on the other hand, there is a clear separation of the public and the private, and the administrative apparatus takes the form of a 'bureaucracy'. Modern states, then, are headed by rulers who claim clearly circumscribed powers within a framework of laws that have been consciously and deliberately enacted and which can, therefore, be changed in exactly the same way. Modern states have defined systems of rules from which their claims to legitimacy are derived. 'This system of rules constitutes the "legal order", and the political community is regarded as its sole normal creator' (1914: 904). That is to say, modern states are legitimated by virtue of a legal framework that they have themselves initiated. This legal framework also enters into the constitution of property and privileges and is an important element in the formation of class and status relations.

Weber's discussion of the state, then, offers a paradigm for the analysis of authority and the formation of command situations. These structures are not, however, limited to the political sphere of the state, but occur in all authoritarian organisations.[34] They arise wherever there is a structure of authority, and are particularly characteristic of the structures of bureaucracy that have developed in modern business enterprises.

Conclusion

Weber's tripartite model of social stratification has much to offer as a framework for empirical investigations. I have tried to show that this framework centres around the recognition of the interdependencies of the economic, the communal and the authoritarian spheres of action, from which will emerge class, status and command situations. *Class situations* comprise those causal components in individual life chances that derive from the differentials of power that are inherent in sheer possession and market relations and that establish domination by virtue of a constellation of interests. *Status situations* comprise those causal components in individual life chances that derive from the differentials of power that are inherent in the social estimation of honour within communities and that give rise to domination by virtue of prestige. *Command situations* comprise those causal components in individual life chances that derive from the differentials of power that are inherent in the exercise of rulership and administration and that establish domination by virtue of authority.

Systems of social stratification combine all three of these dimensions of power in varying degrees, though three ideal typical forms can be identified. The actual social strata that form the elements of particular systems of social stratification must be seen as clusters of class, status and command situations, linked together through demographic processes of circulation and of informal and intimate interaction. *Social classes* exist where economic mechanisms achieve their fullest extent and class situations are clustered into coherent and systemic strata. *Social estates* exist where communal mechanisms of evaluation prevail over other stratifying factors and status situations are clustered into structured layers. Finally, I have suggested that it is possible to identify *social blocs* wherever mechanisms of authority predominate and command situations are clustered into system-wide strata. It is on this basis that a Weberian approach to social stratification would recognise *class societies, status societies* and *command societies,* as well as various intermediate and mixed societal types. In all concrete cases, however, the three dimensions are combined. A social class in a class society, for example, will be structured by status and authority as well as by class relations, though the specifically class elements will prevail.

Weber's remarks on parties may be understood in this context. The actual groups that enter into contest and conflict with one another are *not* themselves social classes, social estates, or social blocs, though they may pursue interests that are generated in class, status, and command situations. Parties are organised social groupings that are concerned with power *per se.* They are not confined to any one specialised sphere of action, but operate within all spheres of power. Parties – political parties, trade unions, professional organisations, employers' associations and so on – are the collective agents whose actions are central to social integration. Social classes, social estates and social blocs are the structures that connect these collective agents with underlying economic, cultural and authoritarian processes of system integration.[35]

The Weberian distinctions that I have set out in this chapter provide the basis for a comprehensive approach to social stratification, but they are not, by themselves, sufficient. Weber points the way, but he does not himself undertake the journey. Indeed, Weber's methodological position led him to be very sceptical of the need for extended theoretical discussions in advance of empirical research. There is a great deal to be said for this kind of scepticism, but the position that I wish to advance is that a degree of theoretical systematisation is essential if empirical research is to be fruitful. Indeed, theoretical systematisation and empirical research go hand in hand, the development of one contributing to the development of the other. In order to see how the Weberian conceptual framework may be further developed, then, it is necessary to go beyond Weber's own work and to draw on the ideas of those who have explored in greater detail the three dimensions of social stratification. I begin this task by looking at the work of Marx and the mainstream of orthodox Marxism, which has developed a very powerful conceptualisation of class relations and of their connection to the economic dynamics of capitalist societies.

3

Class, Property and Market

'The history of all hitherto existing society is the history of class struggles' (Marx and Engels 1848: 79). Thus runs what is, perhaps, the best-known statement about social stratification – perhaps the most famous statement in the history of the social sciences. It was with this phrase that Karl Marx and Friedrich Engels set out their thesis that the mainspring of historical change was to be found in the formation and the conflict of classes. But what did they mean by 'class'? Despite its centrality in their theoretical work, neither author undertook a sustained examination of its meaning. Towards the end of his scholarly career, Marx did draft a chapter on classes for his work on *Capital*, but the chapter – like the book – was never completed. My aim in this chapter is to show how Marx used concepts of class and class situation and how these ideas were developed by Marx and by the mainstream of Marxists after his death. My aim is to show that the Marxian analysis of class is compatible with the views that were later set out by Weber, and that it constitutes an essential element in any comprehensive approach to social stratification.

The context for Marx's discussion of class was the 'materialist' approach to history that he and Engels set out in their critical considerations of the philosophies of Hegel and Feuerbach. For Marx and Engels, social analysis begins not from the abstract 'ideas' of the Hegelian scheme, but from 'real men' in their 'real world' circumstances. Despite the misleading use of the male pronoun, the meaning of this claim is clear. Human consciousness and ideas develop through human action, and the correct starting point for social analysis must be the direct investigation of the material circumstances in which these actions arise. The political and cultural ideas that are employed to understand the world are simply projections or reflections of people's human powers and their material conditions. The core ideas of this materialist critique of Hegel were shared with Feuerbach, but the distinctive contribution made by Marx and Engels was to retain Hegel's historical perspective. In place of Feuerbach's isolated and ahistorical 'individual', Marx and Engels focused their attention on the socially organised and historically specific relations in which these individuals are involved. These socially organised individuals were 'classes', and both writers saw 'economic' relations as the key to the organisation and struggle of classes in modern society. Intellectual ideas have an impact on social life only in so far as they enter into the consciousness and action of social classes.

This strong emphasis on the role of class marked a crucial advance in social thought, though Marx recognised that he had not been responsible for the discovery of class relations. In a letter to the American Joseph Weydemeyer, Marx wrote that 'no credit is due to me for discovering the existence of classes in modern society or the struggle between them. Long before me, bourgeois historians had described the historical development of the class struggle and bourgeois economists the economic anatomy of the classes' (1852b: 139). His own originality, he felt, lay in the fact that he had fused these ideas into a single framework and had added a strong historical dimension to class analysis. He had also harnessed class analysis to a political programme that led him to conclude that human society was developing towards a 'classless' form:

What I did that was new was to prove: (1) that the *existence of classes* is only bound up with *particular historical phases in the development of production*, (2) that the class struggle necessarily leads to the *dictatorship of the proletariat*, (3) that this dictatorship itself only constitutes the transition to the *abolition of all classes* and to a *classless society*. (1852b: 139)

Marx never held a university post, though his life was committed to scholarly work, which he saw as the necessary means for advancing his political goals. He produced a vast mass of research notes, pamphlets and books, only a small fraction of which was published in his own lifetime, and his thoughts on class were scattered throughout these works and in numerous letters and newspaper articles.

Two texts hold an undisputed central position in Marx's output. The *Communist Manifesto*, written jointly with Engels in 1848, set out his model of class struggle in a clear and popular form, while *Capital* explored the economic basis of class relations. The *Communist Manifesto*, commissioned as the political programme for the emergent communist parties of Europe, was one of the very few of his works that Marx was later to feel had stood the test of time and could be seen as something of lasting value. *Capital*, on the other hand, took up the bulk of his adult life, but never achieved a form that was to his own satisfaction, and only its first volume was published in his own lifetime. *Capital* is, nevertheless, the thread that runs through all of his principal works, many of which emerged from his continuing attempts to complete *Capital*. Over his life he produced draft after draft for what he initially saw as a vast conspectus of social theory, and even the posthumously published volumes of *Capital* contain only a fraction of what he intended this to include. It is necessary, therefore, to excavate deeply into Marx's work in order to uncover his views on class and on the links between class relations and the structure of capital.[1]

Of the two authors of the *Communist Manifesto*, it is undoubtedly Marx who was the most original and the most scholarly writer. It was he who gave his name – albeit reluctantly – to the political programme of Marxism. Engels is important in Marxist theory as an early collaborator with Marx, a consistent source of financial support for him, and, most crucially, as his literary and intellectual executor. It was Engels who 'completed' many of Marx's unfinished works and systematised his ideas into 'historical' or 'dialectical' materialism, and it was Engels's vision of the Marxian intellectual project that shaped the development of the orthodox Marxism of the Second International.

Marx and Marxism

Marx's work in political economy began in 1844, following his reading of Engels's critical summary of economic theory (Engels 1843), and he produced a number of research notebooks from which he eventually prepared a draft manuscript (Marx 1844). This manuscript was organised around Adam Smith's identification of three basic classes and their distinct economic locations and property relations in modern capitalism: workers receiving the 'wages of labour', capitalists receiving the 'profits of capital', and landlords receiving the 'rent of land'. Towards the end of 1845, Marx abandoned active work on this manuscript in order to work with Engels on a critique of an influential group of German philosophers (Marx and Engels 1845).

Marx continued to read widely in economics and politics, intending to write a major work that would integrate the subjects into a single framework of social theory. This intellectual task was to dominate the rest of his life, though it was never to be completed. In preparation for this task he again joined with Engels to write the methodological foundations for this work (Marx 1846). Neither this work nor the earlier manuscript were put into final form, though Marx claimed that they had served the important purpose of 'self-clarification', and they remained virtually unknown until their publication almost 100 years later.[2] Following this work of self-clarification, Marx might have been expected to push forward with the production of his projected work, but he again broke off from his researches to produce two shorter works that were concerned with immediate political problems. In both these works (Marx 1847; Marx and Engels 1848), and most notably in the *Communist Manifesto*, Marx worked through a number of issues of class analysis.

Marx arrived in London in 1849, having been forced to leave Paris and Brussels where he had worked in exile from his native Germany. He immediately took up his task of producing the planned work on social theory, this time envisaged as concerned with 'economics' alone, and he began a long programme of research in the British Museum. Marx found himself grappling with fundamental theoretical issues that he felt unable to resolve, and he threw himself into a major reading programme that he hoped would lead to a resolution of his theoretical difficulties. Not until 1857 did he make what he felt to be the crucial breakthrough, the discovery of a theory of 'surplus value'. This discovery heralded a series of published and unpublished works. In the years 1857 and 1858 he produced a first draft manuscript for his proposed work on economics (Marx 1857; 1858), and in the following year he published the first statements of his new ideas (Marx 1859a; 1859b).[3] The 1859 *Contribution to the Critique of Political Economy* was a provisional statement of the ideas that he continued to develop as the basis for his projected work, now called *Capital*. Between 1861 and 1863 he produced a massive manuscript, from which other draft manuscripts were produced, and in 1867 he finally published volume 1 of *Capital* (Marx 1867).[4] Marx continued to rework his manuscripts, but none of the remaining volumes were completed before his death in 1883.

Marx's consistent plan through the many years of his research was that the first three books in his major work would be concerned, respectively, with capital, landed property, and wage labour.[5] These, it will be recalled, were the three class categories that he had taken from Adam Smith and that he had used to organise his first economic manuscript. Despite his life's work, only the first book – on *Capital* – was ever to appear in anything like a final form. The book was completed by Engels and Kautsky, who acted as editors of Marx's draft manuscripts, and it remains unclear how much of the final text is that of Marx and how much is that of his editors.[6] Although landed property and wage labour are both discussed in *Capital*, Marx seems never to have abandoned his intention to write separate, full-length studies on each of these topics. Thus, Marx's exploration of the economic anatomy of the three great classes that had been identified in political economy was limited to just one of those classes, with the other classes being considered only as they impinged directly on the analysis of the capitalist class (Oakley 1983: 105ff).[7]

After Marx's death, his ideas on class and the economic foundations of class relations were codified into what came to be called 'orthodox Marxism'. The orthodox Marxism of the Second International – described by Kolakowski (1978) as the 'golden age' of Marxism – centred on an acceptance of Engels's systematisation of a philosophical basis for Marxism in *Anti-Dühring* and *Ludwig Feuerbach* (1876; 1888) and his focusing of attention on the technicalities of economic theory. My concern in this chapter is not with the validity – or otherwise – of Engels's systematisation of 'scientific socialism' as a natural science of society, or with the acceptance of this positivistic and mechanistic view in the Marxist orthodoxy. I am concerned only with the particular view of class that was taken from Marx's writings and that was elaborated in the orthodox tradition.

While there were many important intellectual and political differences within the Second International – most notably the dispute over reformism and the emerging division between the 'social democratic' and the 'communist' wings – its leading figures were unified by their shared interpretation of the ideas set out in the *Communist Manifesto* and *Capital*. What differentiated their work from Marx's own was a belief that capitalism was moving into a more 'organised' stage in which large enterprises, monopolised markets and state intervention were increasingly important factors. In this stage of capitalist development the various topics that Marx had intended to discuss in his projected, but uncompleted, work on political economy acquired a much greater urgency. Marx's own work had anticipated the implications of some of these developments – most particularly in his discussion of the joint stock enterprise and its role in the concentration and centralisation of capital – but later Marxists began to explore these themes more systematically.

This chapter will, then, include a consideration of the ideas of orthodox and other Marxists who have remained within the broad framework of class analysis that was set out by Marx. I will give less attention to those who, working within the Marxist tradition, have sought to go beyond Marx's own concepts. The arguments of Wright, for example, have gone beyond property and market and have incorporated considerations of authority into class analysis. These views raise fundamental questions that must be considered at length in a later chapter. The present chapter is concerned with the core ideas of class analysis as Marx would have understood it. I must emphasise, however, that, as with my discussion of Weber, my aim is not to present a textual exegesis. I aim, instead, to reconstruct a coherent approach to class from the work of Marx.

The *Manifesto* model

The historical model of class relations that Marx and Engels provided in the *Communist Manifesto*, in programmatic form, was the cornerstone of their work.[8] It stated in a particularly clear, crisp and didactic form the Marxian view of class conflict, but it left implicit much of the detailed reasoning from which Marx and Engels had constructed their argument. Before looking at the *Manifesto* model, then, it is necessary to explore the wider theoretical ideas from which it came.

Like Weber, Marx began from the idea of the transition from a medieval 'estate' society to a modern 'class' society. In his early critique of Hegel – which pre-dated his work on political economy – Marx used these concepts to reconstruct Hegel's view of the development of modern society (Marx 1843a). Marx followed Hegel's terminology and used the term *Stände* throughout his critical study, but the contexts in which the word is used make it clear that Marx had come to appreciate the sharp difference that existed between the politically organised strata of the Middle Ages (the *estates*) and the economically constituted strata of modern society (the *classes*). After moving to Paris and coming into closer contact with socialist thought, he wrote his 'Introduction' (1843b) to the critique of Hegel and used *Klasse* in preference to *Stand*.[9] By the time of *The Poverty of Philosophy* (Marx 1847) this viewpoint had been made clearer, and Marx referred to the 'abolition' of estates by the bourgeois leaders of the *tiers état*. Engels's later note to the text amplified this point and clarified the contrast between the legally privileged estates and the classes of modern society.

Marx saw the Middle Ages as a period in which there was an identity between the social 'estates' of society at large and the politically organised 'estates' of parliament. Civil society had not been differentiated from political society, and so estate differences could be directly organised in and through the state. In modern society, on the other hand, the 'separation of civil society and the political state as two actually different spheres' (1843a: 72, 73) was a central characteristic. The monarchies of France and Germany had been of critical importance as the crucibles of this transition, centralising the differentiated political power in the apparatus of the absolutist state. In France, the separation of state and civil society had been completed during the Revolution, but in Germany it remained incomplete at the time that Marx was writing (1843a: 80). With this growing structural differentiation, civil classes no longer took a directly political form and became 'private' rather than 'official' groupings. Classes were organised, if at all, outside the sphere of the state and only then sought political representation within it (1843a: 76, 77). Modern societies, then, are organised around a sharp differentiation of the *private* interests of individuals within classes from their *public* status as citizens. There is, Marx said, 'a development of history that has transformed the political classes into social classes' (1843a: 80).

Contrary to what has sometimes been suggested (Elster 1985), Marx did not see the transition from an estate society to a class society as involving the wholesale replacement of 'status' by 'class'. 'Class situation', to use Weber's term, is an aspect of *all* historical societies, including those of medieval Europe. Class divisions existed in pre-modern societies, but they were latent. They were embedded in political and ideological relations that formed them into estates. Bukharin's later commentary on Marx's argument made it clear that class relations had to be seen as general but not necessarily universal elements in human society. They existed in medieval society, but they were contained within 'the legal envelope of the "estates"' (Bukharin 1925: 280). Class relations were obscured in ideological forms and appeared as relations between estates. The fact that classes took the form of estates did not mean that there was a direct one-to-one relationship. Estates might contain two or more classes, and classes might be cross-cut into separate estates. This became particularly marked in periods of change. Bukharin felt, for example, that

> In the French Revolution the *tiers état* was a mixture of various classes, then but slightly differentiated from each other: it included the bourgeoisie, the workers and the 'intermediate classes' (artisans, petty traders, etc.). All were members of the *tiers état* for the reason of their legal insignificance as compared with the feudal landlords. This *tiers état* was the juristic expression for the class bloc opposing the dominant landlords. (1925: 279–80)

What distinguishes the modern from the medieval period is the fact that class situation became the predominant feature of social stratification, pushing all questions of social honour into the background. While the medieval estates had clear legal identities and cultural boundaries, modern class distinctions 'take shape in changeable unfixed spheres whose principle is arbitrariness' (Marx 1843a: 80–1). That is to say, the class relations of modern society are fluid in their boundaries and are determined only by their money, their property and their labour.[10] A class situation involves no distinct cultural, legal or political identity, and exists only as 'an external determination' that no longer relates to people 'as an objective communal being organized according to firm laws' (1843a: 81). Only in modern society do class divisions appear *as* class divisions. Where 'economic' relations have been differentiated from the sphere of the state and from the communal structure of society, 'class' appears as something less central to a person's identity than was their 'status' in pre-capitalist societies. Class appears as a mere contingent, factual attribute of an individual, not as something that is directly constitutive of his or her social being and identity (Sayer 1991).

At this early stage in his work, Marx had no clear ideas about the number of class situations that existed in modern society or about the sources of these class divisions. While making some brief remarks about the 'business class' (of industrial and commercial entrepreneurs) and entering into a longer discussion of the 'agricultural class' of landowners, he made no pretence of undertaking a systematic investigation.[11] He did, however, come to recognise that only those classes that achieve political organisation could become agents of historical transformation. The transformation of a society, he argued, would occur only through the revolutionary action of a class that could mobilise popular support for the emancipation of society at large. The only class that could achieve this was a class that could 'concentrate in itself all the defects of society' by virtue of its subjection to another class (Marx 1843b: 140).

In France, he held, every class had become politically organised, and the bourgeoisie was able to act as a truly revolutionary class that could liberate the whole of society. This was the key to understanding the French Revolution. In Germany, on the other hand, 'every class . . . lacks the consistency, the keenness, the courage, and the ruthlessness' that is needed for 'that genius which animates material force into political power' (1843b: 140). Germany had not broken completely with the medieval political forms that inhibited class action and the bourgeoisie was subordinate to these medieval forms. Thus, revolution could occur in Germany only with the formation of a 'proletariat', and this class was still in the early stages of its development in 1843.

The term 'proletariat' had been taken from the ideas of the communist and socialist writers and activists of Paris, in whose writings it had designated the new class of wage workers in industry that were seen as developing a class consciousness of a specifically socialist kind (Draper 1977: 132). Marx saw the proletariat as a class whose particular interests coincide with those of modern society as a whole: it is a 'universal' class. It is driven to revolution by the extreme poverty of the material circumstances in which its members live, and by their motivation to overcome the degradation and dehumanisation that they experience. Its social conditions represent the summation of all the alien features of modern capitalist society: it is 'a class in civil society that is not a class of civil society'; it is 'a social group that is the dissolution of all social groups' (Marx 1843b: 140). By struggling to liberate itself it must, at the same time, liberate all other classes by abolishing class divisions.

This vision of the revolutionary role of the proletariat – forged during 1843 – was the leading idea that Marx and Engels developed in their joint work. By the time that they wrote the *Communist*

Manifesto, however, they had begun their studies in political economy, and they were able to relate the revolutionary struggles of classes more directly to an understanding of the economic trends of modern society. It was this *Manifesto* model of class that formed the point of reference for their subsequent scattered remarks on classes, property relations, and class conflict. It is also the model that was followed by orthodox Marxists, and by many writers of later periods. I will set out this model with the minimum of comment, in order to bring out the broad features of Marx's argument.

Their starting point in the *Communist Manifesto* was the claim that all societies can be seen as being dominated by a *ruling class* that shapes social development through conflict with subordinate and rising classes. The structure of any society expresses the dominance of its ruling class, and the normal means of social transformation is the revolutionary action of an oppressed class against a ruling class. The opposition of oppressor and oppressed was, then, seen as a universal feature of human history, though its form varied from one society to another. Marx's special concern was to highlight the distinctiveness of modern *capitalist* societies, where he saw the opposition of classes as taking a much clearer form than in pre-capitalist societies. Instead of the 'complicated arrangement of society into various orders' and the 'manifold gradation of social rank' that had characterised ancient Rome and medieval Europe, modern capitalism showed a tendency to develop towards a polarised, two-class structure:

> Society as a whole is more and more splitting up into two great hostile camps, into two great classes directly facing each other: Bourgeoisie and Proletariat. (Marx and Engels 1848: 80)

The political and cultural mystifications that formerly clothed class divisions and that transformed them into a hierarchy of estates were being stripped away to produce a simplified and transparent structure of class relations involving the direct confrontation of the bourgeoisie and the proletariat. The bourgeois class, or capitalist class, had emerged as 'the product of a long course of development, of a series of revolutions in the modes of production and exchange' (1848: 81). The bourgeoisie had emerged initially within the social framework of medieval feudalism as the 'burghers' of the medieval towns. The commercial activities that they undertook within the expanding trading system of the medieval world allowed them to generate a new productive force – 'capital' – that became the basis of their own expansion as a class. Feudal property relations had allowed the expansion of trade and the initial development of capital, but they were incompatible with its continued expansion. The expansion of capital proved to be a powerful social force that was eventually to lead to the destruction of feudal property relations. These relations 'became so many fetters. They had to be burst asunder; they were burst asunder' (1848: 85).

The destruction of feudal property relations liberated the bourgeoisie from the powers that had constrained them and, thus liberated, they could continue to expand the productive powers of capital and so lay the foundations of a new social order. Central to this new social order was the market, the mechanism that allowed the expansion of capital and that was fundamental to the 'economic' structure of capitalist society. With the continuing growth of a market economy, many commercial and trading merchants began to be directly involved in manufacturing, and with the industrial revolution of the eighteenth and nineteenth centuries, the 'industrial millionaires' of 'modern industry' emerged as the contemporary form of the bourgeoisie. The bourgeoisie, then, developed from burghers to merchants to manufacturers, in the process becoming a true capitalist class. At each stage of its development the emerging capitalist class both absorbed the rising members of the commercial and industrialist population and displaced those who were unable to adapt to the new economic circumstances.

The *economic* development of the bourgeoisie was the driving force in its political development. The class had occupied a politically subordinate position in feudal society, but it gradually achieved greater political autonomy until it had

since the establishment of modern industry and of the world market, conquered for itself, in the modern representative state, exclusive political sway. The executive of the modern state is but a committee for managing the common affairs of the whole bourgeoisie. (1848: 82)

This rise to political power had also allowed the bourgeoisie to destroy the status distinctions and gradations that had formerly masked class divisions and had given them some legitimacy. Where class relations had formerly been hidden behind religiously grounded ideas of status honour and moral superiority that obscured their true nature as economic divisions, this was no longer

the case in capitalism. In feudalism, social honour had been attached to particular vocations or professions, but this vocational
status had become a peripheral feature of the division of labour in
capitalist society: 'The bourgeoisie has stripped of its halo every
occupation hitherto honoured and looked up to with reverent awe.
It has converted the physician, the lawyer, the priest, the poet, the
man of science, into its paid wage-labourers.' By stripping away
such conceptions of status and prestige, the bourgeoisie had exposed the cash nexus as the measure of all things: 'for exploitation
veiled by religious and political illusions, it has substituted naked,
shameless, direct, brutal exploitation' (1848: 82). The ideology of
the feudal landlords had been replaced by the ideology of the
capitalist class, reflecting a general historical tendency: 'The ruling
ideas of each age have ever been the ideas of its ruling class' (1848:
102). The traditional religious values of feudalism and its ruling
class of landlords, then, had decayed and had been replaced by the
egotistical and calculative values of the bourgeoisie.

The proletariat or working class emerged alongside the bourgeoisie and is subject to its power. While capital is the economic
basis of the bourgeoisie, the proletariat is founded on wage labour.
In place of the journeymen and artisan craftsmen[12] of the pre-
capitalist period, each with their particular status in the wider community, the bourgeoisie brought into being the modern working
class. This is 'a class of labourers, who live only so long as they
find work, and who find work only so long as their labour increases capital' (1848: 87). Labour becomes a commodity, it is bought
and sold on the market, and individual members of the proletariat
come to be regarded as mere appendages to the machines on which
they are employed to work.

The relationship between the bourgeoisie and the proletariat is
one of exploitation, a relationship in which the bourgeoisie gains at
the expense of the proletariat. Workers produce commodities for
their employers and in return they receive a wage that represents
the absolute minimum necessary to ensure their bare existence and
the reproduction of their labour. The 'surplus' produced by the
worker – the difference between the value of the commodity and
the amount of the wage – is appropriated by the capitalist, who
thereby exploits the proletarian. On this basis, the appropriated
labour contributes to the accumulation of capital (1848: 87, 96–7).

Capitalism was constantly transforming its own structure and
eliminating the vestiges of its past. As a result, its class system
became ever more simplified into a dichotomous, polarised system

of stratification. The opposition of bourgeoisie and proletariat became starker and clearer as other strata found their positions
incompatible with the social relations of modern capitalism. For
example, the 'petty bourgeoisie' of small-scale capitalists – shopkeepers, handicraftsmen and peasants who depend upon their own
personal capital and labour – find themselves increasingly unable
to compete with large-scale capital. Their businesses and their
conditions of life are undermined by the growth of capitalism and
they are 'precipitated into' or 'sink gradually into the proletariat'
(1848: 88, 91). So long as they survive as an 'intermediate' class,
they are a conservative force, but they are destined to be swept
away by the tide of history.

The proletariat is engaged in a continuous struggle with the
bourgeoisie over its wages and the conditions under which it works.
At first, its struggle is disorganised and ineffective, as its consciousness looks back to the supposed benefits that had been enjoyed by
workers in pre-capitalist society. Individual, trade, and local struggles against employers, including the 'Luddite' response of ma-
chine smashing, are undertaken in an attempt 'to restore by force
the vanished status of the workman of the Middle Ages' (1848: 89).
As modern industry and the factory system of production developed, however, so did the political organisation and consciousness
of the proletariat. The class developed from 'an incoherent mass'
into a truly organised class as its members formed trade unions
and political associations to carry on a more effective political struggle against the bourgeoisie. The ability of the proletariat to organise itself politically is, however, limited by the continuing effects of
trade and sectional divisions among workers, but there is a long-
term tendency towards class-conscious political organisation:

> This organization of the proletarians into a class, and consequently
> into a political party, is continually being upset again by the com-
> petition between the workers themselves. But it ever rises up again,
> stronger, mightier, firmer. It compels legislative recognition of par-
> ticular interests of the workers, by taking advantage of the divisions
> among the bourgeoisie itself. (1848: 90)

Just as the bourgeoisie developed to the level at which it could
challenge and overthrow the feudal lords, so the proletariat will
also achieve the kind of political organisation that will allow it to
challenge and to overthrow the bourgeoisie. But this can be achieved
only when the economic conditions are ripe, when the forces of

production can no longer be contained within capitalist property relations. In developing the forces of production, the bourgeoisie expands them to the point at which they become incompatible with the framework of capitalist society itself. Capitalist property relations cease to promote the development of the forces of production and become, instead, obstacles to their further development. In this stage of 'modern industry', through which Marx and Engels thought that they were themselves living,

> The productive forces at the disposal of society no longer tend to further the development of the conditions of bourgeois property; on the contrary, they have become too powerful for these conditions, by which they are fettered ... The conditions of bourgeois society are too narrow to comprise the wealth created by them. (1848: 86)

This had led to periodic commercial and manufacturing crises and to the increasing pauperisation of the proletariat, and it had also brought nearer the final demise of the various intermediate classes. At this point, the class struggle becomes a struggle between a ruling class and a *revolutionary class*. The working class becomes the means through which the property relations of capitalist society can be overthrown and a new basis for the further development of the productive forces can be established. The proletariat is poised to act as the agent of historical transformation, overthrowing the rule of the bourgeoisie and establishing a new social order. In this way, 'the violent overthrow of the bourgeoisie lays the foundation for the sway of the proletariat' (1848: 93). The revolutionary transformation of capitalist society is not, however, seen as a mere matter of political choice on the part of the proletariat. Revolution is a historical inevitability that results from the logic of capitalist development itself. In developing the economy and its productive forces, the capitalist class undermines its own continued dominance:

> What the bourgeoisie, therefore, produces, above all, is its own grave-diggers. Its fall and the victory of the proletariat are equally inevitable. (1848: 94)

Marx and Engels, in common with many other observers of their day, saw the European political upheavals of 1848 as a sign that the revolution was imminent. They concluded their review of the contemporary struggle of classes, therefore, with a discussion of the role that they and other intellectuals might play as the revolution

approached. As the political and economic struggle between bourgeoisie and proletariat approached its climax, they argued,

> a small section of the ruling class cuts itself adrift, and joins the
> revolutionary class, the class that holds the future in its hands. Just
> as, therefore, at an earlier period, a section of the nobility went over
> to the bourgeoisie, so now a portion of the bourgeoisie goes over to
> the proletariat, and in particular, a portion of the bourgeois ideolo-
> gists, who have raised themselves to the level of comprehending
> theoretically the historical movement as a whole. (1848: 91)

Those bourgeois intellectuals who have become convinced of the
inevitability of revolution are able to bring their theoretical insights
to the class struggle and, by allying themselves with the communists, in whatever particular parties they may be involved, they
can represent the interests of the working class as a whole and
push forward the class struggle to its final resolution. Their ability
to represent the general interest of the proletariat, rather than the
interest of this or that section or trade, is due to the fact that 'theoretically, they have over the great mass of the proletariat the advantage of clearly understanding the line of march, the conditions, and
the ultimate general results of the proletarian movement' (1848:
95). Communist intellectuals have a clear understanding of the historical picture that Marx and Engels set out in the *Communist Manifesto* and they are, therefore, able to guide those workers who have
not had the advantage of intellectual reflection on their circumstances. Through their guidance and their practical involvement in
progressive struggles, the communists can help to ensure that the
proletariat brings about the 'forcible overthrow' of capitalism:

> Let the ruling classes tremble at a Communist revolution. The pro-
> letarians have nothing to lose but their chains. They have a world to
> win. (1848: 120–1)

Possession, class and consciousness

My summary of the *Manifesto* model has stayed close to Marx's
own words, in order to bring out the central elements in his
approach to class as a historical force. The *Communist Manifesto*,
however, provides neither a definition of class nor a detailed exposition of the anatomy of the class structure of contemporary capitalism. It is necessary to dig deeper into the Marxist framework for
these aspects of his thought. As is well known, chapter 52 of *Capital* – the chapter on 'Classes' – was not completed, and it exists

only as a fragment of just over one page. Engels reported, however, that part 7 of volume 3, of which chapter 52 forms a part, was virtually complete up to that point. It is possible, therefore, to uncover the outlines of the approach to class that Marx intended to set out in his unfinished chapter.

Marx's basic ideas on class are very similar to those of Weber, who, of course, had the advantage of writing after they had been further developed within orthodox Marxism. For Marx, 'class' had to be seen as referring both to the actual *positions* that exist in a social division of labour and to the *people* who currently occupy these positions. In his analysis of positions, then, Marx was concerned with what Weber was to call 'class situation', while his analysis of their occupants led him towards the idea of 'social classes'.

Class positions, or class situations, are not defined by mere similarities in life chances or revenues. They are understood as the causal determinants of these phenomena and are defined by the 'relations of production'. This latter term designates Marx's most general concept for describing the ways in which production is socially structured in particular societies. At the heart of the relations of production are the particular relations of possession (*Besitz*) through which access to and use of the means of production and human labour are regulated, and Marx saw relations of possession as defining a whole technical organisation of production through an occupational division of labour and immediate work relations. Relations of possession are the basis upon which people are able to acquire a particular type and level of share in the total wealth produced in their society.

Marx tended to describe these relations of possession in legal terms, as being relations of 'property' or of 'ownership', but it is clear that he did not mean to see these relations as exclusively legal in character. He was concerned with the actual social relations that structure production, and he recognised that these were only partly defined by institutionalised legal norms and their associated rights and obligations. Relations of possession are relations of effective control over the productive powers of a society. The virtue of using the word 'possession', rather than 'ownership', is that, despite its legal connotations, it strongly emphasises the factual rather than the merely normative nature of these relations. Legal norms operate alongside political, economic and other social forms as necessary conditions for the actual 'underlying' relations of possession, which remain distinct from their 'surface' conditions (Sayer 1987: 56; see also Anderson 1974: 403–4; Cohen 1978). These underlying relations are, Marx holds, the 'real basis' of the various social forms that make up the institutions and practices of a society.[13]

Class positions are defined by the possession, or lack of possession, of specific means of production and by the consequent function that they imply in the social division of labour (Lenin 1914). Those who do not themselves possess the means of production must nevertheless obtain access to them if they are to acquire the income or the goods and services that they need in order to live. They can, therefore, produce only under conditions that are decided by those with possession of the means of production. The possessors, in turn, are able to require the non-possessors to work on their behalf, and so can become non-producers. They can secure their own livelihood without having to work for it; they can appropriate a portion of what is produced by those who actually do work. Possessors, then, 'exploit' non-possessors by imposing conditions under which the non-possessors receive only a part of what they produce. Under these conditions, a 'surplus product' – the difference between the total amount produced and the amount that is required by the producers – can be appropriated, in whole or in part, by the possessors of the means of production. Through this 'exploitation' of the producers, a class of possessors is, at the same time, a class of non-producers and a class of exploiters.

Classes exist, therefore, in all societies where there is a legal framework of property relations that allows the differentiation of possessors from non-possessors, and where there is also a division of labour that allows the producers to produce more than is needed for their own subsistence. Marx saw possession as necessarily a binary relation – people either possess the means of production or they do not – and so he saw the relations of possession in a society as defining two basic or fundamental class positions.[14] This division between the class of possessors and the class of non-possessors is fundamental to a society's mode of production, and the dichotomous class structure is reproduced so long as the mode of production is reproduced.

All systems of production must be seen as historically specific systems with specific forms of possession. The particular relations of production that structure capitalist society, for example, are not universal, eternal categories. They arise from the specific forms under which production takes place in modern society and are the result of a historical process of development (Marx and Engels 1846: 43). The forms that are taken by the relations of production vary considerably from one society to another, and Marx traced the process of structural differentiation through which these relations came to take a specifically 'economic' form in capitalist society. For much of human history, he held, 'economic' relations were not distinguished from other social relations, as they were thoroughly embedded in the wider social structure. In these societies, production took place in and through kinship and other communal relations, rather than being organised in a distinct and structurally separate sphere of activity. With the separation of a distinct public sphere of 'state' activity from these more diffuse communal relations, however, a larger process of structural differentiation was initiated. The 'political' relations of the state came to be distinguished not only from the structures of kinship and community, but also from the sphere of 'civil society', a sphere of activity that is regulated by 'private' rather than 'public' relations. This civil society was brought into being through the struggles of the bourgeoisie against feudal landlords, and is a sphere of action where the bourgeoisie are able to pursue their propertied and market-oriented interests without direct political interference. The bourgeoisie, then, bring into being a structurally autonomous sphere of market relations; production takes a specifically 'capitalist' form. Market relations and trading activities are, of course, long-standing features of human society, and they constitute what Marx termed 'simple commodity production', but it is only with their generalisation throughout a society that they form a capitalist mode of production. The generalisation of these relations between the thirteenth and the sixteenth centuries in England and other European societies gave them the kind of structural autonomy that makes it realistic to describe them as forming an 'economy', understood in the sense of a distinct sphere of social activity and social relations.

Bourgeois social relations are rooted in a very specific structure of *private property* that first came into being within the feudal structures of medieval society and that subsequently developed with the growth of civil society (Marx and Engels 1846: 79). Once they are fully established, however, these bourgeois relations provide the dynamic mechanism for modern society. It was the emergence of a structurally autonomous economy that

> set in motion a wholly new social dynamic of self-sustaining growth and accumulation based on the improvement of labour-productivity generated by the imperatives of competition. (Wood 1991: 7)

Marx shared the view of Locke and the classical economists that capitalist society was organised around relations of possession that correspond closely to the legal form of individual private property. The bourgeois, private property relations that are at the heart of modern capitalist society, then, are those of *personal possession*.[15] These relations of personal possession define the basic class positions of the bourgeoisie and the proletariat. Bourgeois class situations involve personal possession of the means of production, but not of the labour power that is required for production. This labour power must be employed in a labour market. It is by virtue of their personal possession that members of the bourgeoisie also occupy specific command situations in which they exercise authority over their employees and their use of the means of production. Proletarian class situations, on the other hand, involve no personal possession of the means of production and so proletarians must sell their own labour power on the market. Their lack of property involves a parallel exclusion from authority in the workplace. For Marx, then, command situations were so closely associated with class situations that it was unnecessary to distinguish them from one another. Relations of authority in the economic sphere were always secondary to and derived from the relations of possession that defined class situations. In recognising that class and command are empirically entwined in this way in the capitalist societies of his day, however, Marx failed to appreciate the need to make the analytical distinction that was drawn by Weber and that, I will show, is fundamental to a broader comparative investigation of social stratification.

Proletarian class situations are those of people

> who depend for their living on the sale of their labour-power, and are unable to secure an income except by resigning all claim to the product of their labour. The proletariat is made up of workers who are shut off from direct access to the means of production, and live by the alienation of the only commodity they possess – their power to produce wealth by labouring upon machines and materials which they do not own. (Cole 1948: 109)

Bourgeois class positions, on the other hand, are those of people whose personal possession of the means of production provides them with the opportunity to benefit from the labour of proletarians by exploiting them. A bourgeois class has personal possession of machinery, factories and other means of production, while a proletarian class possesses nothing and so must sell its labour on the market.

It was through relations of possession, then, that Marx identified the dichotomous structure of class situations in any society, and the basic class situations of capitalist societies were defined by relations of personal possession that divided bourgeois from proletarian class situations. Marx was also concerned, however, with the actual collectivities that are formed by the occupants of class situations. The word 'class', that is to say, had a dual meaning, referring both to class situations and to social classes. Social classes exist when the occupants of class positions form collectivities that are organised around their shared interests in enhancing the advantages and reducing the disadvantages that result from their particular class situation. A social class is a collectivity rather than a mere logical or statistical aggregate: the members of a social class form a system of individuals in 'constant mutual interaction' that is 'of long duration and constant, being present as long as the whole continues to exist' (Bukharin 1925: 85).

The basic bourgeois and proletarian class situations, it may be said, define large aggregates of people who may be expected to develop the cohesiveness and solidarity that defines them as social classes. As Bukharin put it:

> A social class . . . is the aggregate of persons playing the same part in production, standing in the same relation towards other persons in the production process, these relations being also expressed in things (instruments of labor). (1925: 276, emphasis removed)

Unlike Weber, Marx did not *define* social classes in demographic terms. While he did not deny the relevance of demographic processes of circulation and interaction to social class formation, he did not consider them at any great length. Instead, he focused his attention on the economic foundations of social classes. What Marx did show, however, was that a social class begins to develop only as interconnection and interdependence are established among its members. The burghers of the medieval towns, for example, freed themselves from feudal restrictions and entered into relations of production that distinguished them from other classes, but it was only as trading and transportation links brought the various towns into closer contact with one another that their 'common conditions developed into class conditions' (Marx and Engels 1846: 72).

Marx tended to assume that there was a one-to-one relationship between class positions and social classes, and he saw the dichotomous structure of basic class situations underpinning a dichotomous structure of social classes. The structural contradiction between bourgeois and proletarian class situations in a capitalist society, for example, is expressed in the opposition of a capitalist class to a working class. From the dichotomy of basic class situations, then, Marx derived an image of the polarisation of social classes. In capitalist societies the basic social classes are the bourgeoisie, or capitalist class, and the proletariat, or working class. These social classes are rooted in the basic class positions of a capitalist mode of production. Propertied industrial capitalists and propertyless industrial workers are integral to the productive process of an industrial, factory-based society, and it is their struggle that provides the main dynamic of modern, capitalist society. Workers and capitalists are the occupants of the basic class situations that express the fundamental economic 'contradiction' of modern society.

Class situations were seen as structural positions that embody characteristic causal powers (Savage et al. 1992). These causal powers are the causal components in life chances that were emphasised by Weber in his approach to class situation, and Marx saw them as determining the capacities that the occupants of class positions have for social class formation.[16] The formation of social classes around specific class situations depends on the causal powers inherent in those class situations and the historically specific conditions that allow or deny these causal powers to be exercised. It was mainly in considering these historical conditions that Marx referred to the processes of social class formation that were central to Weber's analysis. In discussing the peasantry, for example, Marx held that the isolation of peasant households from one another and their consequent limited opportunities for interaction with one another set limits on their ability to form themselves into a true social class (1852a: 124).

Unfortunately, Marx did not pursue the question of the demographic formation of social classes. His assumption of a one-to-one relationship between basic class situations and social classes led him to see these processes as being of secondary importance in shaping the contours of class struggle. However, he provided no compelling evidence in support of his assumption, and I will show that he introduced a number of qualifications to the basic dichotomous model that make even more necessary a consideration of the demographic processes of circulation and interaction through which the occupants of class situations are formed into social classes. While the causal powers associated with class

situations may, indeed, contain the *potential* for social class formation, social classes are likely to arise only where demographic processes give effect to them. The failure to incorporate demographic
processes into the Marxian model is one of its major analytical
limitations.

This dichotomous imagery was initially qualified by the recognition of class 'fractions'. Marx held that the basic social classes of
a society may not appear in their pure form and may, instead,
appear as their constituent 'fractions'. These are based in narrower
and more specific class situations than the basic class positions of
which they are fractional parts. Although Marx gave little systematic attention to the lines of economic differentiation that might
lead to the formation of class fractions, it seems clear that specific
types of capital and specific forms of labour power constitute the
most likely lines of fracture. Thus, the basic capitalist situation may
be divided into industrial, banking, or commercial 'fractions', while
the basic proletarian position may be divided along the lines of
skill or labour market participation. These class situations comprise the varying 'endowments' or 'market capacities' that people
are able to use and that define the specific 'optimisation strategies'
that give them specific class interests (Elster 1985: chapter 6).

The actual social classes of a society may, then, form around the
basic class positions or around one or more of their fractional elements. In an investigation of French society in the 1850s, Marx
suggested that a financial bourgeoisie was separated from an industrial bourgeoisie and a mainstream proletariat was separated
from a 'lumpenproletariat' or underclass (1850; 1852a). Marx identified the financial and industrial fractions of the bourgeoisie on
the basis of their different orientations to capital and the optimisation strategies that these involved. Financiers held a rentier or
speculative orientation, while industrialists held an entrepreneurial
or production orientation.[17] Both fractions, however, relied on the
personal possession of capital to generate their economic opportunities in the market and so can be considered as the occupants of
a similar basic class position. In some circumstances, then, differences in capital and in orientation to its use may be bases for the
formation of fractional social classes, while in other circumstances
these fractions may be formed into a single bourgeois social class.

Fractional divisions in the class situation of labour occur when
a division of labour, in which the sellers of labour power are
distributed among a multiplicity of tasks, involves different kinds
and levels of skill that are associated with differential rates of

productivity (Hunt 1970; Cohen 1973; see also Mackenzie 1976). Skilled and unskilled workers, for example, may be said to occupy distinct class situations wherever these skill differences are the bases of distinct orientations and interests that result in substantial differences in their life chances.[18] These skill differences may also be associated with ideological differences that Weber would regard as differences of status situation within the proletariat. Allen (1977), for example, has argued that differences of market situation among proletarians involve the ideological organisation of labour into distinct 'occupations', each with a specific 'status'.[19] This allocation of status reinforces class divisions:

> Workers in high status jobs tend to have higher earnings, shorter and more congenially distributed working hours, better working conditions, longer holidays and more social amenities in general than jobs ranked below them. These distinctions spill over into educational and job opportunities and lifestyles in general and tend, therefore, to be reinforced by them. (Allen 1977: 67)

Conceptions of occupational status and their consequences, therefore, can reinforce the differentiation of market situations within the proletariat and can sharpen the segregation of distinct labour markets with their specific mechanisms of recruitment, training and control.

Fractional class situations have sometimes been seen as bases for the formation of 'intermediate' social classes that lie 'between' the principal social classes of a society, but Marx's own discussion of intermediate social classes concentrates on those that can be defined as based on internally 'contradictory' class situations.[20] These class situations combine elements of both of the basic class situations of a society. Those who are involved in running small businesses, for example, own their means of production and may employ other workers, but they also work directly on their own account. This is the case for many builders and decorators, shopkeepers and others that occupy what Marx called 'petty bourgeois' class situations. The petty bourgeoisie are, in a sense, both bourgeois and proletarian at the same time. This class situation is internally 'contradictory' by comparison with the basic class situations, and it may become the basis of the formation of intermediate social classes with distinctive social characteristics. While the term 'intermediate' should not be taken as indicating that these social classes necessarily occupy a strictly 'middle' class position, it does indicate their particular advantages and disadvantages and their irreducibility to either of the basic social classes.

Class situations and social classes, then, can be 'basic', 'fractional' or 'contradictory', but these distinctions are not the only ones that Marx used in the analysis of class relations. Societies are rarely, if ever, organised around a single set of relations of production. They are the outcome of complex historical processes and will combine, to a greater or lesser degree, various relations of production, in whole or in part. One mode of production may be of primary importance in the overall structure of the society, but there may be secondary forms of production that have a significant effect on class divisions. The emergence of capitalist societies from their feudal predecessors, for example, did not result in the immediate disappearance of feudal relations of production. Elements of the former mode of production survive and may persist for some time, albeit in forms that are altered by their subordination to the newly dominant capitalist relations of production (Mackenzie 1976). Alongside the basic, fractional and contradictory class situations associated with the dominant relations of production, then, it is necessary to consider secondary class situations that may, at any particular time, form the basis of distinct social classes. For example, Marx saw the peasantry in modern capitalist societies as 'survivals' from the feudal past, and he saw the small artisans as surviving elements of small commodity production. Peasants and artisans, as occupants of secondary class situations, were gradually losing their distinctive class character. The relations of production on which they were based were being progressively eliminated, and their members were, in consequence, being absorbed into the mainstream of the proletariat, or its fractions.

The most important of the secondary or 'transitional' social classes that Marx identified in modern capitalism was the class of big landowners. The famous unfinished chapter 52 of *Capital* volume 3 (Marx 1864–5), where Marx had intended to set out his views on class in full, began with a recognition of the 'three great classes' – wage labourers, capitalists and landowners – that had been identified by Adam Smith. This has led some commentators to see Marx as having abandoned his dichotomous model of basic classes, but this was not the case. Marx was, indeed, pointing out that modern capitalist society contained three 'great' social classes, but one of these was a particularly strong, cohesive and well-entrenched 'transitional' social class. This was made perfectly clear in the manuscripts for the so-called *Theories of Surplus Value* (Marx 1862–3)

Relations of possession	Class situations		
	Basic	Fractional	Contradictory
Primary	1	2	3
Secondary	4	5	6

Figure 3 A typology of class situations

that Marx was working on at the same time as the various volumes of *Capital*. Capitalists and wage labourers, he argued, are the basic social classes of the capitalist system. They are 'the sole functionaries and factors in production, their relation and opposition being a result of the very essence of the capitalist mode of production'. Landlords, on the other hand, derive their productive importance not from capitalist relations of possession but from 'property relations handed down to capitalism' (cited in Bukharin 1925: 283). The non-capitalist relations of possession on which landlords depend, and from which they derive their ground rent, are incorporated as secondary elements in a system of production that is shaped by the dominant capitalist relations of personal possession.

The class structure of a society, then, is a complex matter that reflects its particular combination of relations of production. Figure 3 sets out a reconstruction of Marx's typology of class situations. The principal axis of a class structure is defined by the basic, fractional and contradictory class situations of its dominant relations of possession (types 1, 2 and 3 in the figure). Where societies have secondary or transitional relations of possession, these will also define basic, fractional or contradictory class situations (types 4 to 6 in the figure). The particular social classes of a society will be formed around one or more of these class situations, and complex and quite variable patterns of social stratification will be found when comparing societies. While Marx saw stratification in capitalism as subject to a long-term process of structural 'simplification', whereby secondary relations of possession would be eliminated and the principal axis of class divisions would be reduced to the polarised opposition of its basic social classes, he recognised that, at any particular time, particular capitalist societies are likely to have more than just two social classes.

The *Manifesto* model of class emphasised class struggle as well as class structure, and Marx gave a great deal of attention to the ways in which social classes can become organised into the trade unions, political parties and other associations that give voice to their interests. This issue of collective agency was analysed through a distinction between the 'class-in-itself' and the 'class-for-itself'. Social classes exist 'in themselves' by virtue of the fact that their members occupy similar positions in relation to the means of production. They are aggregates of people who occupy a range of class situations and that have specific economic functions and interests in common. A class-in-itself will have little more than an objective similarity of interests and life chances, a demographic unity, and a rudimentary level of 'class awareness', definite forms of consciousness specific to them as members of that class and that involve a sense of 'difference' from members of other groups in their society. This awareness is limited to a recognition of similarities in attitudes, behaviour and life style with other members of the class, and need not involve a recognition of class membership. Indeed, the class awareness of a class-in-itself may often eschew the language of 'class', it may even involve 'a denial of the existence or reality of classes as much as it may an affirmation of them' (Giddens 1973a: 111). As Joyce has aptly reminded us, 'the consciousness of a class need not be the consciousness of class' (1992: 202).

Class awareness may, for example, involve reference to assumed national, ethnic, religious or other characteristics that imply specific status judgements. What Giddens calls 'class identity' occurs only when the language of class is used as a fundamental element in the construction of individual and collective identities. Higher levels of class consciousness involve a conception of an opposition of interests to those of other classes, a willingness to enter into industrial and political struggles in pursuit of these interests, and, ultimately, a recognition that the realisation of these interests may involve a structural transformation of the existing relations of possession (Giddens 1973a: 112–13). When people have only a minimal awareness of their class membership and of common class interests, they are less likely to engage in collective action of a distinctively 'class' character. Social classes become classes 'for themselves' only when this rudimentary class awareness gives way to a strong sense of community that is expressed in a proper 'class consciousness' and a political organisation that allows it to act collectively on the historical scene. This process of growing class consciousness was seen by Marx as driven by economic change: progressively deteriorating economic circumstances created the conditions in which people would be impelled – as a matter of urgency – to enter into collective action aimed at improving or altering their circumstances. Marx held that, as a result, the development of class consciousness was a cumulative process, the level of class consciousness increasing as a direct consequence of the experience of class struggle. It is through the achievement of such class consciousness that an aggregate of competing individuals becomes a cohesive collectivity: 'The separate individuals form a class only in so far as they have to carry on a common battle against another class; otherwise they are on hostile terms with each other as competitors' (Marx and Engels 1846: 72).

It was in these terms that Marx analysed the consciousness and action of the peasantry. They are, he argued, a mass of people that live under similar social conditions, but they are divided from one another by geography and by their mode of production. Each peasant family is virtually self-sufficient and self-contained: it is not involved in any significant market relations and so there is little interconnection between one village and another. There is no awareness of any common regional or national economic interests. The structure of the class is 'formed by simple addition of homologous magnitudes, much as potatoes in a sack form a sack of potatoes' (Marx 1852a: 124). From this he drew a general conclusion:

> In so far as millions of families live under economic conditions of existence that separate their mode of life, their interests and their culture from those of the other classes, and put them in hostile opposition to the latter, they form a class. In so far as there is merely a local interconnection among these small-holding peasants, and the identity of their interests begets no community, no national bond and no political organisation among them, they do not form a class. (1852a: 124)

This is the central structural problem of the peasantry: it is a demographically formed social class with interests that are distinct from those of other social classes, but it has no communal solidarity, no class consciousness and no political organisation. It is a mere 'mass', it is a class-in-itself but not a class-for-itself. As such, it is particularly susceptible to false consciousness and to manipulation from above. In his study of French politics, Marx held that the peasantry looked to a 'master' who would provide for them, and that they found this in the name 'Napoleon' carried by Louis Napoleon.[21]

The class consciousness of a dominant class, Marx argued, tends to form the dominant ideology of its society. As such, it not only unifies the dominant class by forging it into a class-for-itself, it also shapes the outlook of members of the subordinate social classes. Through its incorporation into the political and cultural institutions of the society it becomes a 'hegemonic' force (Gramsci 1929–35) and sets the basic parameters of discourse. As Marx and Engels famously put it:

> The ideas of the ruling class are in every epoch the ruling ideas: i.e., the class which is the ruling *material* force of society, is at the same time its ruling *intellectual* force. The class which has the means of material production at its disposal, has control at the same time over the means of mental production, so that thereby, generally speaking, the ideas of those who lack the means of mental production are subject to it. The ruling ideas are nothing more than the ideal expression of the dominant material relationships which make the one class the ruling one. (1846: 64)

Instead of developing an autonomous class consciousness, then, members of subordinate social classes may be heavily influenced by the ideas and values of those who exploit them. They develop only a limited class awareness and may be subject to a 'false consciousness' of their real situation. In capitalist societies, for example, workers are continually subject to the distorting influence of bourgeois ideas. For the proletariat to become a class-for-itself, its members must break with bourgeois ideas and develop an autonomous class consciousness that is rooted in its own real circumstances and interests. This autonomous class consciousness allows the proletariat to develop into a properly revolutionary force. Marx held, however, that workers were unlikely to develop a revolutionary class consciousness without the help of intellectuals from outside their class, and this view was taken up in Lenin's (1902) argument that workers could spontaneously develop only a 'trades union consciousness'. This form of consciousness involves an awareness of the need to combine in order to oppose employers and governments over economic issues of wages and working conditions. When workers possess a trade union consciousness, collective action tends to be organised around the sectional interests inherent in specific proletarian class situations. The recognition of class interests is limited to the interests of particular occupations and trades and does not stretch to a comprehension of the interests of the social class as a whole. A revolutionary class consciousness, however, involves a broadening of concerns within the social class, industrially and geographically, and a recognition of the need to transform the relations of possession from which class relations arise. Members of the proletariat, Lenin argued, were so tightly constrained by their position within the capitalist system that their spontaneous consciousness was unable to break beyond the bounds of 'bourgeois' concerns and could contribute little to the development of socialism. This is, of course, a contentious position, and one of the major areas of theoretical and political disagreement within Marxism has been over the issue of whether revolutionary class consciousness can develop spontaneously within proletarian parties, as a result of their members' practical experiences of class struggle, or requires the directing and guiding activities of socialist intellectuals. All Marxists recognised the critical role of party organisation and the role of intellectuals in proletarian parties, but Lenin emphasised the need for a socialist party to play the leading part in guiding the development of class consciousness. The policies and programme of the party itself expressed the intellectual world view of party activists, not the immediate and spontaneous ideas of the workers themselves.

Class consciousness is not simply the current state of class opinion. It is a rationally formed intellectual understanding of the actual structure of class relations and, as such, the class consciousness of the proletariat

> is not a question of what this or that proletarian or even the whole proletariat momentarily imagines to be the aim. It is a question of what the proletariat is and what it consequently is historically compelled to do. Its aim and historical action is prescribed, irrevocably and obviously, in its own situation in life as well as in the entire organisation of contemporary society. (Marx and Engels 1845: 47)

An appreciation of this was more likely to result from intellectual investigations than from the practical experiences of the workers themselves. Only through contact with politically committed intellectuals could the proletariat develop a proper appreciation of their own situation. From this it is but a small step to seeing these intellectuals as the 'vanguard' of the proletariat and, therefore, as legitimately able to speak and act on behalf of the proletariat so long as it remains in a state of false consciousness (see also Lukács 1923). I will return to these ideas in my consideration of the idea of the 'working class' in chapter 8.

The principal conceptual problem in Marx's empirical studies is his assumption that social classes can be seen as historical actors. Marx assumes that a class-conscious class-for-itself can be understood as acting as a class and that this is manifest in the actions of the associations that 'represent' its interests or that constitute its 'leadership'. Such claims about the relationship between social classes as collectivities and 'parties' as organised associations are, as Weber was to show, by no means straightforward. While it is possible to show that particular individuals and groups drawn from social classes act in certain ways, this is a very different matter from asserting that social classes *per se* are acting in that way. A claim, for example, that the Parisian proletariat threatened violence against the Provisional Government of 1848, or that the peasantry supported Louis Napoleon, is far from simple. These statements may, of course, be interpreted as asserting that certain members of these classes threatened violence or supported Louis Napoleon, but this would require Marx to show that the wider membership of the classes could be assumed to acquiesce in the actions of those who act in their name and 'represent' their interests. In fact, Marx produced no such evidence, and Hamilton (1991) has highlighted this as a central theoretical problem in Marx's work.

Some have gone further and have argued that the very idea of 'representation' is logically untenable (Hindess 1987; see also Hirst 1977; Hall 1977). What is clear is that social classes, as such, rarely act, and that the linkage between class situation, social class and party formation is a complex matter for empirical investigation. In studying particular societies, it is unlikely that the actions of parties, governments and social movements can be understood without some reference to the status and command situations that operate alongside class situations and the particular historical circumstances that shape their interconnections.

Economic foundations of capitalist class relations

Marx's (1852b) letter to Weydemeyer had made clear the debt that Marx felt he owed to the classical economists. Not only had they given the concepts of class and class struggle their modern meanings, they had also traced the changing historical forms of class relations and illuminated their 'economic anatomy'. Marx's concern for economic theory, over a period of 40 years, was motivated by his desire to improve upon the theories that 'bourgeois' economists had produced to *explain* class relations. Whether the particular explanations that Marx offered can be regarded as satisfactory is, of course, an important matter, but of far greater importance is his demonstration that historical descriptions of class relations must be related to theoretical explanations of their dynamics.

The classical economists had seen class relations as relations of interdependence and had focused their attention on the distribution of income and wealth among the various classes. Marx, on the other hand, started out from the assumption that class relations were relations of exploitation. In order to understand exploitation, he held, it was necessary to examine the relations of production rather than merely those of distribution. The central inference that Marx drew from this basic idea was that capitalist class relations are integrally linked to patterns of capital accumulation. The structure of class exploitation shapes the direction and the pace of capital accumulation, which, in turn, sets the parameters within which class relations vary.

Marx's views on this matter did not emerge fully formed, but developed piecemeal over many years. His earliest work on economic theory (Marx 1844) had been written under the immediate influence of Hegelian ideas, and he saw class in terms of the 'alienation' that occurred in market relations. Labour, he argued, is a commodity, and the proletarian 'alienates' (or sells) labour on the market and, in so doing, also alienates any control over the products of that labour. The goods and services that are produced during the period of employment become the private property of the capitalist and, by acquiring possession of these alienated products, the capitalist can sell them and so can recoup the money that has been paid out in wages to the workers. Any surplus over and above the costs of production form the profit of the capitalist. Through the alienation of labour, proletarians receive only a part of what they produce and capitalists benefit at their expense. Profit, therefore, results directly from the alienation of labour, and Marx was later to describe this process as 'exploitation'.

Central to Marx's concerns at this stage was the labour market, which he saw as a system of conflict, or competitive relations. It is the laws of supply and demand for labour, he argued, that determine the level of wages and, therefore, the distribution of the social product between workers and capitalists. The supply of labour depends upon the size of the workforce and on the intensity of the competition for jobs among workers. The demand for labour, on the other hand, depends upon the number of employers and the degree of competition among them. The balance that is struck between supply and demand depends upon the level of competition between workers and capitalists. Wherever workers are able to form trade unions or other forms of co-operative association, they can limit the damaging competition that divides them from one another. Reducing or eliminating this competition gives them more control over the price at which they sell their own labour and, therefore, the share of production that goes in profits.

Collective action by trade unions, however, is not an inevitable consequence of capitalist relations. It depended, as I have shown, on the state of class consciousness in the proletariat and the extent to which it had become a class-for-itself. In the absence of strong trade union organisation, wage and profit levels were directly shaped by individual market competition. Wages decline during periods of economic depression, because high levels of unemployment lead to an over-supply of labour, while in periods of growth, on the other hand, the buoyant demand for labour and increased competition among capitalists lead to rising wages (Mandel 1967: 31). The boom–slump cycle of the capitalist economy, then, drives a cycle of rising and falling wage levels. Behind these cyclical fluctuations, however, Marx saw long-term processes at work. With each period of expansion, competitive pressures force some capitalist firms out of business and the total number declines. The number of the unemployed and the poor, on the other hand, increases with each slump. The bargaining power of the proletariat declines, while the smaller number of capitalists are able to secure an ever-growing proportion of the total product as wages fall relative to profits. The result of these tendencies, therefore, is a polarisation of classes and the impoverishment, or 'pauperisation', of the proletariat. Though there is some ambiguity in his remarks, Marx seems to have seen this impoverishment as relative rather than absolute. Even if the overall standard of living of the workers increases as a result of economic growth, capitalists benefit disproportionately from this growth and the gap between rich and poor becomes ever greater in relative terms.[22]

This market-based model of class exploitation was at the heart of Marx's earliest writings on economic matters. While writing the *German Ideology* (1846), however, Marx and Engels came to adopt Ricardo's distinction between the price of a commodity and its 'exchange value'. What Marx recognised was that the exchange value of a commodity on the market was its cost of production and that this was 'the axis around which prices fluctuate' (Mandel 1967:

47). If the price of a commodity exceeds its cost of production for any period, increasing profits will attract new producers. Conversely, if the price remains below its cost of production, then producers will go out of business. This argument – developed at length in *The Poverty of Philosophy* (1847) and in *Wage Labour and Capital* (1849) – significantly enlarged Marx's earlier view on competition by showing more precisely how the underlying historical tendencies were generated.

From this recognition, Marx went on to see exploitation as something that could be explained only in terms of a labour theory of value. The cost of production of a commodity, he argued, was nothing but the labour time that was necessary to produce it. This argument, forcibly stated by Ricardo but abandoned by subsequent economists, was seen by Marx as the key to understanding capitalist society:

> labour is the essence of exchange value, because in a society founded on the division of labour it is the only connecting web that makes possible comparison and commensurability between the products of the labour of individuals who are separated from each other. (Mandel 1967: 48–9)

This labour theory of value became fundamental to Marx's whole scheme, and his crucial innovation was to apply it to labour itself. The value of labour, he argued, is determined by the costs of maintaining the labourer as a healthy and productive worker. This cost falls with increasing productivity and so there is a tendency for wages to fall over time. The level to which wages can fall is ultimately limited by the minimal subsistence requirements of labour (the need for food, shelter, education and so on): wages cannot fall below this level without undermining the ability of labour to reproduce itself. While Marx saw the minimal level of wages as being closely linked to the physical means of subsistence, he also recognised that there was a 'historical' element involved as well. While the physical *capacity* to work may depend upon the input of a particular number of calories to replace lost energy and on the meeting of the basic physical and physiological needs of the human body, the *motivation* to work depends upon the achievement of a particular, culturally defined standard of living (Marx 1867: 275; Mandel 1976: 66–7). In so far as culturally specific consumer goods come to be seen as 'normal' and expected elements in standards of living, the minimal level of wages will reflect these cultural expectations as well as physical 'needs'. There is, it may be said, a 'status' element in wages, as these expectations are determined by cultural conceptions of a 'traditional standard of life' (Marx 1865). The value of labour, then, is not a fixed quantity. The minimum level is set by historically determined subsistence standards, and the maximum level is limited only by the need for capitalists to earn a level of profit that is sufficient to stop them from going out of business. The actual wage level in a particular economy will lie somewhere between this maximum and the subsistence minimum, and will depend upon the relative bargaining power of capitalists and workers and, in particular, on the extent to which they are formed into class-conscious collectivities.

In manuscripts that he wrote in 1857 and 1858, Marx made a further series of innovations that became the basis of the concept of 'surplus value' that he first set out in *A Contribution to the Critique of Political Economy* (Marx 1859a) and that became the cornerstone of his argument in *Capital*. His new argument was that exploitation is possible because a proletarian sells 'labour power' – the capacity to work – and not a fixed amount of labour.[23] In return for the payment of a wage, an employer obtains the use of the labour power of the employee for a specific period of time. The value of the commodities that can be produced during this time depends upon the length of the working period and the intensity of work. The difference between the value actually produced and the value of the labour power that produced it is the 'surplus value' and is, Marx held, the 'secret' of capitalist production. Surplus value – the 'surplus product' in monetary form – is the source of the profit that meets the 'capital' costs of investment in maintaining and improving the means of production and also the 'revenue' that meets the capitalist's own personal consumption (Marx 1867: 738). From this standpoint, 'exploitation' is reconceptualised as the appropriation of surplus value. The proletariat is the source of value, but a part of this value passes into the possession of capitalists.[24] These capitalists, by appropriating surplus value, benefit at the expense of the proletariat. The wealth of the capitalist possessing class results from the production and appropriation of surplus value.

It is not necessary to pursue this economic theory any further, as many of its details have been questioned by subsequent writers (see, for example, Bernstein 1899; Böhm-Bawerk 1896; see the discussion in Kolakowski 1978: 295–6).[25] Recent Marxist work has attempted to construct an alternative theory of class exploitation that does not depend upon a theory of value (Roemer 1982; see also Elster 1985). In Wright's formulation of this view, exploitation is seen as a situation in which inequalities are simply the result of 'a particular kind of causal relationship between the incomes of the different actors' (1985: 65). This causal component in life chances involves those in one class situation gaining at the expense of those in another: classes are systematically advantaged or disadvantaged relative to one another.[26]

This conclusion comes full circle to Weber's argument on the relationship between property and market relations, and it highlights the similarity of thought between Marx and Weber on the economic foundations of class relations. Where Weber rejected the need for any generalised theoretical systems, however, Marx correctly saw the need to employ such theories as attempts to explain the dynamics of class relations and class conflict in particular societies.

The case of the capitalist class

Marx's economic model of capitalist class structure was an attempt to explain the interlinked processes of concentration, proletarianisation and polarisation that he saw as characterising capitalist society. While he was writing the final drafts of *Capital*, however, he tried to update his text by assessing the significance of a number of recent trends in business organisation for the development of capitalist class structure. A consideration of these arguments, and their extensions by later Marxists, offers an important insight into how the Marxist approach can be applied in studies of particular societies. Central to the new trends that Marx considered was the joint stock company, which was being used on an ever-increasing basis as the legal form of business enterprise.[27] These changing legal relations, Marx held, were not altering capitalist relations of production but were reinforcing the underlying trends towards concentration, proletarianisation and polarisation.

The concentration of capital into fewer and fewer units, each of which became a monopoly producer in its markets, led to the ownership of capital, and the power that this represented, becoming concentrated in fewer and fewer hands. Marx saw the move from individual capitalist enterprise to the capitalist joint stock company and the credit system of finance as being central to this process. With the introduction of the joint stock company as the principal legal form of capitalist enterprise business undertakings could be expanded by pooling the resources of separate capitalists. Through the credit system, the monetary resources of a whole society could be concentrated in the hands of capitalists, allowing them to increase the scale of their operations even further through mergers and alliances among joint stock companies. In this new stage of capitalism, the relation of bankers (the controllers of loan capital) to industrial and commercial capitalists (the controllers of productive capital) becomes of critical importance for economic development (Marx 1867: 777–8; 1864–5: 528–9).

This growing concentration of capital, Marx held, would lead to the progressive disappearance of 'intermediate' classes, as their members could no longer secure a livelihood from their small property holdings. Small owners were squeezed out by the large monopolies and became proletarianised, having no option but to resort to the sale of their labour power on the market. Marx also anticipated that skill differences within the proletariat would become less salient as skilled labour was reduced to an unskilled level and all workers became mere elements in the vast 'collective worker' that resulted from the modern division of labour (1867: 468). He also held that the poor would continue to grow as an absolutely impoverished level of the proletariat. The 'surplus population' of the unemployed, irregular and casual workers, the infirm, the disabled and the 'lumpenproletariat' of vagabonds, criminals and prostitutes increased in numbers along with the accumulation of capital (1867: 784ff, 797). In consequence, the class structure becomes polarised around an opposition between bourgeoisie and proletariat:

> Along with the constant decrease in the number of capitalist magnates, who usurp and monopolize all the advantages of this process of . . . [centralisation], the mass of misery, oppression, slavery, degradation and exploitation grows. (1867: 929)

These empirical statements were initially questioned by Bernstein (1899), who questioned Marx's account of the joint stock company. Marx had seen the joint stock company as introducing a differentiation of 'money capitalists' from subordinate managers. In companies, ownership takes the form of company shares, and the money capitalist – the 'mere owner' – is concerned solely with earnings from shares and their transfer through stock exchange dealings. The 'mere manager', on the other hand, plays no part in ownership, but is involved in the day-to-day functioning of the means of production and the employment of labour (Marx 1864–5: 567, 571). The direct link between possession and command had been broken, and authority in the workplace was exercised by those who had no personal ownership stake in the enterprise. It was this separation of possession and command that led Bernstein to argue that the joint stock company involved the virtual dispossession of the capitalist owner. The concentration of capitalist *enterprises* could proceed without a corresponding concentration in share *ownership*. Money capital, in the form of company shares, is spread among a large number of 'investors'. Instead of private wealth being concentrated in fewer hands, Bernstein held, it could be spread among a large number of small property holders who need to take no part in the actual running of the enterprise. Bernstein saw this as a condition for further changes in technology and in the organisation of production that were transforming the class structure. The growth of the managerial function produced large numbers of clerks and managers in new 'intermediate' class situations and a decline in the size of the proletariat. Far from becoming polarised, Bernstein held, the class structures of capitalist societies were becoming more complex.

This revisionist argument was rejected by orthodox writers such as Kautsky (1892), for whom the joint stock company was not revolutionising the class structure but was merely consolidating the existing pattern (see also Przeworski 1977). Money capitalists were able to use the joint stock company to attract mass savings through the issue of a large number of small-denomination shares, but this involved no reduction in their power. The money capitalists remained the principal shareholders and retained full powers of control over the process of production. The debate between the revisionists and the orthodoxy was taken in a radically new direction by the Austro-Marxists, most notably Karl Renner and Rudolph Hilferding. While broadening the philosophical basis of Marxism, they undertook a systematic reconsideration of the actual development of capitalism since Marx's own days, linking the rise of the joint stock company and the credit system to the restructuring of world trade.

Marx had never produced his intended book on world trade, and Hilferding's *Finance Capital* (1910) can be seen not only as an attempt to provide such a book, but also as an attempt to show how world trade had changed since Marx wrote *Capital*. Hilferding started out from the concentration of capital in the sphere of circulation, where banks and other investment mechanisms had used the joint stock form to promote and to expand large-scale industrial monopolies that limited the degree of market competition and, thereby, raised the level of profit. This fusion of banking and industrial capital into monopolistic units of 'finance capital', each controlled by a tight knot of money capitalists, was the basis of more regulated markets and more 'organised' national economies. Nation states became stronger and more centralised, intervening in the economy to support the overseas expansion of the national monopolies. State intervention and imperialism, then, were the two faces of the consolidation of finance capital.

Hilferding saw this structure of organised finance capitalism as producing some significant changes in class structure. Capitalists were no longer entrepreneurs who united possession and command within a specific enterprise. They were mere money capitalists, rentiers dependent on dividends from the 'fictitious capital' that they owned. By becoming money capitalists, they could become 'finance capitalists' by holding controlling blocks of shares. The principal shareholders and directors in joint stock companies were a 'financial oligarchy' involved in the functioning of 'real capital' and who controlled the whole mass of joint stock capital and the banking system. At the same time, the petty bourgeoisie were forced to ally themselves with large-scale capitalists as the price of their own survival. Within the large capitalist enterprises there had been an expansion of management, but the growing numbers of managers, clerks, foremen and technicians undertook the 'function of supervision' (Menshikov 1969) on behalf of the finance capitalists to whom they remained subordinate. There was some disagreement within Austro-Marxism as to whether these dependent white collar workers could be seen as occupying distinctive class situations and were being formed into a new 'intermediate' social class. Renner, at least in his later life, believed that they were, indeed, becoming a new 'service class'. Hilferding, on the other hand, believed that they were subject to a process of proletarianisation.

The ideas of Hilferding, as summarised by Lenin, became the core of the new orthodoxy in Marxist thought and spawned a number of studies of capitalist classes in different countries. Rochester's (1936) study, sponsored by the Labour Research Association and published by the communist publishing houses of International Publishers in New York and Lawrence and Wishart in London, was specifically intended as an application of this model to the American situation, regarded as prototypical for finance capitalism in general. Rochester documented the gradual supersession of entrepreneurial industrial capitalists by finance capitalists from the 1890s. The legal form of the corporation or joint stock company, first used on any scale in the building of the railways, became the basis of large-scale enterprises in mining and manufacturing, allowing enterprises in these industries to draw on the large pools of capital that they needed to meet the growing consumer market. Massive industrial enterprises such as Standard Oil and American Tobacco – popularly termed 'trusts' – came to dominate the economy, and while a number were broken up by anti-trust actions, a spate of mergers in the 1920s re-established some of these monopolies and created new ones: American Telephone and Telegraph, United States Steel, General Motors, Pennsylvania Railroad, and so on.

Critical to this process of monopolisation, Rochester argued, had been the activities of the New York banks, themselves the result of a process of concentration in banking. Initially concerned with government debt, the Wall Street bankers developed practices of investment banking (corporate finance) and commercial banking (short-term loans and overdrafts) through the leading role that they took in the development of the railways, and they applied these techniques to the new industrial enterprises from the 1890s. J. P. Morgan, for example, used his bank to promote General Electric, United States Steel, and many other companies, while the Rockefellers channelled profits from Standard Oil into the National City Bank and then used this to finance mergers in the copper industry and other sectors of the economy. In this way, then, the 'fusion' of banking and industry occurred in the United States:

> The fusion of banking and industrial capital was thus a material fact and gave the basis for the new fusion of interest and the criss-cross of directorships, with bankers of all kinds on the boards of industrial corporations and industrialists on the boards of banks and insurance companies. (Rochester 1936: 29)

Finance capitalists do not depend on personal possession alone. Instead, their power derives from the ability to use other people's money to purchase controlling blocks of shares. By virtue of their control over banks, they are able to control industrial enterprises while having little or no personal shareholding in them. Their control over the banks, however, remains a relation of personal possession, backed up by intercorporate shareholdings and inter-locking directorships. According to later research by Menshikov (1969: 149ff), the organisation of investment banks as partnerships rather than as joint stock companies was the key to the whole system of finance capital: the shareholding and lending activities of the investment bankers and the presence of their partners on other financial boards allowed the possessors of the investment banks to dominate the whole of the American economy.

The leading families of finance capitalists were seen by Rochester and Menshikov as standing at the heads of large industrial and financial groups, clusters of companies subject to common co-ordination through stockholdings, interlocking directorships and other types of intercorporate relation. Morgan, Rockefeller and Mellon headed the leading groups, while secondary positions were taken by Schiff, Warburg, Higginson, Peabody, Harriman, Lehman and other families. Nevertheless, Menshikov argues, holdings by financial institutions (banks, insurance companies, investment trusts, etc.) have grown since the 1930s, and the largest enterprises are increasingly controlled not by specific majority or minority stakes but by the collective blocks held by ten or twenty big financial institutions. This situation of 'joint control' rests on tacit consent among the directors and managers of the institutions to support particular policies for the enterprises that they control. Thus, single-family financial groups, Menshikov argues, will increasingly be replaced by groups controlled by alliances of families (1969: 216–17).

At the heart of each financial group – whether controlled by a single family or by an alliance of families – is a core of tightly controlled enterprises. These are surrounded by other enterprises in which the central family and its associated enterprises are the dominant force, and these, in turn, are surrounded by a large number of enterprises in which the family is influential. As influence is generally shared with other capitalist families, the groups overlap with one another at their outer edges, only the inner cores of controlled companies being distinct from one another.[28]

In the 1930s, Rochester saw the Morgan and Rockefeller groups as epitomising this structure. The core Morgan enterprises included Bankers Trust, First National Bank, Pullman, AT&T, and IT&T, and Morgan interests were dominant in Continental Oil, General Electric, General Motors, and United States Steel. In fact, she suggests, Morgan partners controlled or influenced 444 large enterprises (Rochester 1936: appendix D). The Rockefeller core – Chase

National Bank and the Standard Oil companies – was somewhat smaller, but was the basis on which Rockefeller interests controlled or influenced 288 enterprises. The Morgan group, according to Rochester, comprised companies with highly dispersed shareholdings, 'the most advanced stage' of corporate control (1936: 105, 115). They were not, however, 'managerial' enterprises of the kind anticipated by Berle and Means (1932). They were controlled by the Morgan interests through complex interweaving intercorporate relations. The boards of directors of the leading companies, then, were drawn from these financier groups and from other wealthy capitalist families, such as Ford, Du Pont, Vanderbilt, Guggenheim and others.

Perlo's (1957) study explored American financial groups in the immediate post-war period, while Menshikov (1969: chapter 6) extended this into the 1960s. Menshikov suggested that joint control of groups had become more widespread since the 1930s and that groups also overlapped far more than in the past. There was, he held, a growing interconnection of interests among the members of the financial oligarchy. Aaronovitch (1961: chapter 3) has adopted a similar approach for the investigation of British capitalism. The financial groups in the British economy, he argues, are controlled by alliances of families and they overlap to form an extensive intercorporate system, the groups including those associated with Morgan Grenfell, Lazards, and the Rothschilds.

Rochester saw the major property-owning families in the United States as relatively few in number. They were shortly to be described by Lundberg (1937) as 'America's sixty families'. These families were seen as the core of the capitalist class, which stretched beyond them:

> within the capitalist class there are many gradations of power. And great numbers of comfortable parasites, including some of the wealthiest men and women in the country along with all the smaller investors, take no part in the management of the banks and the corporations from which they draw their incomes. (Rochester 1936: 85)

The active 'managerial' power in the large enterprises was held by the inner group of finance capitalists, the oligarchy of the sixty families, who compete and co-operate with one another in securing the global expansion of the American economy. On these depend the much larger rentier fraction within the class, the section that lives on dividends and interest payments and that takes no active part in running the businesses. Through the use of inter-corporate relations and the manipulation of other people's money, Rochester argued, the financial oligarchy could generate massive incomes for themselves and the other members of their class. What unifies the occupants of these various class situations into a single and cohesive social class, then, is the economic dependence of rentiers on massive diversified portfolios of investment, giving them system-wide economic interests (Menshikov 1969: 206), and the relations of intermarriage and mobility that connect them (Sweezy 1951).

The social class of capitalist owners is the basis of recruitment to positions of political authority, forming the social class into a 'ruling class'. Ever since the foundation of the United States, Rochester argues, capitalist owners have monopolised political power, and with the development of monopoly capitalism, the state 'has been increasingly the instrument of the ruling minority within the capitalist class' (1936: 121). Thus, there is no difference between the two main political parties – Republicans and Democrats – so far as their basic policies are concerned. Both are the tools of the capitalist interests that they represent within the state. Finance capitalists divide evenly, and almost at random, in their support for the two parties, some giving their support, personally and financially, to both of them. Despite some overlap and circulation between positions of political command and finance capitalist situations, few finance capitalists are actively involved in government. More typical is the involvement in political command of corporate lawyers, the relatives of finance capitalists, and the rentiers who depend on the finance capitalists:

> since administrative officials are themselves of the capitalist class or have made a political career through service to that class, they mutually maintain the class character of the government. (1936: 129)

Forms of 'regulation' over business, for example, operate to the advantage of business itself, and not the wider public. The state is kept in line through the lobbying activities of finance capitalists and their business organisations, and by electoral considerations – mass support for the political parties being built up through the propaganda disseminated by media enterprises (1936: 135–6).

A critical issue in Marxist research on the bourgeoisie has been the question of the 'intermediate' class situations occupied by managers, and there is much ambivalence over this. Menshikov (1969), for example, holds that while some capitalists may themselves undertake managerial tasks as employees of the corporations that they control, the great bulk of managers are propertyless. Top managers stand with the capitalists as exploiters, opposed to the subordinate workforce, but as they are not possessors of capital they remain subordinate to the capitalist controllers. He concludes that top managers 'are part of the monopoly bourgeoisie' but 'form a special category whose characteristic feature is that they are in a directly subordinate position to the financial oligarchy . . . Thus, the capitalist top managers are a special component of the contemporary monopoly bourgeoisie' (1969: 91). This implies that the capitalist social class is formed from the three distinct class situations of the finance capitalist, the rentier and the top managers or executives, and to these might be added also those in surviving entrepreneurial class situations.

A number of contemporary Marxists have made further attempts to conceptualise the positions of managerial and clerical workers as 'contradictory' class situations and to see whether they might form a 'new middle class'. Many of these writers, however, have departed from the Marxist concept of class and have stressed the importance of authority relations. Marx had seen a direct link between personal possession and workplace authority in the person of the capitalist entrepreneur, but suggested that this direct link between class situation and command situation had altered in the large business enterprise. Recent Marxists have pursued this idea and have seen the growth of bureaucracy in large-scale business enterprises as establishing forms of authority that exert a separate and distinct impact on the life chances of managers, administrators and clerks. The more influential of these discussions (see, for example, Wright 1976) have attempted to incorporate authority relations into the framework of class analysis itself, rather than seeing the new occupations as resulting from a specific combination of property and authority, of class situation and command situation.

I will pursue these issues in chapter 6, but some preliminary remarks are necessary here. Marx's own model of class recognised a close association between class and command. Personal possession of the means of production was the basis of the class situation of the capitalist entrepreneur, it was the basis of their authority within the enterprise and, through different mechanisms, it was the source of their authority within the state. In formulating his idea of the 'ruling class', for example, Marx fused possession, economic authority and political authority into a single concept. Unlike Mosca and the elite theorists that I will consider in chapter 5, however, Marx did not accord primacy to the political level or to authority relations, and he consistently sought to see the economic aspects of 'class' as a separate analytical element from the question of authority.[29] This 'economic' element he saw as a universal feature of all societies and as the predominant driving force in human history. The ruling class of a capitalist society, for example, was rooted in a specific structure of personal possession over the means of production, and it had to be understood in economic terms as a *capitalist class* that also held industrial and political authority.

The work of Wright and others has departed from Marx's perspective and tends to downplay the difference between possession and authority. This is especially apparent in their discussion of intermediate classes. The contradictory class situations that Marx identified were those in which personal possession of small-scale property was combined with the performance of labour. The new class situations that recent Marxist writers have highlighted, however, are defined not by relations of personal possession but by the occupancy of command situations for which specific skills and credentials are required. This recognition that the command situations of managers and certain other occupations are a principal determinant of their life chances, operating alongside the effects of their class situations, is very important. These command situations, involving the exercise of varying amounts of authority in the administrative bureaucracies of large business enterprises, are, however, conceptually quite distinct from their class situations. By assimilating command situation to class situation, however, Marxist discussions of bureaucracy and authority have lost sight of the very distinctiveness of the Marxist concept of class.

While a comprehensive analysis of stratification does, indeed, require a consideration of both class situation and command situation, along with status situation, these dimensions of stratification must remain analytically distinct from one another. The incorporation of elements of command situation into the concept of class situation can result only in a distortion of *both* concepts. It is to prevent this distortion that I have attempted to clarify the central meaning that Marx gave to class and to relate this to the analogous ideas that Weber built into his conspectus of stratification concepts.

Marxian class analysis, then, can find its place within a wider framework of concepts that makes it possible to see the structure of social classes that exist in capitalist societies as being, in the words of Westergaard,

> a web of inequality, anchored in the prevailing relations of production, and made up of inequality of power, authority and influence, inequality of material conditions and security, inequality of opportunity and of access to cultural as well as to material resources, contrasts between relative autonomy and relative dependence in life. (1977: 165)

4

Status, Community and Prestige

'Stratification, in its valuational aspect . . . is the ranking of units in a social system in accordance with a common value system' (Parsons 1953: 388). This definition of stratification highlights a very different aspect from those that are central to Marxian theories. Instead of economic resources and class conflict, Talcott Parsons emphasised communal values and social ranking. This emphasis on the *normative* aspects of social systems identifies 'status' as the principal dimension of social stratification and is the hallmark of 'structural functionalist' or 'normative functionalist' theory. These theorists have produced a powerful conceptualisation of the differentiation of status situations, uncovering the communal structures in which they are rooted and the shared values that sustained them. The stress on status differentiation, however, involved the development of a particularly one-sided theory in which there is little or no recognition of class or of authority as independent dimensions of stratification. In this respect, normative functionalist theory complements the equally one-sided emphasis on class in Marxian theory. The two theories together have the potential to provide a more rounded understanding of social stratification than either can alone.

Despite their recognition of the importance of stratification by status, the work of the normative functionalists centres on a fundamental paradox. While the *concept* of status is central to their work, the *word* was subtly distorted. Weber's concept of status is most generally referred to by normative functionalists as 'ranking', while the word 'status' is used to designate any objectively defined 'position' in a social system. This has caused unbounded, and unnecessary, confusion. As Gordon has argued in his review of American research on stratification, much confusion would have been avoided if the word 'status' had been used in its original Weberian sense and the more neutral term 'position' had been retained for the more general idea of location within a social system (1950: 174). But this was not to be, and the confusion has continued.

While normative functionalists have typically used the word 'status' in preference to the more neutral term 'position', they have used it in a way that involves no necessary reference to social ranking. Thus, Warner claimed that social positions 'may or may not be ranked as superior or inferior' to one another (1952: 46), a claim that he intended as an analytical statement rather than an empirical description of actual social arrangements. His point was that while social positions may, in fact, be ranked in all known societies, it is, nevertheless, possible to distinguish analytically the *definition* of positions from their *evaluation* and *ranking*. The definition of positions and the ranking of these positions are interdependent 'analytical elements' in social stratification.[1] This analytical distinction allows normative functionalists to focus their attention on ranking as the distinctive element that converts a mere system of positions into a system of stratification.

The confusion of 'status' and 'position' has been made worse by the tendency of normative functionalists to equate ranking (i.e. status relations) with social stratification *per se*. Thus, according to Barber, social stratification comprises 'a structure of regularized inequality in which men [sic] are ranked higher and lower according to the value accorded their various social roles and activities' (1957: 7; see also Parsons 1953: 388). This collapsing of stratification into its purely cultural and communal dimension of social standing left no place for an independent analysis of economic class relations. Indeed, the word 'class' was simply seen as equivalent in meaning to 'stratum', social strata being seen as clusters of similarly ranked social positions. With this theoretical framework, it became all but impossible to investigate the relations between class and status as Weber had defined them. This confusion is striking in Shils's statement that 'Class designates an aggregate of persons, within a society, possessing approximately the same status' (1962: 249).[2]

Normative functionalist terminology	Preferred terminology
status	position
rank	status
class	stratum
(social) stratification	stratification by status
economic stratification	stratification by class

Figure 4　A translation of normative functionalist terminology

It is necessary to cut through this confusing and misleading terminology in order to uncover the core of valuable insights that are contained in the works of the normative functionalists. I will endeavour to use a clearer and more consistent terminology in my discussion wherever this brings their ideas into line with Weber's framework. At some points, however, this would be purely pedantic, and so I have continued to use their own words whenever this is unlikely to cause confusion. Where I have altered their terminology to accord with that of Weber, I have adopted the 'translations' that are set out in figure 4. The left-hand column of this figure shows the terminology used by the principal normative functionalist writers, while the right-hand column shows the terminology that has been taken from the Weberian framework.

Values, norms and positions

Normative functionalism has its origins in the sociology of Durkheim. In his critique of Spencer, Durkheim (1893) argued for a recognition of the centrality of normative elements to social life, holding that the actions of individuals and of groups – and, not least, their rational, 'contractual' relations in the market – are shaped by shared norms and ideas. Durkheim saw these norms and ideas as *collective representations* that may be formed into a *conscience collective*, and he pursued the implications of this insight in his investigations of suicide, education and religion, as well as in his comments on social inequality (Filoux 1993: 215ff). The writer who did the most to articulate this view, however, was the American sociologist Parsons, who converted Durkheim's arguments into a more abstract and general theory of society (see Parsons 1937; 1951;

Parsons and Shils 1951; Parsons et al. 1953). It was Parsons who set out a number of influential statements on the theory of stratification as an aspect of a general theory of social systems (1940; 1953; 1970; see also Tausky 1965). Parsons's writings are dense and obscure, though not, perhaps, so uniquely obscure as they are often depicted. Parsons trained a whole generation of sociologists, who often succeeded in formulating his ideas in a much clearer language than he was capable of doing himself, and it was in the hands of these writers that normative functionalism came to be established as the orthodox consensus of Western sociology in the 1950s and early 1960s (Davis 1948; Merton 1957; Levy 1966; Williams 1960; Johnson 1961).

The distinguishing characteristic of normative functionalist theory has been its emphasis on the crucial significance of values and norms in the structuring of social action. The central contention has been the view that societies are organised around 'a more or less common set of values' and so constitute 'moral communities' (Barber 1957: 2). Social order is seen as resulting, above all, from the effect that these cultural meanings have on the members of a society. The most important elements in a culture are *norms*, the ideal standards of conduct that specify the approved ways of attaining culturally defined goals and that regulate social behaviour. Conformity to norms may occur because they are specifically 'sanctioned' in some way or because socialisation into the common values of a culture creates value commitments and a sense of *obligation* to conform to the norms that they underpin. Where these values are internalised, people identify with the social norms and they are likely to conform to them even in the absence of specific sanctions. Wherever values are not integrated with norms in this direct way, social order becomes more precarious and sanctions become all the more important in producing conformity or deviance.

Paradoxically, this assumption of value consensus has rarely been set out in a clear and unambiguous way, leaving considerable doubt as to the ways in which it is to be taken. At least two contrasting interpretations can be given to the idea that societies rest on common values. The first, and strongest, version of the thesis would hold that 'value consensus' involves the idea that there must be an actual *agreement* over value judgements among the members of a society. A second, weaker version of the thesis would hold simply that the members of a society share a common *recognition* of culturally significant values. The strong version requires that the members of a society agree with one another in all the various value judgements that they make about what is right and wrong, good and bad, desirable and undesirable, and so on. Any ongoing society would, then, have to exhibit such agreement in the value commitments of its members. Members of American society, for example, might be held to agree that equality of opportunity is a desirable state of affairs to promote and to pursue. People act in conformity with the value judgements that they make, and the social integration of their actions is a direct result of the integration that exists in their shared system of values. This strong version of the thesis can, of course, be criticised very easily by pointing to the all too evident existence of dissensus and conflict in ongoing societies and to the difficulties that the thesis poses for any attempt to explain the existence of deviance, opposition and subcultures (see Abercrombie et al. 1979; Wrong 1961).

According to the weak version of the thesis, on the other hand, the members of a society simply share a pool of values and meanings to which they may be differentially committed. Members of American society might, for example, be seen as *recognising* the existence of equal opportunity as a culturally significant value, but they could be positive, negative, or indifferent towards it. The value, nevertheless, forms a part of their shared culture; it is part of the common pool of meanings on which they can draw in constructing their various individual or collective definitions and actions. From this point of view, the values of a culture are analogous to the vocabulary and grammar of a language. Those who share a language recognise a common pool of words and grammatical forms on which they must draw if they are to be understood, but it is not necessary to assume that they all have to say the *same* thing. A shared language allows the formulation of a large number – perhaps an infinite number – of different and mutually contradictory statements. Similarly, a shared culture allows the formulation of a large number of different value judgements.

Normative functionalist writers have failed to clarify which of the two variants of the assumption of value consensus they see as fundamental to their theories. Critics of normative functionalism, on the other hand, have generally taken the strong version as the object of their criticisms. While it must be recognised that many normative functionalist theorists have, in fact, posited the existence of agreement over value commitments in their descriptions of particular societies, it is, nevertheless, the case that most of the central tenets of normative functionalism require only the weaker assumption of a shared recognition of significant values. In what follows, I base my presentation on the weak version of the thesis, unless the writers concerned explicitly state their argument in terms of the strong version.

On the basis of the weak assumption of value consensus, it is possible to see that the degree of cultural agreement within a society that has a common culture may be quite variable. While there may, indeed, be some things about which there is a high level of agreement, forming the basis of a dominant system of norms, there may be other norms that are effective only within particular subcultures or are accepted casually or not at all. Norms that are adhered to only within particular subcultures may run counter to dominant norms and may be strongly entrenched through the application of sanctions within the subculture. On the other hand, some norms that are widely shared may be so generalised that it is difficult for people to draw any specific implications for action from them. There are always strains and inconsistencies in cultures, and particularly in those of complex and highly differentiated societies. Thus, Williams has argued that it is essential to examine 'the collision of semiautonomous institutional systems' within a society and the strains that they create for people (1960: 376).[3]

I have so far used the term 'norm' without explaining exactly what it means. A norm is a rule of conduct that is shared by a particular set of people. Durkheim made it very clear that norms were often unconscious and were to be understood as existing independently of their conscious formalisations. Once again, an analogy with language will help. The speaker of a particular language observes its specific rules of grammar, but is able to formulate these rules only in a vague and incomplete way. The codifications that are found in textbooks of grammar, then, are an attempt to formulate the rules that people normally apply in an unconscious way. In the same way, the norms of a group are distinct from the codifications that are found in systems of law, handbooks of manners, and so on. It is important, therefore, to distinguish between the 'internalised' norms that people follow and their 'external' codifications.[4]

Social 'institutions' are sets or systems of interrelated norms that are rooted in particularly important values and so are general throughout a society. Norms are institutionalised if they are widely regarded as obligatory or are sustained by strong sanctions (Williams 1960: 30, 31). Normative functionalists recognise that social institutions are closely linked to the exercise of power. Williams,

for example, remarks that norms may become partially institutionalised by virtue of a consensus among a 'ruling group' that can
impose them on the rest of a society, though he feels that these
imposed norms are not truly institutional. Shils (1961: 6), on the
other hand, is more prepared to recognise that social institutions
invariably involve a degree of imposition and that the actual or
potential use of sanctions is a normal feature of institutionalisation.
The central values that underpin the leading social institutions of
a society, he argues, reflect the concerns of its dominant group and
tend to override the values and interests of more peripheral groups.

Social institutions are central to social stratification because they
define the various social positions that are the objects of social
evaluation and ranking, and they determine the expected patterns
of behaviour that constitute the life styles associated with these
positions.[5] Social positions – 'statuses' in the words of many normative functionalists – are defined by the reciprocal normative
expectations that people share as a part of their common culture
and that are institutionalised within their society. A social position
is, in Warner's words, synonymous with a 'social location' or a
'social place' (1952: 46). Central to the constitution of social positions are normative expectations concerning the rights and obligations that they entail and that specify the attitudes and behaviour
that comprise the 'role' that occupants are expected to perform
(Williams 1960: 35ff; Merton 1957; Gross et al. 1958).

Positions are combined with one another in determinate ways,
and those who occupy certain positions are likely also to hold
specific other positions. A 'husband', for example, is likely to be a
'man' and may also be a 'father'. A 'factory worker' may also be
a 'non-conformist' in religion and an active 'trade unionist'. Linton
held that it is possible to identify typical combinations of positions
in any society and that these may be culturally recognised as giving individuals a composite, overall 'position with relation to the
total society' (1936: 113). The various positions that people occupy
are the bases of their associations and identities, and institutionalised 'overall' positions are especially important sources of identity.
They are also likely to be the objects of social evaluation by others.
It is for this reason that Parsons (1945) held that it is important to
begin the analysis of a society with an identification of its overarching 'membership roles'. These membership roles comprise specific,
socially recognised combinations of social positions and establish
the socially recognised and available social identities.

In the discussion that follows, I present the normative functionalist model of stratification in terms of the weak version of the thesis of value consensus, according to which shared value commitments comprise a pool of meanings from which dominant, subordinate and other value systems can be constructed. It is in this form that it has the most to offer to a broader conception of social stratification, as it emphasises that a diversity of competing values is likely to characterise any complex society. It recognises that the allocation of status in a society may involve a clash of values rather than a harmonious agreement among its members. Complete agreement over value judgements is merely one particular limiting case. Having said this, it must be recognised that many normative functionalists have slipped, almost imperceptibly, from the weak version to the strong version, to which the theory of status stratification is only contingently linked.

Functionalism, Parsons and the status model

Social stratification by status is a result of the subjective evaluations that people make of one another in terms of the commonly recognised values of their society. This point was initially recognised by Durkheim, who saw the *conscience collective* of a society as defining a 'social classification', a public status hierarchy that derives from the valuation of social positions and activities, that defines people's legitimate ambitions and aspirations, and that makes them content to pursue only those goals that are held out to them by the values of their society. In recognising and according moral authority to social inequalities, a social classification legitimises them (Durkheim 1897: 249–50, discussed in Lockwood 1992: 70–1; see also Lee 1994).

Through a process of evaluation, an assessment of the relative 'prestige' of the members of a society is produced, and status situations occur when these conceptions of prestige are formed into stable, institutionalised rankings (Williams 1960: 89). Thus, 'a judgement of rank made about either the total person or relatively stable segments of the person constitutes the *social status* of that person' (Goldhamer and Shils 1939: 245). Value commitments define status situations, and the pursuit of status motivates conformity to the particular life styles associated with these status situations. A person's standing is measured by her or his 'prestige' and by the 'recognition' or 'deference' (appreciation or derogation) that they receive (Shils 1965: 268–70). It is these attitudes of approval and disapproval that sanction life styles. It is by virtue of this social distribution of symbolic sanctions – an aspect of the social distribution of power – that social stratification becomes central to the social order.

Prestige is 'accumulated praise and censure' (Milner 1994: 23),[6] and the amount of prestige that can be built up is a resource that determines the potency of a person's own acts of appreciation and derogation: approval from those who are themselves high in status is, for example, more salient to those who share the values that underpin this status. Prestige, or social honour, symbolises social standing, and those who stand highest in terms of social honour are also likely to be accorded material advantages. The various symbolic and material rewards that people receive are consumed in various ways, and they can be exchanged or converted into other advantages. Money, for example, can be used to buy access to private education, which can, in turn, provide the attributes of social recognition that advantage people in recruitment to highly valued and well-paid social positions. These patterns of consumption and conversion define particular styles of life, and those who positively value their particular style of life will attempt to further distinguish it from that of others through establishing collective and individual practices and identities that set them apart and that symbolise their prestige. Those who do not value their own style of life, because it is imposed on them and involves specific status disadvantages, may, nevertheless, be constrained to follow practices that distinguish them from others and that symbolise their low status. Their exclusion from alternative avenues of interaction by virtue of the power of those in higher status situations confines them to a life style that is not of their own choosing. Where differences of life style are magnified in order to stress differences of prestige, the reinforced activities of the style of life may themselves become the objects of social evaluation and may lead to an increase or decrease in prestige.

Mousnier, for example, has argued that the standing of a group depends upon the social estimation of various aspects of its style of life:

> its rank, honour, rights, duties, privileges, obligations, social symbols, dress, food, coats of arms, way of life, upbringing, its way of spending money, entertainments, social functions, the profession its members should or should not have, the behaviour its members should display in their relationships with members of other groups in various situations in life and the behaviour they can expect in return, the people they should mix with and treat as friends and

equals, and those they should simply coexist with and with whom they should only mix in the course of their social function or through necessity etc. (1969: 25)

The formation of distinctive styles of life is the initial basis of strata formation, which becomes properly established only when demographic processes of inheritance, mobility and exclusion define solidaristic groups with identifiable boundaries that reflect differences in their styles of life (Eisenstadt 1968: 72ff). When this occurs, styles of life may themselves come to be normatively prescribed, and conformity to these group norms becomes a secondary determinant of status. It is through these processes that social estates are formed.[7]

At its simplest, stratification occurs through the direct ranking of individuals on the basis of their personal abilities and capacities, the activities that they are involved in and the social positions that they occupy (Barber 1957: chapter 2). In societies that are small enough for all members to know one another as individuals, evaluation occurs in direct face-to-face encounters and detailed personal knowledge can be the basis of status differentiation. In such systems of 'interactional status', social rankings tend to be fluid and inchoate, and there are only limited possibilities for the formation of stable and persistent social strata (Lockwood 1992: 85). More complex societies – and especially modern societies – involve far fewer direct face-to-face encounters. Interpersonal encounters become elements in more extended and distanciated social relations, and it is difficult for individuals to acquire the kind of personal knowledge of one another that is required for a system of interactional status. As a result, social positions come to be evaluated independently of their occupants, and individuals are accorded status principally on the basis of the positions that they occupy rather than through personal and direct knowledge.

The social positions that are ranked into status situations are, according to Eisenstadt, those that are 'related to the central spheres and symbols of a society, and which represent the community' (1968: 64). Greatest prestige is accorded to those who participate in activities that are 'central' or most 'sacred' to the shared values of a society:

> members of a collectivity who best exemplify the values implicit in its goals – who are, in a way, *closer* to those values than the typical members – are also, for the most part, those who have the highest prestige and hold, or are admitted to, the most prestigious roles. (1971: 32)

Shils has argued that this evaluation in relation to the central core of 'sacred' values gives a 'charismatic' quality to those individuals and associations that are most closely connected to them (1965: 258; see also Milner 1994: 12, 20). They are seen as somehow 'representative' of cherished values and as epitomising highly rated qualities. This view accords with the claim that values tend to reflect functionally important activities and that, therefore, positions that involve the performance of these activities are likely to have a high social standing (Davis and Moore 1945; Davis 1948).[8] Participation in 'functionally important' activities is, at the same time, participation in activities that are 'central' to the society's values. The argument here is that all societies have to resolve certain common functional problems of survival and continuity, and that those activities that contribute to these requirements will tend to be valued more highly than will others. Thus, Barber has claimed that social positions that are involved in activities related to government, economic production, and other 'functionally essential' activities will generally come to be highly valued (1957: 20). It is because of a 'congruence' between values and functions that systems of stratification are able to contribute to the recruitment and motivation of incumbents of functionally important positions. By establishing value commitments and sanctioning behaviour, members of a society are motivated to acquire the training and skills that are required in order to perform the roles that are associated with functionally important positions. Those who are actually recruited to these positions are motivated to remain in them by virtue of the continuing recognition and other rewards that they receive.

There has been much debate over the 'functional' aspects of the normative functionalist theory of stratification (see the reprints in Scott 1996). It is generally very difficult to identify functional requirements with any precision, and many formulations of the theory overstate the congruence between values and functions. Such arguments minimise the possibilities for change that exist in systems of social stratification. In many respects, the functional theory has proved something of a theoretical dead end. The valid residue of the theory, however, is the claim that variations in systems of status stratification are to be explained by variations in value systems, and that prestige will be accorded to those activities that are *perceived* as being functionally important, regardless of whether this perception corresponds to any objectively necessary conditions of survival.[9] According to Parsons, cultural values accord primacy to a problem, and it is this culturally recognised primacy that defines the 'paramount values' of a society. Other functional problems are accorded a secondary importance and play a less important role in stratification. According to Parsons, the paramount values of modern Western societies concern the 'universalism' and 'performance' criteria of the technical efficiency that is involved in activities related to an 'adaptation' function. It is because of these value standards that such stress is placed on the occupational role, which is especially concerned with this function. The paramount values of the former Soviet Union, on the other hand, stressed the criterion of contribution to 'goal attainment', and this led to a particular emphasis being placed on roles in the state-party apparatus.

Status is essentially a *communal* phenomenon that arises through processes of approval and disapproval that rest upon shared meanings within specific communities. Status rankings are tightest and most systematic when the principal positions of a society are clustered into the kind of 'membership roles' that were discussed in the previous section. The membership role, according to Parsons, is an institutionalised social position that combines distinct, specialised positions together and that defines a person's overall 'membership' of a social system. For Parsons, it is the ranking of membership roles that lies at the core of social stratification. They are the basis for the performance of activities that are culturally defined as of functional importance. In relatively undifferentiated societies, communal organisation takes a territorial form. 'Community' is what defines the relationship of a 'population' to its territory, and norms of 'membership' define what it is to be located in that territory (Parsons 1957: 256, 266ff). In these undifferentiated societies, there is a high degree of consensus and consistency in cultural definitions, the whole of the social structure is highly integrated, and membership roles tend to be very clear-cut. As a result, status divisions are especially sharp. In more differentiated societies, specialised social positions have their focus in distinct spheres of activity, and generalised conceptions of social membership and identity come to be located in the specifically communal structure that Parsons termed the 'societal community'.

The societal community comprises the forms of solidarity and mutual loyalty that are a basis of social integration and of the commitment that people have to the groups of which they are members. It is the basis of social solidarity, that 'form of social bond founded on a feeling of common membership in a group united by some commonality' (Mayhew 1990: 298). In modern societies, the societal community has its focus in a conception of the 'nation', understood as a territorial unit of solidarity that tends to be 'associational' rather than 'primordial' in character.[10] The societal community is not a separate and distinct sphere of activity, but comprises the communal aspects of all social relations. The communal bonds of a modern society connect separate households and places of work into an extensive society-wide network which may be differentiated into distinct residential and work districts, but which has a societal significance. The importance of communal relations, understood as an analytical element in action, is that they constitute the processes of communication through which common-alities are discovered or created and a shared culture is transmitted.

Societies vary quite considerably in the ways in which their membership roles are defined. In some societies, membership is defined on the basis of lineage or birth, while in others it may be political authority or control over material wealth that is of critical significance. In modern capitalist societies such as the United States, for example, Parsons saw membership as defined primarily in and through occupational roles. Specialised occupational roles are inte-grated with one another through the societal community and are the basis of 'citizenship', or full membership, in society. It is the centrality of occupational roles to social membership that leads Parsons and other normative functionalist writers to see status situ-ations in contemporary capitalism as arising primarily from the ranking of occupations.

Social positions, such as occupations, may be the *units* of ranking in a system of stratification, but they are not necessarily the direct *objects* of evaluation and judgement. It is, more typically, the prop-erties and attributes associated with the various social positions that are the real objects of value or derogation in relation to the common values. From this point of view, the status accorded to a social position is the resultant of the valuations that are made of its various constituent elements. Parsons identified these elements as the *qualities, performances* and *possessions* that are involved in role behaviour. Social standing is accorded to social positions on the basis of the particular combination of the culturally significant qualities, performances and possessions that they are assumed to involve (Parsons 1953: 389).

The distinction between qualities and performances was first formulated by Linton (1936) as the distinction between 'ascribed' and 'achieved' status. Ascriptive 'qualities' are personal attributes, such as the age or sex of the expected incumbents of social posi-tions, that are generally regarded by actors as fixed, biologically based and inheritable characteristics.[11] Some positions and activities might, for example, be seen as being exclusively prerogatives of the 'elders' of a tribe, of men rather than of women, or of members of a particular kinship lineage. Achieved 'performances', on the other hand, are attributes that incumbents of positions are expected to have acquired through their own efforts. Whether they are actually attained, rather than inherited, is not important. What is important is that actors regard them *as if* they were matters of individual achievement. Thus, educational credentials or occupational success, even where they reflect familial support, may be regarded as valued individual achievements. 'Possessions', finally, are those transferable objects that can be used as facilities or rewards by the occupants of social positions and to which incumbents are accorded – or denied – rights of use and control. They become, that is to say, the objects of property relations.[12] Possessions are important to the social standing of a person because of their 'expressive', emotional significance as the symbols that are associated with an expected style of life. Those who occupy particular positions are expected to follow a particular style of life, for which specific possessions are required and the ownership of which, therefore, symbolises their status. Possessions are 'status symbols'.

The institutionalised 'scale' of status in a social system, then, consists of the rank ordering of central, functionally valued social positions – and, most particularly, of membership roles – on the basis of normative expectations concerning the qualities, performances and possessions that ought to be associated with them. Parsons recognised, however, that there may often be discrepancies between the institutionalised expectations and the qualities, performances and possessions that incumbents actually have. Individuals may, for example, acquire possessions or educational qualifications for all sorts of reasons, and not simply because they are the expected accoutrements of their status. Qualities, performances and possessions are the outcome of a complex set of determinants and may be seen as having both 'material' and normative significance. The operation of material 'power' relations, Parsons argued, may generate a divergence between the actual distribution of qualities, performances and possessions and the institutionalised scale of status.[13] It may be, for example, that the wealth that a person accumulates through market investments is out of proportion to the wealth that someone in their social position is expected to have. Unfortunately, this aspect of Parsons's argument was not at all well developed, and actual, material relations remained a purely residual element in Parsons's scheme. As a result, 'class' is an untheorised and almost unrecognised element in Parsons's work. Although invoked as critical variables in Parsons's (1937) earlier work, political and economic power came to be treated increasingly as residual categories in his theoretical scheme.[14] Lockwood has shown that this analytical failure is rooted in the Durkheimian approach that underlies normative functionalism. He shows that Durkheim did not see status classification as creating material inequalities – it simply recognises and legitimates existing inequalities. For normative functionalists 'the status system legitimates inequalities of power and wealth and serves to integrate the ends of actors by grounding their respective levels of legitimate aspiration' (Lockwood 1992: 83). Durkheim offered no way of explaining these inequalities themselves, and nor have normative functionalists. The material inequalities of class are not treated as structured elements in the theory, except and in so far as they are *normatively structured*:

> Neither 'class' nor 'economic life' is seen as possessing a structure other than that which is given to it by the institutional system. His [Durkheim's] exposition of the sociology of the economic order is almost exclusively devoted to distinguishing the various norms that govern activity and to showing their interrelations. (1992: 80)

In Durkheim and the normative functionalists, the concepts of 'resources', 'possessions', 'power' and 'wealth' were either residual concepts or subject to normative redefinition. Durkheim, Lockwood argues, had invoked these residual concepts to explain disorder – as in situations of 'anomie' – but he had no explanation for them. They were seen merely as random factors that become structured only through their institutionalisation in relation to consensual values.

There is a great paradox in this. If the status hierarchy classifies these material factors, they must *already* be structured. It is not possible for a value system to produce an ordered social classification of things that are randomly distributed. Lockwood concludes, therefore, that the theory of Durkheim and the normative functionalists must be supplemented by another theory that accounts for the 'systematic distribution and redistribution of material resources' (1992: 97). This theory he finds in the Marxian theory of class, to which I would add the Moscavian theory of domination. The normative functionalist analysis of status situation must be complemented by analyses of class situation and command situation.

The existence of paramount and secondary values, especially when combined with an appreciation of the importance of cultural 'strains' and subcultures, highlights the possibility that a society may not have a single, consistent and coherent stratification system. Modern societal communities tend to be 'differentiated publics' (Mayhew 1990: 316), and there may be competing value standards. Parsons held that, in modern societies, positions in the economic, political and other functionally specialised spheres of activity tend to become partially detached from the more diffused and generalised membership position defined by the societal community and so they may not be integrated into a single and coherent structure of status stratification. In these circumstances, there will be a tendency for the stratification system itself to be differentiated into alternative and, perhaps, competing scales of status. The 'membership role' may be the object of a completely different set of values to those that are used to evaluate economic, political, military or other specialised positions. In these circumstances, status becomes multidimensional rather than unitary (Lenski 1952; 1954), and individuals may exhibit 'inconsistent' status profiles: they may, for example, have a high economic status, a low political status, and a moderate educational status. Where the societal community integrates the specialised spheres and guarantees a paramount value system, specialised roles are more likely to be ranked consistently with one another and with the overarching membership role. In these circumstances, it is possible for a 'general prestige continuum' or hierarchy to be established and for social estates to form.

This kind of coherence characterised the stratification systems of the more advanced of the pre-modern societies. Parsons sees these societies as status societies organised around an all-pervasive dominant social estate. The brahmins of traditional India and the nobility of medieval Europe, for example, he saw as dominant social estates whose values sustained general prestige hierarchies that melded differentiated political roles into the more diffuse communal structures of their societies. In modern societies, on the other hand, structural differentiation is seen as having made it much more difficult to sustain either a general prestige hierarchy or a dominant social estate.

Parsons suggested that the paramount values of universalism and performance that are central to modern Western societies make it particularly difficult to sustain a coherent general prestige hierarchy, although he provided no specific evidence in support of this claim. It can be surmised that he saw the diversity of occupational roles and the complexity of the functional activities that they involve as making it highly likely that evaluations of occupational attributes would be inconsistent with one another. As a result, status rankings are much weaker and less well integrated in modern societies than they are in pre-modern societies. There is no general prestige hierarchy and the various dimensions of status evaluation tend to become autonomous from one another. In these circumstances, fragmentation and inconsistency can be prevented only if there are mechanisms of 'inter-larding'. These are 'mechanisms which establish levels of relative equivalence' among the various hierarchies (Parsons 1953: 410; Mayhew 1990). This inter-larding, if it occurs, allows status in one dimension to be 'translated' into status in other dimensions and so allows comparisons of relative standing to be made. This helps to ensure that membership roles will show a degree of 'status crystallisation' or 'status consistency' with other social positions.

Parsons recognised two inter-larding mechanisms. First, he pointed to the market mechanism through which possessions are distributed to various roles. As possessions are central to judgements of status, a market system allows possessions and money to serve as proxies or indicators of status without the need for specialised tasks to be directly compared with one another. Income, for example, can become a yardstick of status in its own right, allowing diverse occupations to be compared in terms of their incomes. Second, he pointed to what he called a 'public communication system', a quasi-market of public opinion through which 'reputation' is distributed in the mass media and other informal channels of communication (Parsons 1953: 411). These two mechanisms, then, allow comparisons to be made through the use of the common currencies of money and public reputation.[15]

Where status situations are more loosely defined and less well integrated through 'inter-larding', stable social estates are less likely to be formed. It is for this reason that Parsons claims that modern Western societies have no single dominant stratum:

one of the most notable features of the American system of stratification is its relative looseness, the absence of a clear-cut hierarchy of prestige except in a very broad sense, the absence of an unequivocal top elite or ruling class; the fluidity of the shadings as well as mobility between groups and, in spite of the prestige-implications of the generalised goal of success, the relative tolerance for many different paths to success. (1953: 431, 407)[16]

Unfortunately, Parsons gave little systematic attention to the conditions that are conducive to the formation of dominant social estates. Indeed, the whole idea of dominance – structures of economic, political and communal power – is untheorised in his work.

Warner and the American case

One of the earliest and most influential attempts to apply a normative functionalist perspective to patterns of stratification in the United States was in a series of studies that were undertaken by Lloyd Warner and his colleagues, and this work serves well to illustrate both the power and the limitations of the normative functionalist approach. In this section, therefore, I will use Warner's studies to show how the status model developed in normative functionalism has been used in investigations of modern societies.

Warner's background was in social anthropology and, having used the ideas of Durkheim and Radcliffe Brown in studies of Australian tribes, he wanted to apply similar ethnographic methods to an investigation of community life in an urban setting. His ethnographic methods required – or so he believed – stable and well-integrated communities, and the long-established cities of New England seemed to provide an ideal laboratory setting for his studies. His urban studies began with a detailed investigation of the New England city of Newburyport, to which he gave the pseudonym 'Yankee City' (Warner and Lunt 1941; 1942; Warner and Srole 1945; Warner and Low 1947; Warner 1963). The Yankee City project was the flagship for a series of studies that Warner coordinated, and it was followed by enquiries into the small rural community of Natchez (Davis et al. 1941), the Midwestern city of Morris, called 'Jonesville' in the project publications (Warner 1949a), and the black ghetto in Chicago (Drake and Cayton 1945).[17]

Where tribal societies are organised around an institutionalised system of kinship, Warner saw modern city communities as organised around their systems of stratification. Each city, he argued, develops a system of stratification that provides the integrative framework for community life in all its aspects. In established communities, a system of 'social classes' provided the sense of identity and belonging that tied people into their community and that structured their relations with one another. Though using the term 'social class' to describe the social strata of modern societies, Warner's specific focus was on the cultural processes of status division rather than on economic divisions. He focused firmly on the ranking of individuals in relation to social norms and their organisation into a prestige hierarchy of superiority and inferiority to which differential rights and privileges, duties and obligations are attached. Social classes, in this sense, arose from the cultural evaluation of economic and other differences – they were a specific combination of 'class' and 'status' elements. Although Warner distinguished what he called 'economic class' from the rank orderings that status relations converted into 'social class', he saw the former as mere nominal categories defined by differences in income, wealth or other economic assets. There was no attempt to weigh the relative importance of class and status in social class formation, and certainly no attempt to assign primacy to class. 'Economic' factors were treated, as they were by Parsons, as residual categories in social stratification. Warner's work was an application of the idea that status evaluation was central to social stratification and that the social classes of modern societies were, at heart, communal, cultural groupings.

'Social classes', then, are real social groups, not mere nominal constructs invented by sociologists. According to Warner, the critical element is their formation as consequences, intended or unintended, of the subjective evaluations that people make of one another in their everyday encounters. Through these evaluations, people come to accept one another as equals or to regard others as 'superior' or 'inferior' to themselves. Occupancy of a particular status situation, then, depends upon acceptance or rejection by others:

> To belong to a particular level in the social-class system of America means that a family or individual has gained acceptance as an equal by those who belong in the class. (Warner 1949b: 23)

In the study of Morris, Warner and his colleagues devised a method that, they felt, would allow them to reconstruct the stratification system by uncovering the processes that lay behind status allocation. It was assumed that those who interact with one another within a locality will evaluate the participation of others in those activities and groups that they value. The research method

that Warner termed 'evaluated participation' was intended to uncover the implicit and taken-for-granted procedures that are used
by people in their everyday interactions, the purpose of the method
being to reconstruct a 'map' of the strata that actually exist in a
community (1949b: 36ff). This method involved obtaining a large
number of rankings and ratings of named individuals by those
with whom they interact or to whom they are known. From these
rankings, the implicit social imagery of actors could be recon-
structed. The patterns of agreement and disagreement in rankings
disclose the 'class' categories that people 'see' as constituting their
society. This imagery, Warner held, corresponds closely with the
actual structure of social classes that resulted from their actions
and social relations. The aim of the method, Warner wrote, is to

> devise techniques of rating which will translate the criteria and judge-
> ments of the informants (townspeople) into explicit, verifiable re-
> sults which will correspond with the class realities of the community.
> (1949b: 38)

Warner held, then, that there is a close congruence between the
social classes that are formed from social evaluations and the social
imagery or 'social perspective' that people employ in their evaluations of one another. Americans operate, he argued, with an image of the 'class' system that they use to organise their relations
with one another. 'Social classes', then, were seen by Warner
as clusterings of status situations that have a psychological reality
in the minds of their members and of others, and that, thereby,
define the boundaries within which relations of relative equality
are contained.

Through the use of this method, Warner claimed to have uncovered the existence of similar stratification systems, mainly six-
stratum systems, in each of the communities that he studied.
Although these structures were, in part, simply unintended consequences of subjective ranking, Warner held that people did actually recognise and identify the six levels in their social imagery.
They had an understanding of the boundaries of the strata and of
the characteristics of their members, and they employed specific
names and labels to designate these strata. As there were structural
variations in the labels that were used, Warner tried to employ
more neutral designations in his own descriptions of the systems.
The terms he used were 'upper-upper', 'lower-upper', 'upper-

Social class		Approximate % of population		Description
		Newburyport	Morris	
UU	upper-upper	1.4	3.0	Society
LU	lower-upper	1.6		
UM	upper-middle	10.0	11.0	Solid citizens
LM	lower-middle	28.0	31.0	Common man
UL	upper-lower	33.0	41.0	
LL	lower-lower	25.0	14.0	

Figure 5 Warner's social class schema
Sources: Warner 1949b: 11ff; 1949a: ch. 2; 1963: ch. 2; 1952: ch. 1

middle' and so on, as shown in figure 5. These terms are not, perhaps, as neutral as Warner believed, and their value implications have detracted from a proper consideration of Warner's method and argument. So as to concentrate attention on the argument itself, I will abbreviate these labels simply to their initials, referring to UU, LU, UM and so on.

The UU social class is the patrician aristocracy of old wealth for whom 'lineage' was a particularly important ascriptive quality. The families that comprised this social class were closely interlinked through kinship, and their solidarity was reinforced by the ritualised behaviour and code of manners of their style of life. They lived in the largest houses in the most exclusive residential districts, and, as well as deriving an income from investments, they worked as financiers, industrialists and lawyers. The LU social class had many similarities with the UU social class, but these families were 'new', mainly first-generation wealth holders. They were *nouveau riche* and were not fully accepted as equals by those whose status and wealth were more established. In Morris, however, the UU and LU social classes were not distinguished from one another, as the city had not been in existence for a long enough period for a sharp status distinction between 'old' and 'new' families to have emerged. UU and LU in Morris were simply differences of level within a single social class. The UM social class comprised those who ran or owned substantial businesses or who worked in the professions. Below the top families, they formed the solid base of civic leadership and urban politics. The LM social class included those who owned small businesses, together with clerical and white collar workers, some tradesmen, and some skilled workers. The LM and the UL social class of semi-skilled and service workers together comprised what Warner called 'the common man', the great mass of citizens in the urban communities. Finally, the LL social class at the bottom of the hierarchy comprised those predominantly unskilled workers who suffered disproportionately from unemployment and low wages and who were often dependent on welfare. Members of the LL social class tended to fall into poverty and were the social class that later commentators would characterise as an 'underclass'.

As I have already mentioned, Warner claimed that the members of the various strata 'see' these six strata from different points of view. They may construct varying images of their society and so they will have a distinct 'perspective' on the social order. Thus, the UU and LU may identify all six strata and may make particularly detailed discriminations within the top three or four, while the LL and UL social classes may distinguish only three or four strata and may make little differentiation among those at the top of the hierarchy. Members of the UL social class in Newburyport and Morris, for example, tended to distinguish only three broad social classes. Equally, the labels that are given to the social classes tend to vary from one stratum to another. The UU and LU, for example, may be variously labelled by people as 'society', 'aristocrats', 'the 400', and so on. This diversity in social imagery and in the language of stratification brings out the fact that the actual strata that exist in a society are, for Warner, primarily to be seen as the *unintended* consequences of subjective valuations. People evaluate one another in face-to-face and other encounters, and the consistency in the criteria and the procedures that are used in these subjective rankings results in the generation of structurally stable social levels. Those who occupy status situations at each level enjoy a similar social standing and tend to develop a similar style of life. Through intermarriage, mobility and other forms of interaction, the levels are formed into distinct social strata. These strata – which in modern America take the form of social classes – are the real social groupings in which Americans live out their lives. Differential location within this system of stratification results in differential awareness of the social strata. Despite this recognition of diversity, Warner held, nevertheless, that there was a basic consensus in American communities and that, with slight variations, the same pattern of stratification and social imagery prevailed in all American towns and cities.[18]

Not all normative functionalists have seen social strata in such exclusively status terms. Some have recognised that people evaluate one another on the basis of their economic circumstances and that the social class boundaries of a modern society will involve both 'class' and 'status' elements. Economic conditions remain a residual category, but they are seen as being required in any comprehensive investigation. Williams, for example, took far more account of these residual categories than did Warner when he discussed the demographic formation of social classes in modern societies:

> If persons of like economic circumstances associate among themselves, interact frequently, intermarry – and do not interact frequently on an intimate basis with persons of a different economic level or occupational grouping – everything we know about human behaviour tells us that over a period of time these persons will become increasingly bound together by cultural consensus, by awareness of common interests, by interpersonal attachments and understandings, and by an increasingly shared total pattern or style of living. (Williams 1960: 125)

Whatever their basis, however, Warner saw that status divisions were a crucial element in the formation of social classes in modern society. The social classes were, however, cross-cut by further status divisions that were rooted in ethnic differences. These did not, in general, establish sharp and impermeable ethnic barriers, however, and Warner accepted the common view that America could be considered as an ethnic 'melting-pot' (Warner and Srole 1945: chapters 1 and 5). The principal exception that Warner saw to this fluidity in ethnic relations – and he recognised it as being a major exception – was the division between 'black' and 'white' communities, which involved sharp 'caste' boundaries.

'Castes', according to Warner, are closed social groups based on *ascribed* status characteristics from which systematic advantages and disadvantages flow. There are rigid barriers to the movement of people from one caste to another. In consequence, it is possible for the ranking of social positions to occur largely *within* each caste and, therefore, for each caste to comprise a distinct system of stratification within the overall stratification system. There were, Warner held, separate black and white systems of stratification in many American cities, and especially in those of the southern states. The 'white' systems in ethnically heterogeneous areas were similar to those found in Newburyport and Morris. In the 'black' systems (sometimes termed the 'colored' or 'Negro' systems), on the other

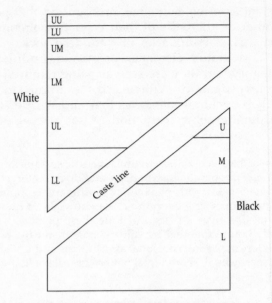

Figure 6　Caste and class in America

hand, there had been very little internal status differentiation until the early twentieth century. During the twentieth century, however, 'black' systems had tended to become more differentiated, and a distinct black middle class had developed. Some African-Americans, then, had a higher social standing within their own communities than some white Americans had in theirs: the black middle class stood, in a significant sense, 'above' the poor whites. Despite this shift, the caste barrier persisted and members of the black middle class were excluded from equal participation with the white UM and LM social classes and they suffered distinct disadvantages. The black middle class had a standard of living that was below that of most members of the white middle class, although its life style had come closer to that of their white counterparts. Warner depicted this diagrammatically as a shift of the 'caste line' from a horizontal to a diagonal position (see figure 6).[19]

In their study of Chicago, Warner's associates reported that the caste line persisted, but that the dynamism of the large city had opened up greater opportunities for African-Americans. The black ghetto had evolved into a three-stratum stratification system, comprising U, M and L social classes (Drake and Cayton 1945).[20] The African-American stratification system formed an extended social pyramid in which the three levels were cross-cut by further

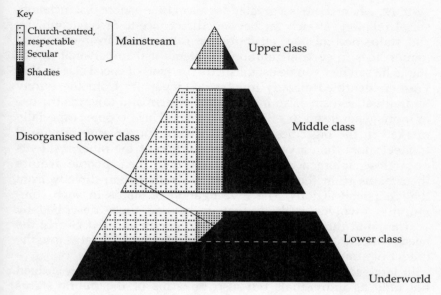

Figure 7 Stratification in the Chicago ghetto

status divisions. There was a church-going minority of 'respectable' families in each social class, separated from a secular mainstream and from deviant strata of 'shadies', whose involvement in shady or illegitimate activities allowed them to rise up the system in material terms. The shadies were closely linked to the underworld and were an especially important element in the L social class (see figure 7).

Paramount values and national status

Warner's approach to stratification was particularly appropriate for small communities, where it is possible for individuals to evaluate one another in face-to-face encounters, and Warner gave little attention to the ways in which social *positions*, rather than *individuals*, are ranked in the larger and more impersonal arenas of the big metropolitan centres and national societies. In small-scale social systems, people are directly judged for their actions in face-to-face contexts, giving rise to distinctive 'interactional' status systems. Valuations may be somewhat variable and inchoate, resulting in particularly fluid patterns of social stratification. In larger-scale social systems, where there is a greater degree of time–space distanciation, social relations stretch far beyond direct face-to-face encounters, and status becomes an 'attributional' rather than an interactional matter. It is in such attributional systems that impersonal public status hierarchies can be established. The kind of social classes that Warner identified already involved a departure from the purely 'individual' esteem of an interactional system and towards the use of more generalised 'positional' rankings. This becomes especially marked in the big cities, where it is difficult for any individual to meet more than a very small proportion of the other residents on a close, interactional basis. In the city, then, people acquire their status from their social positions, rather than directly from their personal actions. The investigation of status in such communities involves methods that go beyond those described by Warner, and the study of the Chicago ghetto showed clearly the need to incorporate more impersonal assessments of status into the model of stratification.

In large-scale, urbanised societies, then, individuals are judged not only as individuals but also in terms of the public status hierarchy of the national system. Such systems have become increasingly important features of the development of modernity. In his critique of normative functionalist theories, Lockwood shows their limitations by uncovering some of the implications of the increasing importance of attributional status systems in modern societies. He holds that interactional status is especially salient for people, as judgements in face-to-face contexts are likely to have a greater emotional significance for people's self-identity than do the more remote and abstract attributional judgements which they experience in more public and impersonal settings (Lockwood 1992: 85–6; see also Scheff 1990).[21] Status situations that are generated through the public evaluation of positions have less salience for people and so are unlikely to be bases of collective mobilisation:

> Only exceptionally does an extension of social horizons occur on such a scale and with such an intensity that it is sufficient to diminish the concern with parochial social standing and situational justice and to mobilise sentiments around wider collectivities. (Lockwood 1992: 89)

Status in modern societies, then, tends not to be an independent basis of collectivity organisation and tends to play a secondary, supporting role to economic class. Such issues are not, however, pursued by normative functionalists, although they have attempted to explore the social processes at work in the attributional status systems of large-scale national societies. Parsons, for example, has explored this issue in relation to the paramount values of societies. The paramount values of American society, he argued, involve a sharp break with the particularistic-ascriptive values of 'traditionalism', and they correspond very closely to the 'universalism-achievement' values that he saw as stressing activities concerned with the 'adaptation' function. Williams (1960: 423, 469–70) summarised this pattern of values as involving a focus on the 'worldly, instrumental activism' that is associated with achievement and success in the world of work and in other disciplined activities. The secondary values of the society are, in order of importance, those concerned with cultural commitment and motivation (the 'latency' function), those concerned with loyalty and solidarity (the 'integration' function), and those that promote system goals (the 'goal attainment' function). The values of universalism-achievement are tempered by the effects of these secondary commitments, and it is the whole complex of paramount and secondary values that shapes status judgements.

The 'modern' complex of universalism-achievement values is the basis of the characteristic 'looseness' of the status system, and these values prevail wherever a structurally differentiated economy becomes an important and autonomous feature of social life. Modern societies are characterised by the structural segregation of work from the domestic sphere of the household. Work is organised into distinct 'occupations', each of which is contracted for in a labour market, is carried out within formal, 'bureaucratic' organisations, and receives rewards that depend upon the specific terms that are agreed between employer and employee (Parsons 1956: 23; 1958: 113; 1960: 148). In such societies, the paramount values identify *occupational roles* and their social attributes as the primary objects of status evaluation.[22] Occupational achievement, regarded as an 'individual' rather than a family matter, becomes the primary basis of status allocation.

The values of universalism-achievement generate a ranking of occupations in terms of the skill, income and authority that are associated with them, as these are the attributes that are central to the values of modern societies (Shils 1968: 279). In the words of Williams:

In American society, broad occupational groups are evaluated according to a definite pattern that places at the bottom of the prestige scale manual labor and unskilled personal service involving direct

personal dependence upon superiors. Above this level the prestige
of occupations seems to follow roughly the degree of skill presumed
to be entailed and the size of the income derived. The authority over
persons inherent in a given occupation further modifies the rank
order. (1960; Williams cites North 1947 and Welch 1949 in support
of this view)

Within the occupational system, 'status is a function of the individual's productive "contribution" to the functions of the organizations concerned, hence of his [*sic*] performance capacities and
his achievements on behalf of the organization' (Parsons 1953: 421).
It must not be assumed, however, that occupational prestige is the
outcome of a monolithic consensus. Parkin's critique of studies of
occupational prestige has shown that these evaluations of occupations tend to reflect the judgements of those who occupy dominant
class situations. The occupants of dominant positions, he holds,
'seek to ensure that the main attributes of their own positions
become widely accepted as the appropriate criteria for allocating
honour' (1971: 44). It is their views that become institutionalised in
the criteria of ranking that provides the framework within which
occupational prestige can be assessed. Indeed,

> the social and political definitions of those in dominant positions
> tend to become objectified and enshrined in the major institutional
> orders, so providing the moral framework of the entire social
> system. (1971: 83)

Parsons saw the centrality of occupation and occupational prestige as bringing about a decline in the significance of property and
creating an increasingly open and 'classless' structure. On the one
hand, the 'upper class' of entrepreneurs and old wealth (Warner's
UU and LU social classes) declines in significance:

> Members of these families have retained elite position but broadly
> through their own occupational or occupation-like achievements
> rather than on a purely ascriptive basis of family membership . . . The
> basic phenomenon seems to have been the shift in *control* of enter-
> prises from the property interests of founding families to manage-
> rial and technical personnel who as such have not had a comparable
> vested interest in ownership. (1953: 431–2; see Williams 1960: 121–
> 4; Parsons 1949)

There has been a separation of ownership and control in industry,
argues Parsons, and this destroys any lingering relevance that a

Marxist view of the capitalist class may have had. As a result of this separation, Warner's UU social class is forced into a secondary rather than a primary location, and its main base becomes local rather than national. There is no longer a cohesive ruling class of entrepreneurial families. At the upper levels of the class system are found those in entrepreneurial, managerial and professional occupations that form a broad and diffuse top stratum, with several loosely integrated components. At the same time, manual working class families are declining in numbers and are adopting more 'middle class' attitudes and values.

Individuals are generally members of 'family households', and Parsons – contrary to the conventional picture of him – gave considerable attention to the part played by gender divisions in occupational status judgements. It was the differentiation of an occupational sphere of predominantly male activity, he argued, that transformed the position of women and confined them largely to the domestic sphere of the family. So long as the differentiation persists, it is central to patterns of status division. In these circumstances, there is 'a whole set of forces making for relative segregation of the sex roles, and in general to "shunt" the feminine role out of primary status in the occupational system or competition for occupational success or status' (Parsons 1953: 423). Gender divisions within the family are the most important of these forces: 'women, regardless of their performance capacities, tend to be relegated to a narrower range of functions than men, and excluded, at least relatively, from some of the highest prestige statuses' (1953: 423). This sex-role segregation ensures that husband and wife do not compete with one another for occupational attainments and so ensures that the solidarity of the family is not disrupted by the operations of the economy (1940: 79–80). For women, largely excluded from paid work in an occupation, 'the primary status-carrying role' is the 'pseudo-occupation' of the housewife (1942: 95; 1943: 191–2):

> The woman's fundamental status is that of her husband's wife, the mother of his children, and traditionally the person responsible for a complex of activities in connection with the management of the household, care of children, etc. (1942: 95)

Membership roles are gender divided: men enter occupations and women enter the pseudo-occupation of 'housewife'. Domestic labour is seen as a pseudo-occupation because it is not contractually defined and is not recruited through a labour market (see also

Oakley 1974). A married woman's status, therefore, tends to be derived from that of her husband: 'the most fundamental basis of the family's status is the occupational status of the husband and father' (Parsons 1942: 95; Barber 1957: 75).[23]

The various members of a family household all tend to be accorded the same status in the larger society:

> The family as a unit has a certain order of 'reputation' in the community. Its members share a common household and therefore the evaluation of this in terms of location, character, furnishings, etc. in the system of prestige symbolism. They have a common style of life. (Parsons 1953: 422)[24]

It is this specific combination of kinship and occupational status that Parsons, rather confusingly, termed 'class status', a form of stratification that is quite different from that found in premodern societies. In modern societies such as America, the 'family-occupation-income complex' lies at the core of social stratification. The occupational role is the focus of economic class relations as well as communal status relations, and it is this which makes it feasible (if confusing) to talk about occupational differences as involving a differentiation of 'class statuses' and to see the interplay of class and status as being expressed in 'social classes' of the kind described by Warner.

Occupational role and occupational attributes, then, are central to the language and imagery of status in societies that are organised around the values of universalism-achievement. This does not mean, however, that there is a perfect consensus over the actual 'scale' of stratification. There may be consensus over the language and meanings that are to be used in status judgements, but there may not be any consensus over the actual evaluations that are made. Thus, in societies which recognise the centrality of skill, authority and income, for example, some people may stress 'skill' above 'authority', while others may regard 'income' as being more important than 'skill'. More radically, some members of a society may introduce alternative but generally subsidiary criteria of status that run counter to the common stress on occupational role. Aristocratic groups, as Warner found in Newburyport, may stress the importance of 'old' wealth alongside a recognition of achieved occupational income.

There is also a tendency for the attributes that are associated with the performance of occupational activities to achieve a degree of autonomy in the determination of status. Wherever the exchange value of an object is represented by its monetary value in the market, the monetary remuneration accorded to a position tends to be seen as a measure of its 'reputation' in the societal community. In these circumstances, evidence on income may be used as an indicator of status, and people may pay less attention to where the income comes from and whether its size corresponds to the prestige of the occupations. Wherever income distribution does not correspond perfectly with status valuation – where, for example, it is determined by 'non-normative' factors – the use of income as an indicator of status will lead it to become a secondary criterion of status in its own right. That is to say, if income is seen as a proxy for status, then high status may be accorded to those with high income, however this income is gained. This is compounded by the fact that income differences are generally apparent from observation of expenditure and consumption patterns, rather than from direct observation of the income itself. Expenditure derived from inherited wealth or illegitimate earnings, for example, may be incorrectly perceived as due to income from a high status occupation and so may earn people status that they would not have received on a purely occupational basis.

In this way, the determination of income and wealth by elements of class situation may lead to these *effects of class* becoming *marks of status*. Barber, like Warner, sees this relation between class situation and status situation in terms of a distinction between 'economic stratification' and 'social stratification' (1957: 50ff). While I reject this terminology (see figure 4), the distinction itself is undoubtedly apt. Unfortunately, as I have shown, normative functionalists tend to treat 'economic' factors as residual variables. It is important to analyse the relation between the causal determination of life chances by the 'economic' processes of property and market relations on the one hand, and by evaluations of social status on the other. Weber, I have already shown, held that class and status divisions will often coincide with one another, and Barber is in complete agreement on this point, so far as the contemporary United States is concerned. He holds that 'Between these two kinds of stratification there is likely to be a large degree of correlation', though he adds that 'there is also likely to be some inconsistency between the two' and that the identification of any inconsistencies is an important aspect of the analysis of stratification (1957: 51–2).

This interdependence of class and status has been explored outside the normative functionalist framework by Parkin, who has argued that status and market situation operate together to determine the life chances that derive from occupations. The result of this is the observed close correspondence between occupational prestige and the various material rewards that people enjoy (income, job security, promotion opportunities, etc.). This correspondence may not be perfect in each case, but there is an overall congruence (Parkin 1971: 30–1). Where occupation is the principal basis of status evaluation, there is clearly a close association between class situation and status situation. Occupational roles are the outcome of property and market relations, and the specific status attributes of these roles become closely linked to market and work situations. Market mechanisms help to ensure the 'interlarding' of the various status hierarchies. In these circumstances, the prevailing pattern of status evaluation will correspond closely with the differentiation of class situations. Changes in status situations will be partly driven by the same economic changes that affect the structuring of class situations. The 'occupational transition' by which modern societies have come to include declining numbers of manual workers and increasing numbers of service workers, for example, will affect the status of both manual and service occupations, as will changes in the relative incomes of these occupations.

The determination of life chances by class situation in modern societies is, therefore, *reinforced* rather than undermined by status evaluation, and the allocation of status accords a degree of legitimacy to the inequalities that result from the operation of property relations and market forces. As Goldthorpe and Hope (1974) have shown, popular evaluations of occupations concern the 'general desirability' of occupations in terms of those attributes that constitute the class situations of households.[25]

The principal exception to this, as it was for Warner, derived from the effect of ethnicity on status. Thus, Parkin has stressed that, in addition to the effect of status as a reinforcing factor to class situation, there is an independent effect of status on life chances where factors such as ethnicity are involved:

> Status ranking associated wth historically rooted ethnic factors is functionally unrelated to the occupational reward system, so that it is not perhaps surprising that we should find serious discrepancies between class and status positions. (1972: 37)

For Parsons (1966), ethnicity – like religion – is an ascriptive status that is rooted in dense and 'primordial' communal ties. Primordial relations are those that are regarded as 'natural' and with which people identify on a purely emotional basis. Primordial societal communities are structured around race, territory, language, kinship or religion and so have a specifically 'ethnic' character. Modern societal communities, such as that of the United States, however, have become increasingly pluralistic: they are differentiated into numerous collectivities in which individuals have voluntary membership, and each individual participates in a wide variety of collectivities. The modern societal community is 'civil' rather than primordial, as it is structured by self-consciously constructed relations rather than by purely emotional commitments. The societal community is no longer organised around dense primordial ties and is, instead, structured by a concern for rational, universal considerations (Alexander 1990). In these circumstances, ethnic and religious identities cannot sustain their primordial and all-encompassing character; they tend to become merely one of the plural group memberships that make up a person's total social status. As a result, there is an 'increasing looseness in the connections among the components of total social status' (Parsons 1966: 715). This fragmentation of ascribed master statuses is reinforced by the tendency to institutionalise a status of 'citizenship' that, with its emphasis on the equality of membership rights, runs counter to ascribed status.[26]

The main blockage to the inclusion of African-Americans as full citizens of American society has been the extreme disadvantages that they have experienced, compared with other ethnic minorities. Early American society had a high degree of civil solidarity, as a result of the absence of a feudal aristocracy. This was associated, however, with a strongly developed sense of WASP (white Anglo-Saxon Protestant) ethnic identity in the dominant strata. Migration of non-English Europeans in the period 1820 to 1920 was, therefore, associated with a degree of status exclusion towards these newcomers; and discrimination against former slaves and their descendants, and non-European migrants, was especially marked (Alexander 1990). The eventual inclusion of African-Americans rests on a prior extension of the social rights of welfare, health and education that would help to offset these disadvantages. It is the failure of status inclusion to occur that results in the continued status of African-Americans as 'second-class citizens' and the perpetuation of 'caste' divisions between the white majority and the black minority.

Where there is a close association between class situation and status situation, as Parsons anticipated to be increasingly the case in the United States, the strata that are formed will be what I have called, following Weber, 'social classes': not only are they principally structured by differences in class situation, but the status evaluations and 'status groups' that arise will reinforce class differences and help to make the language of 'class' a most appropriate vocabulary in popular images of social stratification.

I have tried to show both the power and the limitations of the normative functionalist approach to stratification. Parsons and writers influenced by his Durkheimian approach have constructed a clear and systematic understanding of status stratification that enlarges on the ideas set out in chapter 2. They have shown, in particular, how status divisions are grounded in communal structures of cultural values and how subjective evaluations give rise to social hierarchies and social strata. Although they have shown how status is entwined with economic differences in the formation of occupational prestige gradings in modern societies, however, their treatment of economic differences is inadequate. Economic elements are purely residual within the normative functionalist scheme, being treated only in so far as they are normatively structured. What is missing from their account of stratification is the kind of understanding that Marxists have provided of class situations and their relation to the dynamics of the economy. If Marxist theory has ignored 'status' and normative functionalists have ignored 'class', perhaps they may both make a contribution to the more comprehensive approach to social stratification that I seek to develop in this book.

5

Command, Authority and Elites

'History is the graveyard of aristocracies' (Pareto 1916: 1430). With these words, Vilfredo Pareto staked his claim to be propounding an anti-Marxist theory that was, nevertheless, alive to the centrality of conflict in social life. In Pareto, however, the key to history was to be found in the struggle of ruling minorities ('aristocracies') and not in the struggle of economic classes. It was in the powers of rule, of authority, that Pareto and his contemporary Gaetano Mosca found a principle of sociological analysis that was, they felt, more realistic than a focus on the economic relations of class or ideological conceptions of status. Pareto, Mosca and certain of their followers developed a powerful understanding of how authority relations were involved in the formation of ruling minorities – 'elites' – and they moved towards an analysis of command relations of the kind that I have set out in my discussion of the third dimension of social stratification. Weber's analysis of domination and authority gave him an acute understanding of the formation of ruling minorities in the top command situations of political, economic and other hierarchies, but, for all his insights, the conceptualisation of ruling minorities was one of the least developed parts of his sociology. It is in the works of the Italian theorists Mosca and Pareto that an analysis of command situations can be found that can properly complement the analyses of class situation and status situation that I have developed in the previous chapters.

The importance of ruling minorities had first been recognised by Machiavelli, who had suggested that all structures of political

authority established a separation between a minority of *rulers* and
the majority that they *rule*. The rulers that exercise sway over a
people, Machiavelli argued, have a specific *virtù*, a spirit or will to
power that drives them to struggle with others in order to achieve
dominance in their society. In the works of Mosca and Pareto this
view was converted into a political sociology that interpreted history as the result of power struggles, of the clash between rulers
and ruled and of the rise and fall of those competing ruling groups
that have come to be described as 'elites'.

This view of elites stands in a larger tradition of thought on the
centrality of conflict and struggle in social development. This
broader tradition has often been described as 'social Darwinist',
but it raises broader issues than the 'Darwinist' label implies. A
more accurate designation of this tradition might be 'conflict theory'.
A key figure in shaping this tradition was Herbert Spencer, whose
evolutionary views centred on the idea of 'the survival of the fittest'
in the struggle for life, and it was the melding of Spencer's views
with the contemporary biological ideas of Darwin that influenced
the thought of a whole generation of social thinkers. Marx's emphasis on the role of class struggle in history had, of course, a
major impact on this viewpoint, and Marx (1859b) himself had
pointed to the parallels between his own ideas and those of Darwin. Marx, however, had sought to uncover the economic anatomy
of social struggles, and it was other writers – non-Marxist and anti-
Marxist – who developed a looser framework of 'conflict theory' in
which political struggles played a central part. The most systematic and influential statement of this conflict theory was set out by
the Austrian writer Gumplowicz, whose direct influence on better-
known writers has today been largely forgotten.[1]

Gumplowicz (1875; 1883; 1885) saw the social process as an
outcome of the competitive struggle of ethnic, class and other social groups. The competition of these social groups for economic
resources, he argued, leads to conquest and to the formation of
states, which he saw as the political mechanisms through which
dominant groups are able to establish a more secure basis for the
exploitation and oppression of subordinate groups. States expand
through conquest, and so militarism and warfare must be seen as
the principal forms of inter-state relations. According to Gumplowicz, the military conquerors who establish or seize state power
will always constitute a *minority* that subject the majority of the
society to their rule. Minority rule is a feature of all stages of human

history, though the forms that are taken by minority rule can vary considerably from one society to another. In the modern nation state, for example, Gumplowicz saw political parties as being the principal organs for the expression of group conflict, and these parties were, in turn, seen as dominated by a minority of leaders. Gumplowicz claimed, however, that political minorities did not hold exclusive sway. Modern societies were marked by a clash between the political minorities (in the spheres of government and the military) and the industrial and financial minorities (in the economic sphere).

In a related viewpoint, Tocqueville (1835–40; 1856) had seen modern democracy as embodying a paradox. He held that the elimination of the traditional privileges and prerogatives of the medieval estates and guilds had created a system of formal equality, but that 'intermediate' groups had disappeared. There was no longer any counterweight to prevent the tyranny of a minority over the majority. Somewhat later, Tocqueville's compatriot Le Bon (1895) turned his attention to the subordinate majorities – the 'masses' or the 'crowds' – who figured as major actors on the historical scene. 'Crowds' were understood as large-scale national and class groups as well as relatively small-scale 'mobs', their key characteristics being the possession of collective consciousness and group solidarity. This idea of the 'mass' or crowd as an amorphous aggregate developed after the French Revolution to describe the populace outside the dominant strata. It referred to the 'ordinary' people in a democratic political system, and Le Bon paid particular attention to the ways in which leaders are able to use group psychology to control the masses by stirring up irrational drives that could be obscured by presenting them as political ideals. These political ideals were 'myths' that masked struggles for power. This emphasis on political myths was developed most systematically by Sorel (1906) in his formulation of a conflict theory of political development.[2]

While Weber's analysis of domination was influenced by these kinds of views on group conflict, it was the Italian writers Mosca and Pareto who fully developed them and introduced the key concept of the 'elite' to conceptualise the historical role that had been played by ruling minorities. The arguments of Mosca and Pareto have their immediate roots in the conflict theory of Gumplowicz, and it was on this theoretical basis that they sought to develop the specific insights of Machiavelli. They highlighted the centrality of the state and its apparatus of political power, and they saw what they called 'political classes' as the principal groups involved in the struggles of history. The terminology of 'political class' and 'elite' was deliberately used in preference to the Marxian concept of 'class' in order to emphasise that politics was not to be reduced to economics. Economic power, they argued, was important, but it was not all-important. Despite this opposition to Marxism and to economic reductionism, there remain great similarities between their historical studies and those of Marx. What differentiates them most sharply is that, for Mosca and Pareto, political struggles were accorded an autonomy that verged on a complete independence from economic factors.

Mosca and Pareto were contemporaries of Weber. Pareto entered academic life as an economist in the 1870s and produced his major work in sociology – the *Treatise in General Sociology* – in 1916, while Mosca worked as a political sociologist and produced two versions of his key text on *The Elements of Political Science* (1896; 1923). Both continued to be intellectually active until the 1920s, and Pareto dabbled with support for Mussolini, but they were little known outside Italy. Indeed, their work had few direct heirs abroad in the years immediately following the publication of their studies. Their principal works were not translated into English until the middle and late 1930s, at the same time that Lawrence Henderson was popularising Pareto's general sociology (1935; 1941–2; see also Homans and Curtis 1934). Karl Mannheim (1932–3; 1935) drew critically on Mosca and, after his arrival in England, he joined a small discussion group on modern culture that gave rise to T. S. Eliot's *Notes Towards the Definition of Culture* (1948) and Mannheim's own *Freedom, Power and Democratic Planning* (1947). Most important for the subsequent development of elite theory was the work of James Burnham (1941), who constructed a powerful interpretation of political struggle from what he termed a 'Machiavellian' standpoint. A related argument, which seems to owe little to Burnham, however, was that of Cox, who set out a concept of 'political class' that he contrasted with social estates and social classes. A political class for Cox was 'a power group which tends to be organized for conflict' (1948: 154), and he drew explicit parallels between his own work and that of Mosca. Cox's work, however, had far less impact on subsequent research than did that of Burnham.[3] In this chapter I will present the arguments of Mosca and Pareto themselves, and I will show how their ideas – as developed by Burnham – became the basis of an influential interpretation of the Soviet social system.

Mosca and the political elite

Mosca's work employs a number of terms to describe ruling minorities. In his earliest works on political struggle (1884; 1896) he had used the term *classe politica*, while in his mature work (1923) he preferred the term *classe dirigente* (see Albertoni 1985: 16–17). This change in terminology reflected a growing awareness that the *classe politica*, which he saw as a specialised ruling minority concerned with government, formed a part of a larger *classe dirigente* that embraced all ruling minorities in the political, economic, religious, and other spheres. These terms have usually been translated as 'political class' and 'ruling class', respectively, but these are confusing terms in a comprehensive account of social stratification that employs 'class' in a Marxian sense. The word *classe* was not used by Mosca in anything like the Marxian or Weberian sense of class, and it is preferable to avoid using the word 'class' to designate what are specifically authoritarian groups rather than economic groups. I propose, therefore, to follow Pareto's terminological innovation and use the word 'elite' in place of Mosca's word *classe* wherever he refers to a category of people that are organised around the exercise of authority.[4]

While *classe politica*, then, can be translated as 'political elite', *classe dirigente* poses more difficulties. The Italian word *dirigente* is closest to the English word 'directing', with which it has a common root. It can be used in a number of ways that involve a sense of controlling, guiding, leading, or steering. To direct something is to determine its movements, and this core idea has been extended to the idea of guiding through instructions or commands. A closely related word is 'rule', which means sway, government or dominion, a term that implies the existence of a framework of order or 'rules' in terms of which sway is exercised. By comparison with 'directing', 'rule' implies a more structured or institutionalised relationship. The word 'rule', then, seems to be the most appropriate way to translate Mosca's idea, and it also emphasises the connection with Weber's analysis of authority and command. I propose, therefore, to use the terms 'political elite' and 'ruling elite' to translate Mosca's two key terms.

Mosca's concern was to establish what he termed a 'realistic' rather than a purely constitutional classification of the forms of political domination. The Aristotelian typology of monarchic, aristocratic, and democratic constitutions, he argued, had to be rejected

on the grounds that it was simply too superficial. A realistic, structural approach to politics would show that

> In all regularly constituted societies in which something called a
> government exists, we find that all authority is being exercised in
> the name of the entire people, or of an aristocracy, or of a single
> sovereign . . . but besides that fact we find unfailingly another: the
> political elite or, rather, those who hold and exercise the public power,
> will always be a minority, and below them we find a numerous
> class of persons who do never, in any *real* sense, participate in gov-
> ernment but merely submit to it: these may be called the ruled.
> (Mosca 1884, cited in Meisel 1958: 32–3)

This, then, is the nub of Mosca's position. The holding and exercising of 'public power' is the basis on which rulers and ruled are to
be identified, and the rulers will always form a minority, no matter
how democratic may be the doctrines and ideals that they draw on
to legitimate their power. The 'political elite' comprises the organised core of participants in the exercise of political authority. This
elite 'performs all political functions, monopolizes power and en-
joys the advantages that power brings' (Mosca 1896: 50). Its power
derives not from its communal or economic position but from its
organisation in relation to the public power of the state. A division
between the political elite and the subordinate majority is a universal feature of human history because it is an inevitable consequence
of social organisation:

> the dominion of an organized minority, obeying a single impulse,
> over the unorganized majority is inevitable. (1896: 53)

Although Mosca defined the political elite in relation to the exercise of power in and through the state, his reference to the 'organisation' of an elite introduced an element of ambiguity into his
analysis. On the one hand, a political elite may be understood as
involving positions in the organised political power hierarchy that
is the state. This was the sense that Weber implied in his discussion of rulers and ruled. The state is an organised social grouping
with a structure of authority in which those in the top command
situations can be defined as a political elite. On the other hand,
however, Mosca implied that those who participate in the exercise
of political power constitute an elite because they have addition-
ally organised themselves for collective action in pursuit of their

interests. It is the organisation of the occupants of the positions, rather than the organisation inherent in the positions themselves, that forms the elite and makes their dominance inevitable. Mosca seems, in fact, to have wanted to make *both* claims, without realising that the claims are, indeed, quite distinct. He might almost have been claiming that elites exist 'in themselves' as top command situations within hierarchical organisations, and that they exist 'for themselves' when they are organised through communal and associational relations for collective action. These two features of elite organisation will be discussed more fully in a later part of this chapter.

Elites have various attributes or skills that allow them to use their power more or less effectively, and Mosca believed that it was important that the attributes that are held by elite members should actually correspond to those that are needed for the effective exercise of political power. If this is not the case, they will be ineffective and may be unable to continue in power (Mosca 1896: 65). It is important, then, to look at how open elites are to the acquisition of new attributes and skills. The attributes that are required for the effective exercise of power must be made into a conscious principle of recruitment. Where positions of command are acquired through inheritance, by virtue of their birth or lineage, this does not occur and it is likely that the attributes held by elite members will diverge from those that are required. In these circumstances, the required skills may be concentrated in the hands of those who are excluded from membership of the elite because they were born into the wrong families.

Mosca developed this idea through an analysis of the relationship between political elites and 'social forces'. The social forces are those social and economic categories of people on whom the society depends because of their particular abilities or aptitudes, and a political elite may be more or less representative of these social forces. Unless it is able to absorb or to incorporate powerful social forces, bringing into the running of the state the necessary social attributes that they possess, a political elite may be challenged by those who are excluded from political power and who do possess these attributes or abilities. Political elites that strive to secure their own survival, then, must ensure that they remain representative of the wider society. A political elite has to retain a degree of 'openness' if it is not to ossify and face a challenge from those whose aptitudes and skills are more effective.

The social forces that Mosca identified include the military, the clergy, the wealthy, and the intelligentsia, each of which may, under specific social conditions, have a critical significance for social development. The social forces are organised around particular command situations that lie outside the sphere of the state proper.[5] They hold positions of command in military, religious or economic hierarchies and they have achieved a degree of organisation within their own sphere that allows them to develop a will to increase the scope of their authority. These social forces become politically relevant whenever they develop 'the aptitude to command' (Mosca 1884, cited in Meisel 1958: 46) but are excluded from actual command within the state. For this reason, threats to an existing political elite occur whenever those who hold positions of authority within major social organisations are excluded from the exercise of political power in the state. The continued exclusion of those social forces that have the aptitudes required in the state will result in conflict and struggle:

> When an elite contains all the dominating elements of a society, it may act ... with impunity; yet, in the course of centuries, it will have difficulty in keeping dominating elements from forming outside the existing ruling class and in excluding them legally from power without stirring up a struggle. (Mosca 1884, cited in Meisel 1958: 47)

In a fundamental statement, though using the term 'class' rather than 'elite', Mosca added that:

> One might say, indeed, that the whole history of civilized mankind comes down to a conflict between the tendency of dominant elements to monopolize political power and transmit possession of it by inheritance, and the tendency toward a dislocation of old forces and an insurgence of new forces; and this conflict produces an unending ferment of endosmosis and exosmosis between the upper classes [sic] and certain portions of the lower. (1896: 65)[6]

There is, then, a constant struggle and renewal of political elites as they absorb or enter into conflict with those who are outside the elite but who seek to rise into it or to overthrow it.

In the final version of his great work, Mosca (1923) moved from a focus on the 'political elite' to a recognition that the elite in charge of the government is but one element in a wider cluster of command situations. There may be a variety of elites – 'political', military, economic, religious, and so on. At the same time, however,

Mosca continued to use the word 'political' in a broad sense to describe patterns of power and domination of all kinds. He held, for example, that the phrase 'political control' was to be taken in its widest sense as encompassing 'administrative, military, religious, economic and moral leadership' (1923: 329). This remark reflects the same ambiguity over the boundaries of the 'political' sphere that I identified in the work of Weber: is the political sphere to be understood as the sphere of the state (or, even more narrowly, of government) or as the sphere of authority *per se*? Mosca seems to have resolved this ambiguity in favour of the latter position. Confusingly, he also used the word in its narrower sense when referring to the 'political elite' as the occupants of top command situations within the state.

Beyond his remarks on the 'social forces' outside the political elite, Mosca gave no systematic review of top command situations other than those of the state. While all structures of domination give rise to 'elites', Mosca gave no thorough account of these. Mosca's close friend Roberto Michels, however, did set out a remarkably sophisticated summary statement and elaboration of Mosca's mature standpoint. According to Michels, the overall structure of authority in a society included three sections: the 'political' elite in its narrow sense of those in government and the state who are characterised by a 'will to power'; the 'economic' elites whose power is rooted in wealth from banking, insurance and industry; and the 'intellectual' elites who work with 'words, symbols and science' (1927: 106).[7] These three elites 'form circles which, though far from coinciding with one another, have points of intersection' (1927: 107).

Mosca himself anticipated that the political elite and the various elites that exist at the heads of other major structures of authority in a society could become clustered together through demographic processes of social circulation into a particular kind of social bloc that he termed a 'ruling elite'. A ruling elite is an advantaged and powerful social bloc that fuses various specialised elites together into a single structure and that is likely to exhibit what Meisel (1958: 4) called the three Cs of 'group consciousness, coherence and conspiracy'. Through the holding and exercising of power in organised structures of authority, a variety of command situations are established. A ruling elite arises wherever the occupants of these top command situations are unified and show a high degree of communal solidarity. As a minority within its society, it has distinct advantages over other social blocs. Parry has summarised Mosca's claims:

A small group is more readily organised than a large one. Its internal channels of communication and information are much simpler. Its members can be contacted more speedily. As a result, a small minority can formulate policies rapidly, can agree on the presentation of the policies and give the appearance of complete solidarity in its public statements and actions. (1969: 37)

Meisel has pointed out, however, that there is nothing inevitable about the demographic formation of a cohesive ruling elite from the formally constituted command situations:

The fusion of the leader elements may remain incomplete; in that case, the authority of the political class [*sic*] will remain precarious. (1958: 41)

It should be noted here that Mosca's model of the formation of a ruling elite conflated two quite distinct processes. On the one hand, he was clearly referring to the demographic circulation that could unite the occupants of command situations through social mobility, intermarriage, and other networks of informal social relations. On the other hand, however, he also referred to processes of 'party' formation through which specific associations could be established in order to defend and to promote the interests of elite members. Where Weber saw these processes as analytically separate from one another, Mosca conflated them into a single conceptualisation of what might be called, only slightly tongue-in-cheek, an 'elite-for-itself'. It is undoubtedly a major limitation of Mosca's work that he did not properly distinguish or conceptualise the 'party' relations in which elite members may, under appropriate circumstances, be involved.

Mosca's mature work also involved a reconstruction and enlargement of his account of the *legitimacy* of elites. His earlier work had introduced the concept of the 'political formula' through which elites sought to justify their power, and he traced a historical tendency for political elites to rely less and less on *de facto* domination with advances in the level of social development. Those with power, he held, try 'to find a moral and legal basis for it, representing it as the logical and necessary consequence of doctrines and beliefs that are generally recognised and accepted' (Mosca 1896: 70). The political formulas that are used for legitimation, however, are not 'mere quackeries' – 'myths' in Sorel's (1906) terminology. They are real bases of moral attachment, drawing on deeply rooted sentiments. Indeed, the political formula is 'a social force that contributes powerfully to consolidating political organisation and unifying peoples or even whole civilizations' (Mosca 1896: 71). In Mosca's idea of the political formula can be found the germ of Gramsci's (1929–35) later idea of 'hegemony'. For both writers, political and cultural dominance coincide in a 'consensus of sentiments and ideas' that become 'forces of moral cohesion' (Mosca 1923: 481).

Mosca drew a broad contrast between 'supernatural' and 'rational' political formulas, paralleling Weber's contrast between 'traditional' and 'rational' forms of legitimation. To illustrate his point, he referred to the mandarin elite of traditional China and the 'supernatural' basis of their authority:

> The Chinese Mandarins ruled the state because they were supposed to be interpreters of the will of the Son of Heaven, who had received from heaven the mandate to govern paternally, and in accordance with the rules of the Confucian ethic. (1896: 70)

Supernatural forms of legitimation declined with the rise of modernity, and in the modern United States Mosca saw the popular vote in elections as expressing the will of the people and so conferring a more 'rational' legitimacy on the elected authorities.

In place of this contrast between supernatural and rational legitimation, the second edition of his major work (Mosca 1923) introduced a contrast between *autocratic* and *liberal* formulas of legitimation. In autocratic systems, authority is presented as being transmitted from the top to the bottom of a hierarchy. In liberal systems, on the other hand, authority is derived through electoral mechanisms from bottom to top.[8] Alongside these two formulas of legitimation, Mosca identified two patterns of recruitment to elites, which he termed the *aristocratic* and the *democratic*. In aristocratic systems, membership in an elite depends upon direct descent from previous elite members and so membership is hereditary. In democratic systems, on the other hand, there is an open pattern of recruitment and so there is a constant replenishment of the elite from outside (1923: 395). Figure 8 gives a reconstruction of this argument.[9] Types 1 and 4 in the typology are systems in which the pattern of legitimacy is congruent with the mechanism of recruitment, though many actual societies, Mosca held, fall between these two extremes into types 2 and 3. Traditional China, for example, he saw as a system of type 2: an autocratic political formula

Form of legitimacy	Mechanism of recruitment	
	Aristocratic (closed)	Democratic (open)
Autocratic	1	2
Liberal (elective)	3	4

Figure 8   Mosca on elite recruitment

was associated with a meritocratic mechanism of recruitment through competitive examinations. Twentieth-century Britain, on the other hand, he claimed to exemplify type 3, as electoral mechanisms of legitimation are associated with tightly closed mechanisms of recruitment (1923: 396).

Mosca completed his analysis of ruling elites by exploring their forms of internal differentiation. Ruling elites are rarely monolithic, and generally have a complex internal structure. All forms of rule, he held, show 'The formation of a clique, perhaps of two or three dozens of persons, or even as many as a hundred . . . who monopolize the management of the state and occupy the more important offices' (1923: 402). That is to say, a ruling elite – and perhaps any elite – is hierarchically organised into two categories: a 'ruling clique' that comprises 'the supreme head and his [*sic*] immediate associates' (1923: 433), and a 'second stratum' on which it depends. In societies corresponding to type 1 of figure 8, the ruling clique will tend to be a nobility of birth whose members may be engaged in a factional and family struggle among themselves for positions at court. In systems of type 3 and type 4, on the other hand, the cliques will form the nuclei of 'parties'.[10]

Despite his failure to pursue the analysis of parties, Mosca's mature work is compatible with Weber's discussion of modern political parties. The important linking figure between Weber and Mosca is Michels (1911), who drew on the earlier work of Ostrogorski – a writer whose book had been translated into French in 1903 and who had worked within a similar framework of elite analysis to that of Mosca. Michels also drew directly on his friend and colleague Weber, and his particular contribution was to show that political parties were themselves subject to the leadership of a small minority. No matter how democratic they may attempt to be, all organisations involve 'oligarchy'.[11]

Pareto and the governing elite

Pareto was the first writer to popularise the word 'elite' in referring to the idea of the ruling minority (1901; 1902; 1916). The fact that Pareto's major work was translated into English in 1935, four years before the translation of Mosca's study of ruling minorities, helped to ensure that the word 'elite' acquired greater currency than the terms suggested by Mosca. The English word 'elite' has been used to translate a variety of French and Italian words that were used by Pareto. These words included *aristocrazia* (1901: 36), a term that put him very directly in the tradition of Machiavelli. The phrase that he most frequently used, however, was *le classi elette*, which means the class or category of the 'elect' or 'select'.[12] This phrase was translated into French, by Pareto himself, as *l'élite*. This terminological innovation is, in many respects, Pareto's greatest achievement, as the originality of his ideas has sometimes been called into question. Mosca, for example, had claimed that Pareto was simply a plagiarist who had passed off Mosca's ideas as his own. It is clear, however, that the basic ideas of the elite framework had a wide currency at the time and that Mosca and Pareto gave similarly outstanding expression to them. Pareto rightly deserves the credit for introducing the most appropriate terminology for describing ruling groups, even if Mosca's major work on this topic did appear some 17 years before Pareto's. Pareto's work on elites stands as an important and original contribution to subsequent discussions. Indeed, Mosca's own later work showed the unacknowledged influence of Pareto's ideas, and Michels's influential lectures on political sociology described Pareto's analysis of the circulation of elites as 'one of the most remarkable theories of the philosophy of history of recent times' (1927: 63).

Pareto claimed that 'Every people is governed by an elite, by a chosen element in the population', except for very short and unusual periods (1916: 169; 1901: 36). Elites vary in their social composition, this being determined by the degree of mobility from outside their ranks. It is social mobility – or circulation – that plays the central part in Pareto's work. The circulation of individuals in and out of command positions results in the continual rise and fall of elites: 'the history of man [*sic*] is the history of the continuous replacement of certain elites: as one ascends, another declines' (1901: 36).

In his attempt to give a formal definition to the word 'elite', Pareto developed a generic concept that was not limited specifically to the state or to the political sphere. His starting point was to identify elites in all spheres of society, and not merely in those that are related to the exercise of authority. Elites, in this sense, comprise the 'selected', 'chosen', 'ruling' or 'better' elements in a society, and Pareto explicitly followed Mosca's pupil Kolabinska in seeing elites as those who are 'superior' to others in terms of some socially significant criterion (1916: 1421 n. 1). 'Superior' in this context does not mean more useful, ethically better, or more valuable; it simply means that the elite comprises those who have more of some socially significant capacity, ability or resource. An elite comprises those who are the 'best' in each social sphere, and those are the best who have the most resources or the best-developed aptitudes and abilities. Thus, those who have the greatest legal knowledge and powers of advocacy will make the best lawyers and should rise to the top of the legal hierarchy; those with little or no legal competence should remain at the bottom of the hierarchy.

Pareto explored the formation of these elites by examining the relationship between the distribution of aptitudes and the distribution of advantages. He held that individuals can be envisaged as being ranked numerically into hierarchies according to their capacities, abilities and resources 'in every branch of human activity'. Any aptitude that gives people advantages in achieving their goals can be seen in hierarchical terms:

> The highest type of lawyer, for instance, will be given 10. The man who does not get a client will be given one – reserving zero for the man who is an out-and-out idiot. To the man who has made his millions – honestly or dishonestly as the case may be – we will give 10. To the man who has earned his thousands we will give six; to such as just manage to keep out of the poor-house, one, keeping zero for those who get in. (1916: 1422)

Pareto held that this kind of mathematical ranking can be applied to *any* socially valued or significant attribute of individuals. On this basis, then, there would be a large number of dimensions of stratification – legal capacity, wealth, political influence, poetic ability, religious knowledge, criminal aptitude and so on. In an ideal situation, then, the elites of a society would comprise the best in each sphere of activity, those 'who have the highest indices in their branch of activity' (1916: 1423).[13] This would be the basis on which would be recruited, for example, the legal elite, the wealth elite, the poetic elite, and even the criminal elite.

The distribution of skills and abilities within an elite depends upon the degree of 'circulation' or social mobility in the society. Pareto recognised that wherever rewards or formal structures of advantage or disadvantage are allocated to particular tasks and activities, there may be a mismatch between this and the actual distribution of aptitudes. Incompetent lawyers, for example, may establish restrictive practices that monopolise rewards and official posts in the legal system and that exclude those with superior legal skills. If the top positions in the various hierarchies of a society are to be occupied by those who actually are the 'best' people in these spheres, then recruitment to these top positions must allow talented individuals to rise from below. Only in this way can those at the top remain a true 'elite' of the superior or best persons. Pareto held that this occurs under a meritocratic regime of free competition that allows talented individuals to compete for positions to which rewards and recognition are attached. This argument rests upon the application of a market model of supply and demand to elite recruitment. In a meritocratic system, the velocity of circulation – the rate of social mobility – depends only on supply and demand factors. Changes in the demand for particular skills alter the mobility chances of those who possess these skills. An increase in the demand for a skill increases the opportunities open to those with this skill, while a decline in demand for it reduces their opportunities. Skills that are in great supply, even when they are in demand, might not offer such opportunities for mobility as those skills that are in short supply. Under such conditions, a constant circulation of personnel would ensure that the 'best' were always at the top of their respective hierarchies.

Pareto recognised that these conditions of openness and meritocracy do not typically occur in real historical situations and that those who occupy top positions in the institutional hierarchies are often able to establish a degree of closure that prevents the entry of those with particular abilities or talents. This will mean that the elites that are perpetuated may not truly be the 'best' in their various spheres. When this kind of social closure occurs, the actual elites are simply those who are able to monopolise advantages within a particular sphere of action (Meisel 1965).

This move from a *normative* conception of the 'best' to a *descriptive* conception of the 'advantaged' was only partially theorised in

Pareto's work. He undertook no theoretical analysis of the formation of elites in situations other than free competition and meritocracy. Although this kind of theorisation was required by his own
studies – and was specifically developed in relation to authority by
Mosca – Pareto's general remarks were undeveloped. His comments suggest simply that the actual elites in a society can be identified in purely formal and statistical terms as those who happen
to occupy the top levels of the numerous hierarchies that make up
its social structure.

Pareto did recognise that it might be possible to identify an overall
social elite that would comprise the members of all the various
specialised elites, but he also recognised that any overarching social elite was likely to be very diverse in its composition. To make
his work more precise and more useful, Pareto again followed
Kolabinska and distinguished between a 'governing' and a 'non-
governing' section of the overall elite. The governing elite of a
society, he held, comprised those occupants of top positions 'who
directly or indirectly play some considerable part in government'
(1916: 1423). In an earlier work, Pareto had pointed to this group
as the 'elite in control' (1902: 35). Those in the governing elite are
involved, in some way or another, in the government of the state.
Thus, top poets and chess players may form part of an abstract,
statistically defined overall 'elite', but they will not necessarily form
a part of the governing elite. The governing elite, then, comprises
those who actually occupy top command situations in the state
and other strategic hierarchies, regardless of whether these people
are actually the 'best' in terms of the specific skills and abilities that
are required for government. In developing this descriptive concept of the governing elite, Pareto converged, in a largely untheorised way, with the concept that Mosca was to formulate as the
'ruling elite'. Pareto's model of this governing elite in relation to
the overall elite is shown in figure 9.[14]

Pareto's approach to elites involved a purely *ad hoc*, and partial,
listing of social hierarchies, and he made no attempt to theorise why particular 'elites' may have a potential for power and,
therefore, may form part of the governing elite. Those with great
poetic abilities, to the extent that this can be measured in the sense
that Pareto implied, may have considerable power in 'heroic' societies, but they are likely to have little power *as poets* in modern
industrial societies. Top chess players are unlikely to be powerful
in any conceivable society. What is missing from Pareto's work is
a criterion for identifying which attributes, skills and resources
are involved in the exercise of power. Mosca, like Weber, resolved

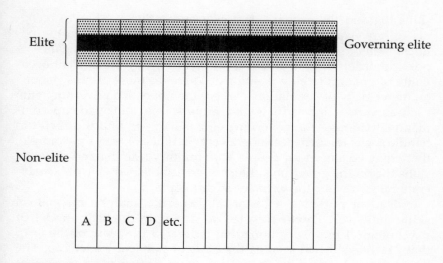

A   hierarchy of wealth
B   hierarchy of legal competence
C   hierarchy of political influence
D   hierarchy of poetic ability
etc.

Figure 9   Pareto's model of the governing elite
Not to scale. The balance in size between the elite and the non-elite and
between the various elements within the elite and the governing elite are
determined empirically and not *a priori*

this problem by identifying elites only in relation to the exercise
of authority, and this criterion can be used to complete Pareto's
argument. The power of the bards in heroic societies, for example,
could be seen to derive from the centrality of an oral tradition to
the legitimacy of authority. Bardic poetry consolidates the oral tradition and gives the bards a power base, but their power is not a
consequence of their technical poetical ability in itself. What is
required in Pareto, then, is an understanding of the centrality of
command situations to the formation of elites. An analysis of command situations would have allowed Pareto to demarcate the 'governing elite' either as the narrowly defined 'political elite' or – as
Mosca did in his later work – the broader 'ruling elite'. Pareto, in
short, failed to use the criterion of power in his abstract model,
despite its centrality to his historical studies and to his concept of
the governing elite.

Membership in the governing elite depends, in the 'ideal' situation
of open recruitment, on the holding of those particular political

skills that aid the exercise of power and influence. Pareto recognised, however, that there may be a discrepancy between the political skills that are 'objectively' required for the maintenance of political order and the actual skills possessed by the current occupants of governing elite positions. Wherever there are restrictions on the velocity of circulation – where members of a governing elite exclude certain individuals and groups from entry to top command situations – the governing elite is likely to find it difficult to handle social disturbances effectively. In times of war, for example, there may be a need for people with military training and strategic skills to join the governing elite, but an established elite of bureaucrats may prevent the entry of such people.

Instead of pursuing a historically specific analysis of political skills, however, Pareto resorted to a simple dualistic model of psychological predispositions that reiterated the view of the *virtù* that Machiavelli had seen as the basis of political leadership. The particular political skills that Pareto investigated were those that originated in the specific 'residues' or sentiments that people possess and that created their psychological predispositions to act in particular ways. The politically relevant residues, according to Pareto, were the sentiment of combination and the sentiment of persistence. Some elite members, Pareto argued, are rich in 'combination' sentiments, by which he means that they have a tendency to innovate and to use their intelligence and cunning in the pursuit of their material interests. Such people rely on persuasion and consent and tend to be relatively 'tender-minded' humanitarians and pragmatists in their policies. Their specific political skills are those of ideological elaboration, coalition-building, and factional manoeuvring. Pareto equated those who hold these particular sentiments with Machiavelli's 'foxes'. Other elite members are rich in the sentiments of 'persistence', or the tendency to consolidate. Such people seek permanence, stability and order, and they are willing to use force and violence to suppress any opposition to their rule. They are 'tough-minded' and doctrinaire in policy, and their specific skills involve the exercise of coercion and repression. Pareto equated these with Machiavelli's 'lions'. Whatever may be the validity of Pareto's psychologistic explanation of the 'residues' that are supposed to be associated with these political skills, the historical value of his typology of styles of political leadership – of the foxes and the lions – can be assessed separately.

Pareto placed great emphasis on the strategies that can be adopted by established governing elite members to limit the extent of social circulation and so to exclude those with specific skills. His discussion

of social closure by governing elites identified only the most extreme strategies, of which he recognised four. First, an established
elite may purge and execute disloyal members and may physically
repress external challengers to their rule. Death, for Pareto, is the
ultimate means of social closure. A less extreme measure of closure
is persecution, through which imprisonment, exclusion from offices, and financial penalties are used to prevent a challenge. Third,
challengers may be exiled or ostracised by putting them beyond
the bounds of the territory of the state. Finally, and most impor-
tantly, elite members may adopt a strategy of incorporation through
which potential challengers are admitted to high office on condition that they consent to loyally serve the existing system (1916:
1787–8, 1796). Pareto made no mention of the more routine, day-
to-day processes through which closure could be achieved, and on
which subsequent writers have concentrated: the use of family and
school background as a filtering device for elite recruitment, for
example, is not mentioned by Pareto. The reason for this neglect,
perhaps, is that, despite his emphasis on the supply and demand
for skills in a political market, Pareto focused his attention, like
Mosca, on those situations in which social forces outside the governing elite are able to pose a direct and confrontational challenge
to the established rulers.

Social closure, however achieved, is the key to social change and
to the rise and fall of elites (1901: chapters 3 and 4). While the entry
of 'new blood' into an elite may invigorate it, the innovative practices that they introduce may undermine the position of established members. If elites remain closed to outside recruitment and
influence, they may end up in a situation where their particular
capacities and sentiments have become irrelevant to their continued power. Unless they change, they are likely to decay. If established governing elites rely exclusively on the extreme strategies of
exclusion that Pareto described, the dominance of one particular
kind of residue is likely to be exaggerated relative to its significance in the population as a whole. In such a situation, 'the road to
ruin is thrown open' (1916: 1797). It is for this reason that revolutions
figure centrally in Pareto's analysis. Decaying elites that are maintaining themselves through ineffective means are likely to be overthrown by revolutions (1916: 1798–9):

> Revolutions come about through accumulations in the higher strata
> of society – either because of a slowing down in class-circulation, or
> from other causes – of decadent elements no longer possessing the
> residues suitable for keeping them in power, and shrinking from the

use of force; while meantime in the lower strata of society elements
of superior quality are coming to the fore, possessing residues suitable for exercising the functions of government and willing enough
to use force. (1916: 1431)

Pareto held that it is possible to measure the balance between the
two styles of political leadership within particular governing elites.
The pattern of history, he argued, shows two distinct kinds of
period. In some periods, social circulation is great enough to bring
about a gradual alteration in the balance between the two styles in
the governing elite. In other periods, social closure by an established
elite excludes certain skills and produces a revolutionary reaction
and overthrow of the established elite by their rivals (Pareto 1902).

Elites of 'foxes', he argued, will tend to restrict circulation through
mechanisms of social closure that are aimed at minimising the effects
of social mobility on the interests of their membership. Elites of
'lions', on the other hand, are more likely to allow circulation to
take place. It is possible to imagine, for example, an elite of foxes
facing a gradual accumulation of political and social problems that
require repressive measures and that are increasingly difficult to
handle with their particular skills of cunning. If the governing elite
does not recruit those who are skilled in coercion, those lions who
are excluded from power may form themselves into what later
writers have called a 'counter-elite' that mobilises the masses in
order to overthrow the established governing elite. The lions, when
established in power as the new governing elite, will take the necessary measures to re-establish public order and political stability.
Pareto held, however, that the new elite of lions will itself, in the
long run, face an accumulation of political and social problems that
require the skills of cunning that they lack. They will, in these
circumstances, open their ranks to the foxes and social circulation
will result in the gradual replacement of the lions by the foxes.
When this has occurred, the whole historical cycle begins again.
Political change is a continuous cyclical process of evolutionary
and revolutionary periods.[15]

Bureaucracy, technique and the managerial elite

Weber had identified a central element in the 'rationalisation' of
the modern world as being the growth of that rationalised form
of domination that he termed 'bureaucracy': complex structures of

formal administration that are organised around hierarchical structures of 'rational' authority. In a similar vein, Mosca (1896) had charted the transition from direct, personal authority to 'bureaucratic' forms of authority exercised through salaried officials. The growth of bureaucracy centred on an alteration in the basis of power in large-scale political and economic associations. Elected or hereditary political leaders and the owners of commercial and industrial businesses were increasingly exercising their powers indirectly through hierarchies of civil servants and managers who owed their positions to appointment rather than to election or to ownership. The modern nation state and the large business enterprise had become organised around the exercise of delegated authority by salaried officials who were legally separated from the means of administration and who each had a particular expertise, specialisation and sphere of responsibility.

This alteration in the mechanisms of power in large-scale associations was seen by some commentators as pointing to possible changes in patterns of elite recruitment. Weber (1918a) himself had suggested that it was necessary to explore the possible rise of rule by officials (*Beamtenherrschaft*), but the most systematic early statements of this possibility were those of Michels (1911), who held that the growth of bureaucracy was undermining democratic leadership, and of Veblen (1919) and Berle and Means (1932), who saw property ownership as being undermined by the growth of bureaucracy in large businesses. These writers suggested that those with delegated authority based on administrative competence could usurp the powers that were formerly exercised by politicians and owners and could become a new 'managerial' elite.

This possibility, for many, seemed close to realisation in the emerging 'bureaucratic' structures of the Soviet Union, and the classic statement of the argument – that of James Burnham (1941) – arose from discussions over the future of the Soviet form of industrialism. Marxist and non-Marxist writers had recognised that fundamentally new forms of political and economic organisation were developing in Russia during the 1920s and 1930s, and for many people these were harbingers of change in the West itself. Marxist discussions of the Soviet experience in its Stalinist period culminated in Trotsky's study of *The Revolution Betrayed* (1937), where he highlighted the great achievements of the Soviet system but set these beside its bureaucratic 'distortions'. The extreme unevenness of its industrialisation had left many areas of the economy in a backward state, reflecting, he argued, the extreme stagnation of the Russian economy before the Revolution. The Soviet Union, he claimed, had moved the economy into a 'preparatory stage'; it was a 'transitional regime' that was preparing the way for a socialism that had yet to be achieved (1937: 26, 52, 240–1). During this transitional period, however, it had become a 'degenerated worker's state', combining an increasingly socialised economy with a centralised, bureaucratic and authoritarian political system.

Far from withering away, the Soviet state had been significantly strengthened. Bureaucracy and a centralised system of control had been expanded, and the bureaucrats had become entrenched as a new and powerful social group: Russia had become dominated by a 'ruling bureaucracy' (1937: 87). This bureaucracy, claimed Trotsky, was the basis of Stalin's rise to power. Stalin was 'the indisputable leader of the Thermidorian bureaucracy' (1937: 93) that hastened the degeneration of the Bolshevik party into a mere adjunct of the state bureaucracy. The regime had become 'totalitarian' (1937: 99), totally dominated by its new 'ruling stratum'. This stratum, comprising up to half a million people in the 'commanding upper circles' of the Soviet Union and its republics, had been formed in the bureaucratic hierarchies of the state, the trade unions, the co-operatives, and the party, and was supported by 'a heavy administrative pyramid with a broad and many-faceted foundation' (1937: 32). This whole bureaucratic hierarchy comprised about 15 per cent of the population.

This strengthening of the state power and of bureaucracy was also apparent in the fascist societies of Germany and Italy, but Trotsky distinguished these regimes from the Soviet case. Bureaucracy under fascism, he argued, was the servant of private, monopolistic business. In the Soviet Union, on the other hand, the state bureaucracy was the ruling social power itself. 'It is in the full sense of the word the sole privileged and commanding stratum in the Soviet society' (1937: 235). Its source of power was state property, which it had made its own and from which it excluded the mass of workers from any effective control. The state bureaucracy did not, however, hold property in the form of stocks and shares that could be passed on to their heirs by its individual members, and so it was not a system of 'state capitalism'. It was, on the contrary, 'recruited, supplemented, and renewed in the manner of an administrative hierarchy, independently of any special property relations of its own' (1937: 236). It was the administrative power of command *per se* that formed the basis of its social position.

Trotsky had attempted to comprehend the emergence of a new,

bureaucratic ruling minority from the standpoint of a Marxist theory that continued to recognise the importance of property relations. This attempt to theorise the relationship between property and bureaucracy in the formation of elites was carried further by the Italian theorist Bruno Rizzi in a book published two years after Trotsky's (Rizzi 1939). Rizzi nudged forward the debate by depicting a shift from the *ownership* of property to the *control* of property as the basis of dominant groups. The new 'ruling class' of the Soviet Union depended upon its collective control of state property, and it headed a new system of 'bureaucratic collectivism'. According to Rizzi, however, the Soviet experience was but a manifestation of a much wider process that he termed 'the bureaucratisation of the world'. The enhanced power of the state in all the advanced societies had led to the expansion of bureaucratic hierarchies, and the regimes of Nazi Germany and fascist Italy, and even Roosevelt's New Deal America, could be seen as moving towards bureaucratic collectivism. Rizzi's book was not published in full, and its suppression confined its influence to Trotskyist circles. Trotsky himself rejected Rizzi's view that the ruling stratum could be designated as a 'ruling class', but James Burnham – who had split from American Trotskyist circles and had begun to abandon Marxism after the German–Soviet pact of 1939 – set out his own views in a form that was strikingly similar to that of Rizzi (Burnham 1941).[16] From his base in the Philosophy Department at the University of New York, he produced *The Managerial Revolution* (1941) and, a year later, a reconstruction of the 'Machiavellian' origins of these ideas in the works of Mosca and Pareto (Burnham 1942).

Burnham began by reconstructing what he took to be Marx's position on the origin of class relations, and he saw this as rooted in the same broad framework that lay behind the conflict theory of Gumplowicz and Mosca.[17] All societies, he argued, are characterised by a 'struggle for power'. There is 'a particular, and relatively small, group of men [*sic*] that *controls* the chief instruments of production' and that can be described as 'the socially dominant or ruling class' (1941: 56):

> The instruments of production are the seat of social domination; who controls them ... controls society, for they are the means whereby society lives. (1941: 97)

A 'ruling class' has the power to prevent any access to the means of production by other members of the society, and it has the ability to secure a preferential treatment for itself in the distribution of the wealth and privileges that are generated in the system of production. In capitalist societies, as Marx had argued, the ruling class is a capitalist class that has its base in its individual ownership of the means of production. This is a class of employers that exploits the labour of the propertyless proletariat. It is the opposition of capitalist and proletariat that defines the structural distinctiveness of capitalist society (1941: 16). For this ruling class, then, 'control is exercised in terms of the typical property rights recognized by modern society' (1941: 58). Commanding positions in the economic system are derived from relations of individual private property in the means of production.

The capitalist class had had to struggle for power against the 'feudal lords' that dominated medieval society, and capitalists secured their social position only when the power of this class had been broken. The rise of the capitalist class, then, involved 'a great deal of fighting and wars to break the physical power of the feudal lord, and the propagation on a mass scale of new ideologies suited to break the moral power of feudalism and to establish social attitudes favorable to the bourgeois structure of society' (1941: 60). Burnham argued, however, that capitalist society, like the feudal society before it, was itself breaking down as a result of a new struggle for power. The agents of social transformation were not the proletariat, as Marxism had anticipated, but 'the social group or class of the *managers*' (1941: 68). By the First World War the emergence of this new 'class' was a clear and recognisable historical fact, and Burnham held that the managers would, in the following 50 years or so, establish the foundations of a new 'managerial society' in which they would be the ruling class.

In his analysis of the rise of the managers, Burnham gave far greater attention to relations of domination and control in the economic sphere than had Mosca or Pareto, who had concentrated on relations of political domination. The rise of the managers was apparent, Burnham held, in the economic sphere, where the increasing scale and complexity of industrial production meant that greater importance had to be attached to the technical direction and co-ordination of production. This task had become highly specialised, often requiring some degree of scientific training, and it had become organised into bureaucratic structures. This was the sphere of 'management', and the managerial class comprised the large numbers of people who filled the bureaucratic hierarchies of the modern business enterprise (1941: 76). Drawing on the work of

Berle and Means (1932), Burnham held that managers were increasingly replacing capitalists as the leading force in industry. The mass of shareholders had been effectively excluded from power, and the managers were well advanced in their struggle against the 'finance capitalists', who retained a powerful, entrenched position. Many managers had to undertake subordinate managerial tasks linked to the expansion of capital and profit-making, but this had ceased to be an essential feature of industrial production. Industrialism was breaking loose from capitalism. The days of the finance capitalists were numbered, and the managers would soon hold exclusive sway. Indeed, capitalist property relations had already been abolished in the Soviet Union, and they were on the verge of abolition in Germany and elsewhere:

> The position, role and function of the managers are in no way dependent upon the maintenance of capitalist property and economic relations (even if many of the managers themselves think so); they depend upon the technical nature of the production process of modern production. (1941: 86)

The power of the capitalist was everywhere on the wane. The 'managerial revolution' was in full swing.

Burnham saw the rise of the managers as also being characteristic of the political sphere. States and public bodies had become more bureaucratised, and – most significantly – states had extended their control over 'private' economic enterprises. States were no longer limited to the support and maintenance of a system of private enterprise; they intervened at many more points in the system of production and, in many cases, had taken over the ownership of industrial concerns. Burnham held that

> the universal tendency, in the world economy as a whole and in that of each separate nation, is toward the relative extension of governmental enterprise at the expense, necessarily, of private. (1941: 111)

Those who run the expanded public bureaucracies of the state are 'managers', concerned with tasks of technical direction and co-ordination and, increasingly, with social planning. The distinction between 'private' and 'public' managers becomes impossible to make (1941: 100–4). In a managerial society of the kind that was emerging in the modern world, there is full state control in all areas of society, and the new 'class' of managers owes its position not to individual property ownership but to its technical indispensability in the bureaucratic hierarchies of the state. These managers control the process of production and form the leading element in the new class, which encompasses also the partially distinct set of bureaucrats concerned with armies, police, court, prisons, and so on.

The societies that were most advanced in the move towards managerialism – Russia, Germany and Italy – were all 'totalitarian' in form, but this was seen by Burnham as a passing feature of their transitional stage of development. Once the new form of society was fully established, the need to suppress capitalist elements would disappear and the managerial societies could become more democratic in character. Totalitarianism in Russia, for example, reflected the backwardness of its pre-revolutionary structures and was a political response to the particular crises that it faced in the 1920s and 1930s. There was, nevertheless, already a powerful class of Russian 'managers': directors in the concerns, the trusts and the collective farms, officials in the principal ministries and commissions, and their associates in the military, police and political hierarchies (1941: 209). Similarly in Germany, Nazism and Hitler's rise to power expressed its transition from 'decadent capitalism with managerial intrusions' to a truly managerial society. This process was less well advanced than it was in Russia, but Germany was following the same path, albeit under different ideological forms (1941: 225). The advance to managerial society was least marked in the United States, but even there the New Deal showed an incipient form of managerialism (1941: 244).

Djilas, Voslensky and the communist case

For Burnham, I have shown, the Russian experience was especially important in the development of the theory of the managerial revolution and the rise of managers as a ruling elite. Undoubtedly the most influential and compelling illustrations of this theory have also taken the Soviet Union as their point of reference. In order to illustrate the uses of the argument, therefore, I will take the works of Djilas (1957) and Voslensky (1980), though I will concentrate on those specific elements that they add to the general theory.

Djilas was a Yugoslav communist, who criticised contemporary trends in actual communist societies and spoke out in favour of the reform of these systems, for which he was jailed. Djilas held that Trotsky had been the first observer to see the bureaucratic distortions of the Soviet system, but that he had been unable to see the full implications of this development. Trotsky had seen bureaucratic degeneration as a transient stage, whereas Djilas, like Burnham, saw it as a new and stable form of 'class' society.

The communist Revolution had occurred, argued Djilas, in response to the failure of capitalism to generate an industrial take-off. The party itself had taken a highly centralised form – both organisationally and ideologically – in preparation for the Revolution and because of the need to build the industrial foundations of a new society, and this centralisation had persisted after the Revolution. One of its earliest steps had been the nationalisation of industry and the establishment of a system of collective ownership. While this abolition of private property was seen by the revolutionaries as involving the abolition of class relations, Djilas held that the result was not the establishment of a classless society but the birth of a 'new class' of rulers, a ruling elite.

Control over property, according to Djilas, is the basis of 'ownership', which may take a number of different legal forms. The state property of the communist system was controlled by the bureaucracy of the party and the state, which therefore became a new class of owners. By virtue of its control over state property, then, the party bureaucracy was the new ruling and exploiting class (1957: 35, 54):

> The new class may be said to be made up of those who have special privileges and economic preference because of the administrative monopoly they hold. (1957: 39)

This emergence of the new class of rulers was not, however, the result of bureaucratisation *per se*. The roots of the new class were to be found in the Bolshevik party, which was specifically formed as a party of professional revolutionaries, and it was from this group of revolutionaries that the new class emerged. It established its power in a one-party system. The core of the new class was, therefore, the party bureaucracy, which headed a much larger apparatus of power. It had gradually consolidated its position through the establishment of strict authoritarian control over recruitment to its highest levels. The new ruling elite was open at its lower levels, but mobility within it was dependent upon complete loyalty to the party and its power (1957: 61). Its top circles were highly restricted in their recruitment, including only those who had demonstrated their loyalty over the course of their career in the party. Having been established as Stalin built his own power base as the head of a dependent and loyal party bureaucracy, by the 1950s – when Djilas was writing – the ruling elite no longer had the need for such autocratic leadership and felt more secure with oligarchic 'collective leadership'.

Other societies had their politicians and bureaucrats, but only the communist regimes had party bureaucracies that had been nurtured in the organisational structure of a party of professional revolutionaries. This revolutionary tradition legitimated the position of the party within the state and led party members to see themselves as a special and privileged group. They accorded themselves advantages, such as higher incomes and enhanced opportunities for advancement, and because of this and their shared control over the property of the state, they developed a consciousness of their position and entered into a struggle with the other strata of communist society.

This emphasis on a new 'class' or ruling elite of loyal party bureaucrats exercising collective control over the means of production has recently been enlarged in an influential study undertaken by Voslensky (1980), a study that first made popular the use of the word *nomenklatura* to designate the new social bloc. Voslensky traces the ruling elite of Soviet society to Lenin's cadre of professional revolutionaries, who organised themselves into a tight faction that exercised firm supervision and discipline within the Bolshevik party. Following their seizure of power during the 1917 Revolution, they established a strong and centralised system of control over the whole society, seeing this as a condition for transforming it in a socialist direction. As a result, they had to build a large state and party apparatus whose key positions of command were held by those who sought careers as bureaucrats.

Voslensky sees Stalin as the key figure in the building of this new stratum, as he established processes of selection and recruitment that operated through political qualification and personal sponsorship. This system of recruitment was monitored by a new department of the party's Central Committee, responsible directly to Stalin. This department monitored appointees at all levels of the party and the state, its 'recommendations' being all but mandatory. The lists of 'acceptable' candidates and, therefore, the body of those who owed their positions to its recommendations were termed the *nomenklatura*. During the Stalin purges of 1936 to 1938, Voslensky argues, the *nomenklatura* finally achieved dominance over the surviving old guard of Leninists. The *nomenklatura* had become a new ruling elite – indeed, it is tempting to say that the Stalinist 'lions' had replaced the Leninist 'foxes'.

This *nomenklatura*, according to Voslensky, remained the ruling elite of Soviet society until the 1980s. The core of its power base was the top of the KGB and the military apparatuses and the military-industrial complex of the armaments industry, and these were buttressed by the propaganda agencies. Its power culminated in the Politburo and its Secretariat, at which point the various chains of sponsorship formed a series of factions tied together by interests and patronage. Voslensky holds that, by the Brezhnev era, this ruling elite had reached a stage where the children of its members were beginning their own careers and were being especially fa-voured in recruitment. The elite was increasingly able to reproduce itself from its own numbers, recruiting from outside only where absolutely necessary. The 'lions' had established effective closure.

Voslensky said nothing about the long-term viability of the sys-tem, though a reading of Pareto or Mosca would have suggested that the ruling elite could not sustain itself for long if it became too closed to the incorporation of new skills and abilities. It is open to question whether the transformation of the Soviet system under Gorbachev and its subsequent collapse can be seen as a result of the pressure of excluded social forces.

I have concentrated on outlining the central arguments of Mosca and Pareto, and the extension of this work in Burnham. Taken together, these writers provide a set of tools for expanding on Weber's brief and rather undeveloped remarks in his analysis of authority of the relations of 'rulers' and 'ruled'. Mosca was un-doubtedly the most sophisticated and historically informed of the three. Pareto's work is certainly more conceptually precise – and it introduces the word 'elite' itself – but his systematisation led him into ambiguities and premature attempts at theoretical closure. A reconstruction of Mosca's work using the term 'elite', as I have tried to provide in this chapter, offers the best possible basis for advance in the study of elites, and a basis from which the remain-ing elements of Pareto's schema can be assessed in the light of their empirical value. Burnham's contribution was to explore in some depth the link between the elites and bureaucracy, seeing bureau-cratisation as enhancing the power of a managerial elite. He, like Djilas, however, remained wedded to the Marxian language of 'class', and he failed to realise that the ruling elites that he described could not be seen as equivalent to the social classes that Marx had analysed. They were social blocs, defined by their occupancy of top command situations. The attempt to assimilate authority to class must be firmly rejected.

The arguments of these writers cannot be accepted as they stand, but their conceptual and theoretical works are full of insights that form a central part of the analysis of stratification. Sociological analysis must examine the structure of authority in a society in order to disclose the command situations into which it is structured. Authority within the sphere of the state is the basis of those command positions that may be described as 'political' elite positions. Authority within the economy also defines a set of command positions that may be described, in purely descriptive terms, as economic or corporate elite positions: positions of authority in business enterprises, business associations and federations, and so on. Similar considerations apply to authority within the cultural sphere (e.g. church hierarchies). These command positions may, under certain circumstances, be demographically clustered into the type of dominant social bloc that, following Mosca, I have termed a ruling elite.

This is the case, for example, in societies such as the former Soviet Union. In societies where stratification takes the form of social classes or social estates, an overarching ruling elite will not be found, though the distribution of command positions may still involve the formation of clusters of positions that are linked to class and status situations. The use of 'elite' ideas in the analysis of non-communist societies can be seen in the influential work of Mills (1956), who looked at the ways in which occupants of top command situations in the economic, political and military hierarchies of the United States were welded into a cohesive 'power elite' by virtue of their shared exclusive social background. According to Mills, power to make decisions of national and international importance had come to be focused in the economic, political and military bureaucracies, and the leaders of these institutional hierarchies made decisions with the greatest scope for affecting the mass of the population. It is through the circulation of 'leading men' (*sic*) among the three hierarchies that the power elite emerges as a cohesive and solidaristic social bloc. Baltzell extended this approach and linked it to aspects of Warner's view of social class, looking at the role of intermarriage, informal and intimate interaction and common schooling in forging the members of 'elites' into what he called an 'upper class' (1958: 6–7). His concern was with the ways in which top command situations in business enterprises are associated with particular status situations rooted in 'old wealth' and are clustered into a cohesive social stratum. Domhoff (1967; 1970) has combined the arguments of Baltzell and Mills into a systematic account of the relations between 'elites' and the 'upper class' in the contemporary United States. In his analysis of the British situation, Miliband (1969) has adopted a similar approach, though he draws more heavily on Marxist class theory to provide a context for his investigation of economic and political 'elites'.

In class societies such as contemporary Britain and America, then, economic authority is derived from property and market relations and operates as a secondary, reinforcing factor to these features of class situation. While it is possible to identify economic and political 'elites' in these societies, these exist in a purely abstract and formal sense as top command situations. They are elements in a dominant social class whose life chances depend primarily on property. As I will show in the following chapter, analyses of the authority of managers and top executives in Britain and the United States owe much to the tradition of Mosca and Pareto.

6

Property, Authority and Class Relations

I have argued that social stratification must be seen in terms of the three analytically distinct elements of class, status and command, and I have explored a number of the issues that are raised in studying each of these elements by considering the founding forms of intellectual discourse associated with each of these ideas – Marxism, normative functionalism and conflict theories. In arguing that each of these three approaches can find a place within the framework of ideas that I have derived from the work of Max Weber, however, I am not implying that they can simply be juxtaposed in an eclectic and unproblematic way. This would be absurd. On the contrary, my argument is that the study of social stratification might better be advanced by searching out and exploring the specific areas of intellectual contact that I have highlighted, rather than by pursuing the internal logic of a particular approach alone. The purpose of my 'Weberian' framework is to set out the basis for a new research programme: a return to Weber allows us to advance more firmly beyond him.

Theorists and researchers in social stratification have tended, however, to pursue the particular concerns of their preferred theoretical approaches, and they have tended to talk *past* one another rather than *with* one another. This is particularly apparent in the works of two influential writers who have produced important theoretical statements in the post-war period. Writing as critics of normative functionalist theorists, the arguments of Dahrendorf and Wright are rooted, respectively, in conflict theory and Marxism. The growth of large-scale corporate bureaucracies with massive structures of authority was, for both writers, the central economic trend of the twentieth century, and both sought to explore – in different ways – the consequences of this for the relationship between class and command. They have explored this issue from the standpoints provided by their differing theoretical starting points, and this has meant that they have failed to recognise the important theoretical convergences that mark their works. Indeed, Wright once glimpsed the parallel between his own ideas and those of Dahrendorf, only to reject his own position in a self-critique that reaffirmed his Marxist purity.

For both writers, a 'separation of ownership from control' in large business enterprises had transformed class relations. According to Dahrendorf, the growth of large corporate bureaucracies meant that class relations had to be reconceptualised as relations of authority. Drawing explicitly on the ideas of Mosca, Dahrendorf drew the conclusion that contemporary forms of administration had given birth to new social blocs – 'ruling classes' and 'subjected classes' – that had supplanted the economic classes of Marxian theory. Wright, on the other hand, drew on the renewal of Marxist theory that occurred in the 1960s and 1970s to formulate an internal revision of the Marxian concept of class that emphasised 'authority' as having supplemented – or even replaced – personal property ownership as the basis of class division.

Dahrendorf: authority embraced

In *Class and Class Conflict in an Industrial Society* (1957) Ralf Dahrendorf set out to provide a radical and innovative alternative to both Marxism and normative functionalism. Though he was seen along with Rex (1961) as a leading 'conflict theorist' (Lockwood 1964; Cohen 1968; Binns 1977), this characterisation of his work failed to draw out the very clear and explicit roots of Dahrendorf's work in the conflict theory of Gumplowicz and Mosca. This is particularly paradoxical as Dahrendorf had identified his own work, along with that of Aron (1950), as an attempt to draw on and to enlarge the ideas of Mosca (Dahrendorf 1957: 194ff). In much the same way as Burnham (1941), Dahrendorf sought to show that Marxist theory had been appropriate for nineteenth-century capitalism but had now been rendered moribund. Dahrendorf found the reasons for the irrelevance of Marxism in the bureaucratisation of the business enterprise and the nation state. The ever-increasing numbers of managers had achieved enhanced economic and political power, and a 'managerial revolution' had established a new, 'post-capitalist' form of industrial society.

In setting out to demonstrate the inability of Marxism to grasp these social trends, Dahrendorf concentrates his attention on managers in industry. Drawing on the empirical work of Berle and Means (1932), he sees the spread of the joint stock company as having produced a separation of 'ownership' from 'control'. When 'legal ownership' of the means of production is separated from their 'factual control', he argued, the Marxian model of class can no longer be applied. Dahrendorf sees Marxist theory as having assumed that legal property rights and relations of effective control were always combined in the powers of personal possession that were exercised by the class of capitalist entrepreneurs. In the joint stock company, however, the role of the capitalist is structurally differentiated into two new roles: those of the 'shareholder' and the executive or 'manager'. The shareholder is an owner only of shares in a joint stock company. He or she has no legal title to the means of production themselves and has no managerial responsibility for them. The shareholder does not have 'a defined place in the formal hierarchy of authority in the enterprise' (Dahrendorf 1957: 44).

The thesis of the separation of ownership from control rests upon a particular interpretation of the implications of the growth of shareholding. Because of the growing scale of business activity in the twentieth century, it is argued, the number of shareholders in companies has increased and, in consequence, their ability to influence business affairs has diminished. Each shareholder now has so few shares that they can have no real voice in the running of business enterprises. Conversely, managers are salaried officials who occupy bureaucratic posts and who have no financial stake in the share capital of the company. The manager has no property rights in the enterprise that he or she manages. Dahrendorf recognises that certain shareholders may, in fact, occupy managerial posts, and that certain managers may hold shares in their company, but he sees such overlap in social roles as being purely contingent. It is not a necessary aspect of either role, and the particular combination of roles is increasingly unlikely to be found in contemporary societies. The roles of shareholders and managers are quite distinct from one another. The powers of the managers increase just as surely as the powers of the shareholders decline.

The exercise of authority in a business enterprise, therefore, no longer depends upon ownership rights. For this reason, Dahrendorf claims, it is necessary to 'replace the possession, or non-possession, of effective private property by the exercise of, or exclusion from, authority as the criterion of class formation' (1957: 136).[1] While the powers of a manager may 'accrue in part from the property rights delegated to him [sic] by the shareholders, acting either as a group or through an elected board of directors', they derive mainly from 'some kind of consensus among those who are bound to obey his commands' (1957: 44–5). By this, Dahrendorf means that the legitimacy of managerial authority flows not from any legal rights of ownership but from the consent of subordinates. It might be noted that Dahrendorf's view of authority departs somewhat from Weber's. For Weber, legitimacy involved the basis on which claims to obedience are made, and not to the subjective motivations from which obedience actually flows. For Dahrendorf, on the other hand, authority depends on the consent of subordinates for its legitimation. This is an important theoretical shift, and Dahrendorf fails to recognise that it moves his position away from Mosca and closer to the consensus assumption of the normative functionalism of which he is otherwise critical. The ultimate foundation of legitimacy, however, is not an essential part of his theory. What *is* essential is the move away from systems of authority grounded in property rights.

Dahrendorf makes this point by generalising the concept of 'control'. He holds that Burnham had correctly seen that 'the class structure of the industrial enterprise is based on control and not on legal ownership of the means of production' (1957: 90). Control based on personal possession was simply one, historically specific form of class relation. All forms of control over the means of production, he holds, can be seen as relations of authority, and the break with Marxist ideas had to be completed by seeing 'classes' as defined by authority relations. It was the structure of authority relations that gave rise to 'class' relations, and changing forms of authority produce transformations in class relations. Wherever there is authority, there will be 'classes', and a truly general theory of class must take the concept of authority itself as its starting point.

Because of the changing nature of authority roles since the nineteenth century, Dahrendorf argues, the advanced societies of the contemporary world can no longer be seen as specifically 'capitalist' societies in any meaningful sense. Indeed, Dahrendorf has a number of reservations about the use of this term to describe any society. The word 'capitalism', he argues, has a Marxist pedigree and, in addition to its reference to the predominance of private property relations, it implies that economic conditions determine other aspects of social life, that they are the 'real basis' of a 'superstructure' of social institutions (1957: 37). Non-Marxists who have adopted the term 'capitalism' to describe the European societies of the nineteenth and twentieth centuries – and Dahrendorf here cites Weber and Sombart – have tended, whether intentionally or not, to take on some of the economic determinism that he believed to have characterised Marx's theory. For this reason, Dahrendorf prefers to employ the more general term 'industrial society', seeing 'capitalism', shorn of any implications of economic determinism, as simply one historically specific form taken by the industrialising societies of the nineteenth century.

'Industrial society', then, is the most general societal type identified by Dahrendorf, and he acquiesces in the common usage of 'capitalism' to designate industrial societies in which property and market relations are the basis of class divisions. Dahrendorf suggests, however, that the industrial societies of Europe and America have now advanced beyond 'capitalism' to a 'post-capitalist' stage of development. Post-capitalist societies themselves are not all of a single type, and Dahrendorf identifies two sub-types: there is, he claims, the 'democratic' or 'pluralist' form of industrialism found in Western Europe and North America, and the 'totalitarian' variant that existed for many years in Eastern Europe.[2] The democratic variant, on which Dahrendorf focuses his attention, is found in such societies as the United States, Britain, Germany and France. The totalitarian variant was found in Russia and its satellites prior to the collapse of the Soviet Union.

It will be apparent that Dahrendorf's reconceptualisation of 'class' departs from the core meaning of the concept by redefining it in terms of authority. Whatever the merits might be of his empirical conclusions about the growth of bureaucracy, the stretching and redefining of 'class' in this way does not further the understanding of the social world. Paradoxically, Dahrendorf betrays some considerable ambivalence himself over the use of the word 'class' to describe command situations in a structure of authority. These power situations and the collectivities that arise from them are termed 'classes', despite Dahrendorf's recognition that 'the similarity between Marx's and even Weber's concepts of class and our concept of conflict group is but slight' (1957: 203). He sees this, however, as a 'purely terminological' issue, despite recognising that it might cause theoretical and political confusions. He holds that:

> Since there is no other concept that expresses this purpose with equal clarity, one might consider it reasonable to retain the concept of class despite all qualifications necessitated by the arguments against it. (1957: 203)

There is, however, a viable alternative to the terminology of 'class' for describing the phenomena in which Dahrendorf is interested. This alternative is to use the terms 'command situation' and 'social bloc' that I defined in chapter 2. In the rest of this section, I will use Dahrendorf's own terminology of 'class' wherever necessary, but I will try to indicate how his arguments could usefully be recast and clarified by using this alternative terminology. In summary, my reformulation of Dahrendorf's position would see him as claiming that 'class situation', in the sense that Marx and Weber saw it, had become a redundant theoretical concept because relations of private property and the market had been superseded by relations of authority as a result of the separation of ownership from control and the growth of bureaucratic administration. The occupancy of command situations in these expanding structures of authority has become the most significant causal component in individual life chances in advanced, post-capitalist industrial societies.

The relevance of the concept of 'command situation' to Dahrendorf's argument is apparent from his definition of authority as a structure of social relations within which there is a definite probability that specific commands will be obeyed (1957: 166). Authority relations exist within all 'authoritarian associations' (*Herrschaftsverbände*), by which Dahrendorf means forms of organised social action that are structured by the exercise of 'imperative co-ordination'.[3] Authoritarian associations include business enterprises, states, churches, trade unions, political parties, and clubs, all of which have a structure of executive power. Despite this recognition of diversity, however, Dahrendorf draws back from any implication that there could be a vast mosaic of command situations, arguing that, for all practical purposes, states and business enterprises are the most salient sources of social division. This *ad hoc* solution leads Dahrendorf towards a similar position to that of Pareto, though he fails to make the important distinction that

Pareto saw between 'governing' and 'non-governing' positions of command. His focus on the business enterprise and the state does, however, point to this solution as an implicit and untheorised condition of his argument.

The command situations of the state and the business enterprises of an industrial society are clustered into collectivities that Dahrendorf calls 'classes' or 'conflict groups'. What he seems to mean by this is that they are formed into more or less cohesive and solidaristic social blocs with specific capacities for involvement in collective action. Command situations are clustered into what he calls, following Ginsberg (1934), 'quasi-groups', rather than organised groups of a 'party' type. However, Dahrendorf gives little attention to the demographic processes of circulation through which this clustering might occur. Indeed, his remarks on the issue of stratum formation are limited to some isolated suggestions about the impact of practices and patterns of recruitment and mobility on the emergence of cohesive and homogeneous social blocs (1957: 188). For the most part, Dahrendorf simply assumes that it is reasonable to see the diversity of command situations within authoritarian associations as being organised around a simple fault line that divides 'ruling groups' from 'subjected groups'. Following Mosca, Pareto and Aron, Dahrendorf sees the incumbents of top command situations as forming 'elites' (1957: 193–4). Elite social blocs are the most important social blocs in any society in which authority relations take the primary place in social stratification.[4]

Elites and other social blocs are quasi-groups with 'latent interests' that comprise the possibilities of action that are involved in the specific roles that are occupied. Shareholders, for example, have different interests from executives and from manual workers, and the interests of government politicians differ from those of civil servants. These interests are 'latent' whenever the occupants of the roles are unaware of them, but they are, nevertheless, real constraints on individual action. Incumbents of similarly located positions, then, will have shared interests, but they may have no consciousness of these interests and, therefore, no organisation or cohesion as actual social groups (1957: 180). Where people do become aware of their latent interests, transforming them into the 'manifest interests' that are subjective, 'psychological' realities for the actors concerned, they have the bases for true collective action. It is only manifest interests that can become the basis of support for the programmes of organised 'interest groups' such as trade unions and political parties. Interest groups have programmes and goals, forms of organisation, and personnel, and they are recruited from quasi-groups to pursue specific manifest interests. Those interest groups with which Dahrendorf is concerned are those that arise from 'interests related to the legitimacy of relations of domination and subjection' (1957: 181). These are the groups that enter into the most significant social conflicts, they are the Weberian 'parties' that are the agents of social change.

Dahrendorf pays considerable attention to the conditions under which the members of social blocs are able to form themselves into one or more interest groups. I have explored this aspect of his theory elsewhere (Scott 1995: chapter 5), and I will not repeat that discussion here. In broad terms, however, he sees this as depending upon the specific organisational aspects of the interest group itself – the nature of its programme and its form of leadership – and the general framework of civil and political rights that allow, or preclude, the participation of bloc members in political and economic organisations.

Having constructed a general model of authority relations and social blocs, Dahrendorf examined the specific form of stratification found in post-capitalist societies. Central to this system of social stratification, he argues, are the occupational roles that are formed around the various command situations of the state and business enterprises. Hierarchies of authority in post-capitalist societies take the form of hierarchies of occupations. Authority is fundamental to the determination of life chances, and so the occupational structure becomes a structure of rewards, of advantage and disadvantage. It is also through the occupational structure that authority relations articulate with differences of status. The social blocs of post-capitalist societies, then, are clusters of occupational roles whose occupants have similar life chances (1957: 70), and Dahrendorf investigates changes in post-capitalist social stratification through examining changes in occupational structures. Since the nineteenth century, Dahrendorf argues, there have been a great many changes in the occupational division of labour. At the same time, there have been changes in the articulation of command and status and in processes of stratum formation, the result of which was to 'institutionalise' definite limits on the extent of inequality. Dahrendorf identifies three major transformations in the occupational system: the decomposition of capital, the decomposition of labour, and the growth of intermediate occupations. Alongside these, he recognises two processes of 'institutionalisation': the institutionalisation of citizenship and the institutionalisation of social mobility.[5]

The decomposition of capital (1957: 41–8) is a consequence of the 'separation' of ownership and control in the joint stock company. As I have already shown, this was the starting point for Dahrendorf's move from a theory of property to one of authority. As a result of the separation of ownership from control, he argues, the entrepreneurial role of nineteenth-century capitalism underwent a structural differentiation into the two separate roles of functionless property holder and propertyless executive. Owners of shares became irrelevant to the process of production, which came under the control of salaried managers. These new propertyless executives comprise the 'functionaries without capital' of Renner's (1953) 'service class' and they are recruited to enterprises on the basis of their specialised education or their administrative competence, not because of their ownership of property. As a result, they have very different attitudes and outlooks from those of the old entrepreneurs and the rentier shareholders.

The decomposition of labour (Dahrendorf 1957: 48–51) is the corresponding process through which the role of the unskilled labourer, characteristic of nineteenth-century factory capitalism, has been differentiated into semi-skilled and highly skilled work roles as a consequence of advanced and science-based technology. Highly skilled workers exercise greater autonomy and responsibility and have been required in great numbers by the more complex technology of the advanced engineering industries in which their skills and expertise bring them close to engineers and supervisors. Semi-skilled workers are also required to exercise greater autonomy, for which they are trained 'on the job'. This differentiation of work into skilled, semi-skilled and unskilled occupations corresponds with a hierarchy of income and prestige. Manual workers show a great diversity of life chances, and Dahrendorf believes that 'it has become doubtful whether speaking of the working class still makes much sense' (1957: 51).

Between the occupational categories of the executive and the skilled worker there has been a massive growth of 'new' occupations whose members cannot easily be assimilated to either category. These salaried non-manual workers – clerks, shop workers, doctors, secretaries, civil servants and so on – comprise a highly diverse 'occupational salad' (Mills 1951) that lies somehow 'between' capital and labour but does not form a single category. They have often been described as a 'new middle class', but Dahrendorf holds that they actually comprise two quite distinct groups. The larger group consists of those occupations that have been differentiated from or are closely linked to entrepreneurial and executive positions and that are involved in the exercise of delegated authority. The other group consists of those who are excluded from the exercise of this authority and occupy subordinate positions. These two groups are termed, respectively, 'bureaucrats' and 'white collar workers' (1957: 55). Because of their latent interests, bureaucrats tend to align themselves with the ruling groups, while white collar workers are aligned with the subjected groups.

These changes in occupational structure are seen as being shaped into patterns of social stratification in a context that is determined by the institutionalisation of social mobility and of citizenship. Education has become the principal means of occupational allocation, and, as a result, people's occupations are no longer so directly determined by those of their parents. In consequence, the expectation and the reality of social mobility have been institutionalised (1957: 57–61). Inter-generational and intra-generational occupational mobility has increased with industrialisation, and is now at a very high level. Only at the very top and bottom of the occupational hierarchy, Dahrendorf claims, is there still any significant degree of self-recruitment to occupational positions. As a result of these changes in patterns of social circulation among occupations, stratum solidarity and conflict have declined, and individual competition has increased (1957: 60; see also Dahrendorf 1965). The extension of the status of citizenship (1957: 61–4), and especially of the social rights of citizenship, has limited the growth of inequality and has resulted in a certain degree of equalisation in the life chances of those in different occupations. The welfare and redistributive policies in which the social rights of citizenship are embodied, together with rising real wages, have brought about greater equality and an increased ability for all members of post-capitalist societies to participate in the mass consumption and new consumerism that is the correlate of social citizenship. Dahrendorf cites the work of Adorno and Horkheimer (1944) on the culture industry as supporting his view that these changes have led to a greater uniformity in life styles and, correspondingly, a diminution in status distinctions.

Social mobility and social citizenship, then, have altered the shape taken by social stratification. The differentiation of the occupational structure has loosened the boundaries between social strata and has changed their contours. The institutionalisation of social mobility and of citizenship has created an 'open' and relatively equal structure in which differences of income and life style among social strata are minimised. As a result, the social blocs of post-capitalist societies are not to be seen as sharply bounded, cohesive or polarised social groups, and they are less likely to form themselves into tightly organised interest groups.

Dahrendorf has paid most attention to the top levels of the stratification system, to top command situations and the social blocs into which they are formed. The holders of authority are described variously as the 'political class', the 'ruling class', and the 'elite', but Dahrendorf generally uses the more neutral term 'ruling groups'. While taking on much of Mosca's argument, he rejects the assumption of the Italian writers that ruling groups necessarily form a minority within their society. The delegation of authority through an extensive bureaucratic hierarchy, he argues, means that many people are able to participate in the exercise of authority and so may be considered as members of the ruling group (1957: 195). The subordinate groups, similarly, are seen not as a residual 'mass' but more positively as 'subjected groups'. This conception of 'ruling groups' as large groups, rather than small minorities, and the emphasis on the openness and looseness of social stratification, are associated with a recognition of divisions within ruling groups. The social bloc that dominates a post-capitalist society, he argues, may be fragmented into relatively distinct and competing sub-groups. In particular, Dahrendorf points to a distinction between economic and political ruling groups as a common line of social division.

This division of economic and political rulers follows from the 'institutionalisation of industrial conflict', a process that has involved the separation or 'isolation' of industrial from political conflict. Industrial relations and industrial conflict are 'confined within the borders of their proper realm and robbed of their influence on other spheres of society' (1957: 268). On this point, Dahrendorf is completely at odds with Burnham, whose views on industry he otherwise shares. The rulers of industry and those who are subject to their authority within the economy are not formed into political parties that enter into open political conflict with one another. Indeed, the whole political sphere is autonomous from industry and is the locus of distinctive authority relations of its own.

Within business enterprises, Dahrendorf argues, the division between those with authority and those without means that 'incumbents of positions of domination and subjection' are 'united in two conflicting quasi-groups with certain latent interests' (1957: 251). The ruling group in the economy comprises the executives and bureaucrats of industry, while the subjected group comprises the mass of the workforce (including white collar workers). Thus, the ruling group extends beyond the narrow category of executives – the 'managerial elite' – to include the whole administrative hierarchy:

> the industrial bureaucrats or, as Renner calls this group, the 'service class', stands as a whole on this side of the borderline which separates the possessors of authority in an enterprise from the subjected workers, both manual and white-collar. By virtue of their positions, bureaucrats are members of the ruling class of industry and share its latent interests. (1957: 256)

Bureaucrats are, in short, a part of the dominant social bloc in the economy, while manual and white collar workers form a subordinate social bloc. These social blocs are not, however, involved in the kind of conflict and struggle that Marx had depicted for the bourgeoisie and the proletariat. The institutionalisation of industrial conflict has limited the extent of their struggles. Conflicts of interest that are generated in the labour market have been recognised and granted a degree of legitimacy by giving them a particular legal definition through the establishment of rights of collective bargaining, negotiation and arbitration. As a result, a normative framework of 'rules of the game' was established for industrial conflict, and this has allowed industrial relations to become 'democratised' (1957: 64–7, 257–67). Economic divisions do not spill over into the political arena.

The state has a structure of authority in which the occupants of some roles have the right to issue authoritative commands and those of other roles are subject to this authority (1957: 290). This is the division between the rulers and the 'mere citizens' of the state. The core of the ruling group – the 'political elite' – comprises ministers, parliamentarians and judges, but it also includes all bureaucrats and white collar workers in the service of the state. By contrast with industry, Dahrendorf argues, the gradation of authority and responsibility in the state is such that the white collar workers cannot be excluded from the social bloc of those who exercise authority. The ruling group in the state – the 'political ruling class' – is more inclusive and more diverse than its industrial counterpart (1957: 297). The subject group in the state also plays an important part in Dahrendorf's model of post-capitalism: 'The citizens of a democratic state are not a suppressed class, but they are a subject class, or quasi-group, and as such they constitute the dynamic element in political conflict' (1957: 297). It should be noted that the subordinate group in the state is not completely separate from that in industry. It includes, of course, those in subordinate positions of authority within the state, but it also includes all those *outside* the apparatus of the state who are subject to its authority. The 'mere citizens', then, include most of those in the ruling and subordinate groups in industry. What differentiates most citizens from the subordinate industrial bloc is an institutionalised separation of concerns and activities, not any difference in actual personnel. The degree of overlap in composition and recruitment between the industrial and the political spheres is a matter for empirical investigation that Dahrendorf sees as having no direct implications for the institutionalised separation of the two aspects of social conflict.

It will be recalled that Dahrendorf identifies two variants of post-capitalism, and the discussion so far has concerned principally the 'democratic' or 'pluralist' variant. Many of the underlying processes are also found in the 'totalitarian' variant, but this is seen as having a number of important differences. The principal differences between the two societies involve the relationship between political and economic authority and the pattern of recruitment to the political elite. In the 'pluralist' form of post-capitalism, the government is democratically elected, the political elite is responsive to 'veto groups' and power is generally more diffused (1957: 304–5). Dahrendorf's views on this echo those of Kornhauser (1953; 1959), whose work was influential for the whole 'pluralist' approach to political sociology. The institutional separation of political from industrial conflict means that the managerial elite, as the leading element in the industrial ruling class, must lobby and pressurise the political elite from the outside (1957: 302):

> Leadership in the state does not imply leadership in industry, in the army, or in other associations, nor does exclusion from authority in one context imply exclusion in all others. (1957: 317)

In totalitarian situations, on the other hand, the political elite is drawn from a larger social bloc and claims to rule in its interest. Political authority and industrial authority are superimposed. In a similar vein to Djilas (1957), Dahrendorf sees a totalitarian society as headed by a monistic 'ruling class'. By contrast with the 'freedom' that characterises pluralist societies, totalitarian societies are closed and oppressive.[6]

Social class	% of population
Elite	1
Service class	12
Old middle class	20
Working class elite	5
'False' middle class	12
Working class	45
Lower class	5

Figure 10   Social classes in Germany, 1965
Source: Dahrendorf 1965: 92

Dahrendorf's aim was to construct a general model of authority relations and social blocs in post-capitalist societies, but he did not completely ignore the question of how this model was to be applied to particular societies. He did not expect there to be a one-to-one relationship between the general and the concrete, but he did expect his model to highlight the key social divisions in particular societies. The only society to which he gave any sustained attention was Germany (Dahrendorf 1965), though he did not fully reconcile his account with his theoretical work. Following Geiger (1932) he examines the social strata that are formed on the basis of the differentiated market and command situations that are embodied in the occupational structure. On this basis, he presents a scheme of seven social classes, as shown in figure 10. In this scheme, the overall 'elite' comprises the occupants of the leading command positions in the various institutional orders and, as I have shown, he sees this as being a diverse collection of separate 'elites' with little coherence or collective consciousness. The managerial and the political elites he sees as being most important. The service class consists of those groups that he has defined as 'bureaucrats', while the white collar workers who occupy subordinate positions in the structure of authority are described as a 'false middle class'. Independent entrepreneurs in large and medium-sized businesses, who still depend on the personal ownership of property for their control over the means of production and their authority over their employees, make up the 'old' middle class. Although Dahrendorf says nothing about the matter, it may be assumed that he would draw on his general model and see the service class and the white collar class as likely to divide into their industrial and political fractions in any social conflicts, the industrial fraction uniting with the managerial elite and the political fraction with the political elite. Subordinate manual workers in Germany are said to fall into three separate social classes that are distinguished largely by their command situations and, to a lesser extent, by their market situations. The 'working class elite' comprises foremen and craftsmen whose work situation involves them in a degree of autonomy or authority, while the 'lower class' consists of the 'unemployable' lumpenproletariat that Dahrendorf would later (1992) see as forming an 'underclass'. The great bulk of manual workers, however, form a single 'working class'. Once again, the general model would suggest that skill divisions would be important within the 'working class' and that its social conflicts would be divided into industrial and political concerns.

Wright: authority denied, and reinstated

In chapter 3 I looked at some of the disagreements that arose within the Marxist tradition as attempts were made to explore the consequences of joint stock enterprise for class structure. The joint stock company seemed to involve an alteration in relations of personal possession that transformed the capitalist class and introduced new 'intermediate' class situations. Much of the debate on these issues, however, has been dominated by those outside the Marxist tradition who have espoused the thesis of the separation of ownership from control on which Dahrendorf drew in his investigation of 'post-capitalism'. Recent Marxism, however, has reinvigorated this debate by attempting to draw on Marxist interpretations of this same process. The conceptual tools for this work were developed within the framework of structural Marxism by Althusser and Balibar (1968), and it was those who drew upon their work – most notably Poulantzas (1968; 1975), Carchedi (1975a; 1975b) and Wright (1976) – who developed novel interpretations of joint stock enterprise.[7]

According to all three writers, contemporary capitalism was 'organised' or 'monopolistic' in form, by contrast with the liberal, competitive capitalism of the nineteenth century with which Marx had been concerned. Central to their concerns was an attempt to understand the growth of the intermediate occupations that have generally been described as a 'new middle class'. Marx himself had glimpsed the growth of these intermediate occupations and had interpreted them on the basis of their 'unproductive' character (Marx

1862–3; see also Nicolaus 1967). The proletariat comprises those wage earners who perform productive labour: they generate surplus value and so contribute to the expansion of capital (Marx 1862–6: 1041; 1865–78: 209–11). 'Unproductive labour', on the other hand, is undertaken by earners who are paid by a deduction from 'revenue' rather than from capital. A domestic servant, for example, is paid from the personal income of an employer, and so the servant's wages do not form a part of the variable capital of a business enterprise. Unproductive labourers, then, occupy a distinct class situation from that of the proletariat.

These relations of production are, however, unusual. Despite the large numbers of domestic servants that there were in Victorian households, the 'intermediate' occupations that seemed to pose such a problem for Marxist theory were those found in the offices and counting houses of capitalist enterprises and the state, not those found in a domestic or personal service capacity. Poulantzas (1975), nevertheless, tried to use Marx's idea of unproductive labour to define the class situation of a 'new petty bourgeoisie'. While he faced great problems in showing that clerks, bankers, insurance agents, and others in the service and commercial sections of capitalist enterprises were 'unproductive', he had more success in his claim that workers in the state occupied a distinct class situation. Those who work in the civil service, the police, the education and health services, and other sectors of the state, are paid from tax revenue rather than from capital and so can more plausibly be treated as 'unproductive' workers.[8] Their dependence on the tax capacity of the state, rather than the immediate profitability of an employing enterprise, Poulantzas argued, gives them class interests distinct from those of the proletariat.

Carchedi and Wright rejected this solution to the question of the intermediate occupations, but they also found unsatisfactory the attempts of the Ehrenreichs (1979) and others to conceptualise them as lying 'between' labour and capital. Their solutions, independently arrived at, consisted of seeing those in the intermediate occupations as 'both' labour and capital. They were a distinct 'class' – neither bourgeois nor proletarian in the conventional sense, but having characteristics that combined elements of both of these class situations. This was what gave them their 'intermediate' position within a basically dichotomous class structure of the kind described in figure 3.

At the most general level, it was accepted, the capitalist mode of production comprises just two basic classes: the capitalists, or bourgeoisie, who own the means of production; and the workers, or proletariat, who are excluded from this ownership. But the capitalist mode of production rarely, if ever, appears in this pure form, and the class situations that are found in actual capitalist societies will be more complex than those of the general model. The first element of complexity recognised by Carchedi and Wright is that which results from the coexistence of capitalist and non-capitalist relations of production in the same society. These are the secondary or transitional relations of production that Marx identified. Wright defines the relations of simple commodity production, for example, as those in which 'petty bourgeois', self-employed producers own the means of production but do not employ others and so lack any effective control over labour power. The basic classes defined by capitalist relations of production are consistent 'controllers' or 'non-controllers' of the means of production. The bourgeoisie, for example, had full powers of control over capital, in the form of their control over both people and machinery. The proletariat, on the other hand, were excluded from effective control and were subject to the control of the bourgeoisie. The petty bourgeoisie, defined by the relations of simple commodity production, showed an inconsistent profile by virtue of their lack of control over the labour of others. The actual liberal capitalist societies of the nineteenth century showed such a combination of relations of production, and they continue to describe important aspects of class relations in contemporary capitalism.

The most striking innovations made by Carchedi and Wright, however, were the attempts to look at the transformation of capitalist relations themselves and the ways in which these generated new intermediate class situations. These transformations were seen as involving a differentiation in the previously simple structure of ownership relations, and in these circumstances the conventional Marxian typology of class situations becomes inadequate. The differentiation of ownership relations alters the class situation of the bourgeoisie and generates the new class situations of the intermediate occupations.

While their terminology differs, the basic ideas of both writers are similar. Wright, for example, distinguishes the 'legal ownership' that is involved in property relations from the 'economic ownership' that constitutes actual control over the means of production. Relations of legal ownership are defined by the legal title to physical objects and financial securities, in so far as these are relevant to the production of goods and services. Formal, legal entitlements to machines, commodities, stocks and shares, for example, are all involved in the legal ownership of the means of production. Relations of economic ownership, on the other hand, are relations of effective control over capital in the process of production. This control over investment and resources gives people the power to assign the means of production to different uses and to dispose of their products. In the liberal capitalism of the nineteenth century, legal and economic ownership were united in an undifferentiated relation of ownership: legal rights of ownership were directly expressed in the powers of economic ownership. This was the basis of the personal possession that was exercised by the capitalist entrepreneur. The two basic classes of such a capitalist mode of production in its liberal, private or competitive stage – the bourgeoisie and the proletariat – are defined quite simply as the owners and non-owners of the means of production (Wright 1978: 68; Carchedi 1977: 83–4).

The increasing use of joint stock forms in business, however, allows the legal relations of ownership to be differentiated from relations of effective control. As had been argued by the theorists of the managerial revolution, the legal ownership rights of shareholders are quite distinct from the actual ability to control the means of production and to appropriate their products. In the early stages of joint stock capital, of course, this need involve no real departure from personal possession, as can be shown through a slight digression from Wright's own argument.

A capitalist entrepreneur who adopts a corporate form of business may retain all or a majority of the shares in the company and so may continue to unite legal ownership and effective control. The introduction of the joint stock company, then, may merely involve a shift from *direct personal possession* to *indirect personal possession*. Instead of owning the assets directly, the entrepreneur owns all or a majority of the shares in a company which, in turn, owns the assets. In a situation of direct personal possession, an individual or a family owns a factory or a workshop and uses these personal assets to generate the profits from which an income is derived. Both ownership and appropriation are direct and immediate. In a situation of indirect personal possession, on the other hand, an individual or family owns a majority of the shares in a joint stock company and so is able to continue to enjoy effective control over the operations of the company from which a dividend income is derived. The legal form of the joint stock company, then, intermediates between the personal owner and the actual operations of the means of production, and personal possession takes a more indirect form.

Wright shows little awareness of this possibility, though it is an important first step in the process with which he is mainly concerned. Of much greater interest to Wright are the consequences that follow from the need for large-scale enterprises to draw on ever larger pools of capital in order to finance their activities. The joint stock company allows capital to be mobilised on a scale that is beyond the resources of most individuals and families. Shares are sold ever more widely through the stock exchange system, and there is a progressive dispersal in share ownership. In these circumstances, many individuals who own company shares have none of the powers of effective control. Workers, for example, may acquire company shares in small numbers, but these will have little or no impact on their class situation. Carchedi, like Dahrendorf and the managerial theorists, sees this process as a separation of ownership from control in which share ownership becomes irrelevant to business operations. The shareholders, Carchedi (1977) argues, 'fall outside the capitalist production process: they have no function to perform within this process'. Shareholders are functionless property holders. Wright, on the other hand, holds that legal entitlements may continue to play a part in effective control and can continue to be an essential element in 'bourgeois' class situations:

> Not all individuals who own stock are part of the bourgeoisie, but all occupants of bourgeois class locations own substantial quantities of stock. (1978: 70 n. 62)[9]

The legal ownership of stocks and shares, then, may still allow people to participate in effective control, but it is not, in itself, a *sufficient* condition for this control. In the latest version of his position, Wright (1989) has further explored this interdependence of legal ownership and economic ownership, recognising that individuals may, simultaneously, be both the owners of share capital, from which they derive a dividend income, and the occupants of business directorships, for which they receive a salary. Their life chances may be determined, at one and the same time, by two distinct causal components, one rooted in property and the other in authority. This recognition of the importance of authority was integral to his view of effective control.

The full differentiation of legal ownership and effective control means that control over the means of production can no longer take the form of personal possession. With the differentiation of 'shareholders' from 'directors', the latter owe their control over the means of production to their appointment to top command positions in a business enterprise rather than to the inheritance of property. This process is taken a step further when effective control itself is differentiated into relations of appropriation and relations of immediate authority in the system of production. With the growing scale of production, it becomes impossible for the controllers of large enterprises to exercise their powers of control to the full. They are forced to delegate many of their powers to 'managers' and their subordinate clerks, who can actually put the means of production to work on a day-to-day basis (Wright 1978: 68).[10]

This argument rests upon the idea that capitalist enterprises have undergone a transition from personal possession to 'impersonal possession', and a further digression from Wright's argument will, again, clarify the trends that are under consideration (see the fuller discussion in Scott 1985). Indirect personal possession ceases to be possible when an individual or family holds less than a majority of the shares in a company, though minority holdings may allow them to continue to retain a substantial involvement in the running of the business. As shares become more widely dispersed, however, no individual or family stands in a position of effective control, and the directors are no longer responsible to substantial personal possessors. The culmination of this process occurs when the bulk of company shares come to be owned not by individuals but by other companies – by banks, insurance companies, pensions funds, and other industrial companies. In such a system of *impersonal possession*, there is a complete dissociation of the class situation of the rentier from that of the executive. The rentier occupies a propertied market situation, deriving an income from portfolio investments in a wide range of corporate and other stocks and shares. The rentier, typically, has no substantial stake in any particular company. The executive, on the other hand, occupies an acquisitive market situation, deriving an income in the form of a salary but also occupying a key command situation in a business undertaking. In the terminology that I have used in this book, the life chances of the executive are determined by the interplay of market situation and command situation, with market situation playing the primary role.

It is this development from personal to impersonal possession that lies behind Wright's own argument, though he casts it in a

Supervision	Self-employment	
	Yes	No
Yes	Bourgeoisie	Managers
No	Petty bourgeoisie	Proletariat

Figure 11   Wright's initial four-class schema

different form and makes it the basis for an unhelpful redefinition of 'class'. The differentiation of shareholders, directors and managers that occurs in systems of impersonal possession alters the basis on which class relations are produced and reproduced. Shareholders are themselves corporations or financial 'institutions', though some individual shareholding rentiers survive, and the mechanisms of personal possession are no longer central to the structuring of class situations.[11] Wright holds that directors and managers owe their life chances not only to their specific market situations as financially or technically qualified labour, but also to the command situations that they occupy in the service of capital. The authority that they have within their employing organisations becomes an important determinant of their life chances, and Wright attempts to incorporate these command relations into his very definition of 'class'. Directors and managers occupy distinct 'locations' because of their positions of command at, respectively, the top and the middle levels of the expanding corporate hierarchies, and Wright saw these positions of command as constituting the specific features of their class situations. It was through reflecting on the rising significance of authority relations that Wright attempted to theorise the 'contradictory' character of certain 'intermediate' occupations as having the characteristics of *both* labour and capital. Some occupations, he held, fall into more than one of the basic classes: some class locations have a multiple class character and so may be 'contradictory' rather than coherent.[12]

His first attempt to develop this idea involved an elaboration of his simple three-class schema. In this class schema – not published at the time, but later used in a study of income distribution (Wright 1979) – he cross-classified employment relations with supervisory relations to generate a four-class schema (see figure 11). The bourgeoisie and the proletariat occupy basic class situations, while the petty bourgeoisie occupy secondary class situations defined by the relations of the small-commodity mode of production. In contemporary capitalism, however, it is the directors and top corporate executives that comprise the bourgeoisie, not entrepreneurial capitalists with personal possession. The directors of a company, who own virtually none of its share capital, nevertheless have collective control of the means of production. They control the means of production without having personal possession of them (Wright 1980: 338). The class situation of the managers, however, is ambiguous or contradictory in that it involves them simultaneously in both bourgeois and proletarian relations. Managers are wage earners whose command situations involve them in the exercise of authority as one aspect of what Carchedi called the function of capital. This is the 'work of control and surveillance' that is involved in ensuring that production takes place in such a way as to expand value (Carchedi 1977: 64). By virtue of their role in the technical process of production, however, managers are also involved in the 'work of co-ordination and unity' that is an integral part of the organisation of labour. Managers, then, are involved in both the function of capital and the function of labour.

The typology in figure 11 is defined by the cross-classification of 'supervision' with 'self-employment'. The concept of supervision corresponds directly to the idea of involvement in relations of authority that establish positions of command, but 'self employment' fits less well with Wright's intentions. While the petty bourgeoisie may, indeed, be self-employed, this is not generally the case with directors and top executives, who are employees of their organisations. Even entrepreneurial capitalists with indirect personal possession cannot truly be regarded as 'self-employed' in any meaningful sense. Wright himself recognised that there were many problems with his interim solution, not least the fact that it dealt only with 'managers' and ignored many other intermediate occupations.[13] In the revised version of his argument, which is now its best-known form, he replaced 'supervision' and 'self-employment' with Balibar's categories of ownership and control. This allowed him to recognise that bourgeois class situations involved 'economic ownership' of the kind that has already been discussed, and to classify the various intermediate occupations by the degree of control that they have over the means of production (Wright 1978: 68–9). An occupational position may, for example, have minimal 'economic ownership', but partial control over the physical means of production, and full supervisory authority over labour power. This differentiation of control relations was the basis of the 'contradictions' that structure the class locations that lie between the basic class situations of the bourgeois, the proletarian, and the petty bourgeois.

Wright recognises three of these contradictory locations in contemporary capitalist societies: 'managers and supervisors' occupy contradictory locations between the bourgeoisie and the proletariat, 'small employers' occupy contradictory locations between the bourgeoisie and the petty bourgeoisie, and 'semi-autonomous workers' occupy contradictory locations between the proletariat and the petty bourgeoisie. Managers, for example, have full or partial authority, but they lack full powers of appropriation over the surplus produced. The senior managers that are closest to the bourgeoisie 'are generally characterised by limited participation in economic ownership', while middle managers exercise a limited degree of authority but have only minimal powers of appropriation. Supervisors, on the other hand, are completely excluded from both appropriation and command over the physical means of production, but they do exercise a limited degree of authority over the labour power of others. Small employers, like the petty bourgeoisie, have full powers of appropriation in their small businesses, but they differ from the petty bourgeoisie in that they are employers of labour. Finally, semi-autonomous workers are those who have a certain degree of control over their own immediate conditions of work but who are not involved in the employment of others or in the exercise of any authority over them.

The unambiguous and the contradictory class locations are the building blocks of Wright's mature class schema for modern society (see figure 12). His schema assumes, however, a one-to-one correspondence between class situations and economic class categories. The concept of 'class location' is used to grasp a range of specific class situations that are not differentiated by Wright in any systematic way. At the same time, he has no conception of demographically formed social classes. Wright's 'classes' are nominal economic categories that are assumed to be homogeneous 'class locations'.

By far the largest of the nominal economic 'classes', he claims, is the proletariat, a basic class that accounts for around half of the economically active population of the United States. This is closely followed in size by the intermediate class of managers and supervisors (about one-third of the economically active

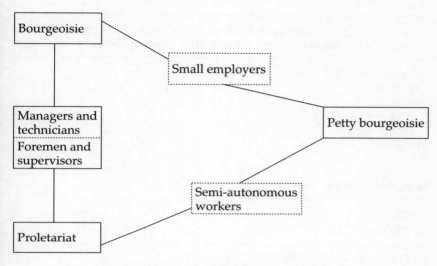

Figure 12 Contradictory class locations
Source: Wright 1978

population), which he sees as being 'at the boundaries of the working class'. The remaining classes are all relatively small. The bourgeoisie – comprising 'traditional capitalist' entrepreneurs and the top directors and corporate executives – forms a minute 1 to 2 per cent of the economically active population. Wright's allocations were intended as rough and ready indications only, and at this stage in his research he provided no reliable way of coding occupations or of allocating particular positions to their correct class location. This class schema, with minor modifications, remained the basis of Wright's work for a number of years, and it became the cornerstone of a large international research project for which more rigorous methods of coding were developed.[14]

During the 1980s, Wright began to work closely with John Roemer (1982), contributing to the development of 'analytical' or 'rational choice' Marxism. These new theoretical ideas led Wright, once more, to modify his class schema. 'Class' remained a term that he saw as involving relations of both 'exploitation' (appropriation) and authority ('domination'), and the main change that he made was to see the class situations of small employers and semi-autonomous employees as reflecting the interpenetration of capitalist relations of production with those of small commodity production (Wright

	Capitalist relations		Small commodity relations	
	Appropriation	Domination	Appropriation	Domination
Bourgeoisie	+	+		
Top managers	+/−	+/−		
Lower managers and supervisors	−	+/−		
Workers	−	−		
Petty bourgeois			+	+
Semi-autonomous employees	−	−	−	+
Small employers	+	+	+	+

+　appropriator or dominator
−　non-appropriator or non-dominator
+/−　both appropriator and non-appropriator or dominator and non-dominator

Figure 13　Wright's later class schema
Source: modified from Wright 1985: table 2.2, p. 50

1985: table 2.2, p. 50). This new version of the schema is shown in figure 13, and the results arrived at when this schema was used to compare the class structures of various societies are shown in figure 14.

This change in the class schema was, however, short-lived. As he worked through more of the implications of Roemer's argument, Wright came to the conclusion that the idea of command situation ('domination' in his terminology) could not be assimilated with an exploitation-based concept of class. The 'contradictoriness' in the locations of managers and others in his schema was no longer their essential characteristic. This contradictoriness had been defined as a contradiction between expertise and authority, and such a view, he held, gave too great an importance to their participation in authority. This effectively marginalised the relations of exploitation which, as a Marxist, Wright wanted to retain at the centre of his analysis. Wright had recognised that his position was moving close to that of Dahrendorf (Wright 1985: 57), and for a Marxist this was too close for comfort.[15] In reaction to this realisation, he denied the very element that Dahrendorf had embraced and he produced

	% of population	
	US	UK
Capitalists	1.8	2.0
Managers	12.4	16.7
Small employers	6.0	4.5
Petty bourgeoisie	6.9	6.0
Supervisors	17.4	9.4
Experts	3.4	4.1
Semi-credentialled employees	12.2	14.4
Proletariat	39.9	42.9

Figure 14 Class locations in the United States and Britain, 1980
Sources: calculated from Wright 1985: table 6.1, p. 195; Rose and Marshall 1986: table 1. The Rose and Marshall data are taken from the estimates that they made using Wright's own coding methods. The categories are simplified from Wright's more differentiated categories

the very converse of Dahrendorf's own solution. Where Dahrendorf had rejected Marx's concept of class and embraced authority as the sole criterion of division in the business enterprise, Wright came to reject his earlier concern for authority and to reassert the exclusive relevance of a purely economic concept of class situation.

Wright developed a view of managers as an exploiting class that lacked capital assets but held 'organisation assets'. This concept of organisation assets referred to the 'coordinated cooperation among producers in a complex division of labour' (1985: 79). Wright sees organisation assets as playing an important part in the analysis of monopoly capitalist societies, and as also being particularly relevant to the former Soviet Union and other examples of 'actually existing socialism'. Entrepreneurial capitalists control both capital and organisation assets, but the development of monopoly capitalism had divided them: rentier shareholders control capital, while managers control organisation assets. In the Soviet Union, the absence of private property and market relations had allowed the organisation of production to become a centralised task undertaken by a complex state apparatus, and state bureaucrats were able to establish themselves as a new exploiting class based on their organisation assets (1985: 78–82; 1983). Managers in capitalist societies, according to Wright, are the wage earners without personal capital who control organisation assets through their occupancy of top command situations. They hold 'positions which are directly involved in making policy decisions within the workplace and which have effective authority over subordinates' (1985: 151). They are distinguished from the subordinate 'supervisors' who occupy the lower levels of the authority hierarchy and who are not involved in decision-making; and they are also distinguished from the capitalists who have ultimate strategic control.[16]

Neither Wright's nor Dahrendorf's theoretical strategy is tenable as a basis for a comprehensive investigation of social stratification. Both Dahrendorf and Wright had recognised the significance of command situations in the determination of life chances and the particular part that they played in determining those of contemporary business directors and executives. This must be seen as a shared recognition of a fundamental shift in the relation between class situation and command situation in actual patterns of social stratification in the twentieth century. This does not mean, however, that class situation can be disregarded, as Dahrendorf sought to do. Relations of exploitation *also* remain as important determinants of life chances. The relative importance of class situation and command situation – and, I might add, of status situation – is a question that can be resolved only through empirical investigation and not by theoretical fiat.

Wright seems to have recognised this in his most recent work. Despite his concern that his own analyses were growing too close to those of Dahrendorf, Wright's denial of authority was both partial and short-lived. Between 1985 and 1989, he stressed his exploitation-based concept of class. He became increasingly uncertain, however, about whether managers merely exercise delegated authority or are able to secure a real autonomy because their powers 'are built into the social organisation of production' (1988: 200). In the face of substantial criticism and of his own doubts, however, he returned to some of the themes of his original conception of managers as occupants of contradictory locations. Organisation assets – powers of command in a corporate structure of authority – were seen as bases of differentiation *within* a managerial class that was defined by its combination of partial economic ownership and participation in the function of capital (1989: 338–40, 347).[17]

This conceptual shift led Wright into serious problems with his analysis of state employees. The concept of organisation assets had initially provided him with a way of discussing the position of state employees in the stratification system. State employees are, of course, not directly involved in the ownership or control of capital and this has posed considerable problems for orthodox Marxist attempts to identify their class situation. By stretching the term 'class' to cover command situations as well as property-based market situations, however, Wright was able to solve this problem to his own initial satisfaction. Just as in the Soviet Union, employees of the state in capitalist societies were seen as being distinguished by the 'organisation assets' that they controlled. Wright was able to see senior civil servants, for example, as occupying an analogous position to managers in industry. Wright was, however, unhappy with this solution, and in his latest work he suggests that the absence of capitalist relations in state employment means that civil servants and other decision-makers in the state do not occupy the same contradictory exploitation relations as private sector managers (1989: 340–3). Wright has begun to outline a concept of 'state relations of production' that takes account of the coercive and fiscal roles of states. Wright holds that

> The state cannot reasonably be viewed simply as a giant corporation in which the material basis of the capacity of 'state managers' to appropriate and allocate surplus is equivalent to that of corporate managers. (1989: 343)

He goes on to introduce a rudimentary classification of command situations within the state, but he does not develop the idea. His few remarks on the senior levels of the state are, however, reminiscent of Pareto, as Wright notes that members of the state 'elite' have mediated links of career mobility with those in capitalist locations and so cannot be considered as a separate, state-based class.

Wright's problems with state employees and with achieving a proper understanding of managers are consequences of his failure to distinguish *class situation* from *command situation*, and of his related failure to distinguish power *situations* ('locations') from the social *strata* into which they are formed. Indeed, Wright has a totally inadequate conception of 'class formation'. Class formation in Wright's work involves two levels of analysis: class structure and class collectivities. Class structure refers to the structurally defined places or locations that exist within relations of production. These class relations involve specific 'structural capacities' that comprise the objective links that arise from the conditions of production, and this structure of relations 'generates a matrix of exploitation-based interests' (1985: 123; 1978: 99ff). These places may or may not be formed into collectivities with specific 'organisational capacities' and the ability to engage in struggle.[18] The structure does not yield a unique pattern of collectivities, and its expression may be modified by numerous intervening factors such as ethnicity, religion, and so on.

Now, this view restates some of the arguments that Marx set out in his distinction between the class-in-itself and the class-for-itself, and it involves all the ambiguities and inadequacies of that position. More particularly, Wright's twofold distinction between class structure and class collectivities conflates the levels of what should be seen as a threefold distinction between class situation, social class and 'party'. Wright looks at the relationship between structurally defined class situations and what Dahrendorf called 'interest groups' that enter into conflict and struggle. He pays little attention to the demographic formation of the social classes from which interest groups recruit their members. Wright requires a far more fine-grained awareness of class situation (and of command situation), an awareness of the ways in which these stratifying situations may be demographically formed into social strata, and an appreciation of the conditions under which parties and other associations may emerge and represent social strata or their fractions.

I have shown that both Dahrendorf and Wright have recognised the increasing salience of command situations in contemporary societies, and that they have both confused matters by conflating 'command' with 'class'. In Dahrendorf this involved redefining class in terms of authority relations; while in Wright it involved subsuming authority in an economic concept of class. Neither writer recognises the need to distinguish these elements analytically before exploring their actual interconnections in concrete settings. Both writers also fail to properly consider the demographic formation of social strata. Dahrendorf recognises that command situations can be formed into 'quasi-groups', but these collectivities get little attention compared with that accorded to the formation of interest groups. Wright does not even recognise the existence of demographic quasi-groups, and he simply assumes a one-to-one correspondence between broadly defined class locations and the economic categories of his 'class' schema. Their ideas can, however, be used in a wider synthesis of concepts, and in the following chapter I will try to show how this is so.

7

Structures of Social Stratification

In this book I have explored the theoretical ideas of a diverse range of writers, but I have looked at them in relation to a particular conceptual framework derived from the work of Weber. Although I have tried to present fair and accurate interpretations of these theoretical positions, which I hope will be valuable in their own right, my main aim has been to show that their underlying ideas – if not their detailed conclusions – are complementary to one another. The many areas of disagreement and incompatibility that mark their works should not, of course, be minimised, but my claim is that their core ideas can be fruitfully employed in complementary ways. Using their ideas together, I hold, it is possible to provide a more comprehensive basis for research on social stratification than can be provided by any one set of ideas alone. My overall argument does not stand or fall on the accuracy of my interpretations of particular writers. Regardless of whether I have correctly interpreted their intentions and achievements, the ideas that I have set out can be seen as the raw materials for developing the theoretical framework that I derived from Weber's sketchy outlines for the analysis of social stratification.

Weber's work sustained a multidimensional approach to social stratification in which class, status and command were seen as analytically distinct, but empirically entwined aspects of the distribution of power and the formation of social strata. This 'multidimensional' aspect of Weber's approach has often been recognised, but it has invariably been misunderstood. For some commentators,

Weber is supposed to have drawn a contrast between class, status and power, while others have remained closer to Weber's own text and have claimed that the dimensions were class, status and party. I have shown that Weber is more correctly seen as pointing to 'command' – and not 'power' or 'party' – as the third dimension of stratification. Economic, communal and authoritarian power are the three forms of social power that give rise to relations of class, status and command (see also Runciman 1989).[1] The distinction between what I have called 'power situations' and 'social strata' is fundamental to my argument. Power situations are structural locations in the social distribution of power and specific causal components in life chances. I have classified power situations into class situations, status situations and command situations. Social strata, on the other hand, are the actual collectivities of people that are formed from the demographic clustering of power situations through the circulation of individuals and through their informal and intimate interactions. I have classified social strata into social classes, social estates and social blocs (see figure 2). Class relations were seen by Weber to involve domination by virtue of constellations of interests in the property and labour markets, and I turned to Marxian theory for an exploration of the dynamics of class. Marx's work on class showed that such constellations of interests resulted from the possession or non-possession of the means of production and that changing forms of class relations reflected the changing forms of possession that characterised particular modes of production. Marx saw personal possession, or the lack of it, as the source of class divisions in capitalist societies, while later Marxists have explored the implications of more impersonal forms of possession for class relations in contemporary capitalism. Status relations were seen by Weber as rooted in structures of domination that occur by virtue of the prestige that is associated with particular styles of life. In the work of Parsons and the normative functionalists this prestige was seen as generated in the 'societal community', and they held that changing patterns of social evaluation and ranking reflected the values through which these communal relations were organised. Changing cultural values in the context of the differentiation of social activities produced variations in status ranking. Finally, command relations arise from relations of domination that occur by virtue of authority. Mosca, Pareto and their followers, I argued, explored the ways that structures of authority and administration are shaped by the development of the state and other bureaucratic hierarchies. Changing forms of administrative authority are the basis of patterns of command that define 'elites' and other social blocs.

Social stratification is a complex set of structures that articulate the levels of analysis that Lockwood (1964) has termed system integration and social integration. 'System integration' involves the systemic interrelations among the structural parts of a social system, most specifically the mechanisms through which economic, communal and authoritarian power relations are organised into structures of domination. Each of the three traditions that I have considered made an attempt to relate the phenomena of power to deeper issues of system integration, seen variously in relation to modes of production, forms of social community and structures of authority. I have shown that 'power situations' – class, status and command situations – have been seen as emerging from the structuring of economic, communal and authoritarian relations, and that demographic processes of circulation and interaction structure these power situations into social strata of various kinds. The forms of individual and collective action that are entered into by the members of social strata are aspects of what Lockwood has called 'social integration': the relations of order and conflict among individuals and groups. It is through the formation of parties, trade unions, associations and other social groups that the members of social strata can contribute to the reproduction or transformation of the very processes of system integration that give rise to their opportunities for action. Social stratification, then, has a central importance in sociology as the connecting link between system integration and social integration.[2]

For each of the three main theoretical approaches that I have considered, I have examined empirical applications that have drawn on their ideas in order to explore patterns of stratification in specific societies. These studies have carried forward the theoretical arguments and have demonstrated the explanatory power – and limitations – of each theoretical approach. Marxist investigations of the American capitalist class showed how economic divisions became the basis for the formation of a social class that was able to enter into forms of political action to become a dominant force within the state. Such analyses, whatever their other failings, did not seriously consider status relations, which Marx had seen as a rapidly disappearing ideological relic of the feudal past. Lloyd Warner, on the other hand, saw status divisions as continuing to play an important part in contemporary patterns of social stratification. Indeed, he held that they outweighed economic class divisions in their significance for consciousness and action. Through his investigations into local social status in twentieth-century America, Warner firmly established the principle that status relations had to be considered in any comprehensive investigation of social stratification. Mills, Baltzell and Domhoff showed how the concerns of Mosca and Pareto could be allied to Marxist issues of class to give a more adequate account of the relationship between economic and political power, while Djilas's 'elitist' view of social stratification in the Soviet Union, on the other hand, demonstrated that the Marxian view of class could not provide a full and complete picture of the distribution of power in Russia and other East European societies. So long as they remained totalitarian 'command societies', their patterns of stratification had to be seen in relation to the distribution of the powers of command through the state-party apparatus.

The works of Dahrendorf and Wright, which I considered in chapter 6, took the argument a step further forward and showed, in different ways, that contemporary capitalist societies could no longer be understood in terms of the classical Marxian model of class. According to Dahrendorf, it was necessary to abandon economic class theory – although he remained attached to the word 'class' – and to focus exclusively on authority relations in all advanced industrial societies. For Wright, on the other hand, an economically based class theory could be broadened out to incorporate an understanding of command relations alongside property and market relations. Wright, I argued, provided the more plausible account, though his insistence that command was to be seen simply as an aspect of class was, I argued, both confusing and unnecessary. This conceptual failure led Wright to reject the possibility of learning from the works of Dahrendorf and Mosca.

Previous chapters have concentrated on outlining the specific features of these theoretical approaches and their various attempts to explore the dimensions of stratification. In this chapter, I return to the overarching 'Weberian' framework in order to draw out the connections among them that have often remained implicit in the earlier discussions. The specific arguments of the previous chapters will not, of course, be repeated. My aim is merely to set out more explicitly the underlying connective ideas and to leave the reader to refer back to the more detailed discussions in the earlier parts of the book. I will, however, draw out some of the implications of the argument by considering the self-consciously Weberian work of Goldthorpe. In his many studies, Goldthorpe has set out a powerful and influential programme of 'class analysis'. I will argue that Goldthorpe's work can be extended and enlarged through a more explicit use of the ideas in the body of this book. The work of Goldthorpe has been the focus of much critical discussion, and I will show that much of this criticism is well founded. I will suggest, however, that he does provide some of the essential tools for an investigation of social stratification and that a reconstruction of his views from within the framework that I have set out can provide a more secure base for sociological research.

Stratification and power situations

Social stratification, it should by now be apparent, is more than just social inequality. Structured social inequalities can occur around a variety of social differences, and they may involve a wide range of resources, capacities and possessions. Such inequalities include those associated with age, gender, sexuality, ethnicity, religion, language, region, and so on. Social stratification occurs when structured social inequalities are systematically interrelated in the way that they shape people's life chances and are involved in the formation of large-scale collectivities that stand in hierarchical relations to one another. The social stratification of a population, then, involves the formation of its members into a system of social strata that are distinguished from one another by their life chances and their life styles and by the particular causal mechanisms that are responsible for these.

Critics of the idea of social stratification have often failed to recognise this distinction between inequality and stratification, claiming that the concept of social stratification fails to properly consider group formation and group conflict (Dahrendorf 1957). For such critics, the metaphor of social stratification ignores the struggle over resources, which they see as central to 'class' analysis (Saunders 1990: 3; Bourdieu 1979: 245). Such objections betray an ignorance of geology, from where the metaphor of 'stratification' was first derived. When properly understood, the geological metaphor of stratification provides a powerful and highly appropriate model of the very processes that these critics wish to emphasise. Geological formations are certainly not akin to the simple, uni-dimensional structures of inequality that critics of the metaphor imply. They are complex structures that are characterised by fissures, faults, folds and intrusions, and that involve complex metamorphic processes. Strata do not simply lie on top of one another in neat layers like a jam sandwich. They are compressed and distorted into complex shapes that can be understood only through painstaking research and with an analytical imagination that is able to reconstruct the processes through which they have been formed. Indeed, it is precisely the *complexity* of geological formations that makes the metaphor of social stratification so appropriate. It is, of course, essential to use the concept in a way that grasps the specific features of the social world, but the model of stratification itself, properly understood, is a powerful tool of sociological analysis.

Social strata reflect the complex processes through which the underlying power situations that people occupy operate, in both reinforcing and contradictory ways, to generate their life chances and life styles. I have identified these power situations as being class situations, status situations and command situations, each of which is to be understood as an aspect of the distribution of power within a society, and as arising from the structuring of power into relations of domination. Each type of power situation results from specific types of social relations. Class situations arise from the property and market relations that establish patterns of domination by virtue of constellations of interests and that result from the rational, calculative alignment of economic interests. Status situations, by contrast, result from the communal relations through which domination on the basis of prestige is established. Finally, command situations are a consequence of the relations of command that are built into structures of legitimate domination.

The analysis of class situations, as they are defined here, has principally been undertaken by Marxist writers, many of whose contributions have been discussed in chapters 3 and 6 of this book. Of particular importance has been the debate surrounding the work of Wright, which has highlighted many of the critical issues in class analysis (see also Abercrombie and Urry 1983). Analyses of status situations have been more diverse in character and have not been confined to the normative functionalist tradition that was discussed in chapter 4. The debate over 'citizenship', for example, has explored the implications of the ideas of Marshall (1949) for the changing forms of status in contemporary societies. For Marshall, legally enshrined citizenship rights were rooted in ideas of participation in the communal heritage of a society and they defined new forms of status division that run counter to divisions of class (Turner 1988; Barbalet 1988). In a different vein, Bourdieu (1979) has explicitly related his idea of 'cultural capital' to Weber's concept of status, and has seen cultural distinctions as providing the basis for a framework of analysis complementary to that of class and 'economic capital'. The analysis of command situations has, perhaps, been least developed, despite the growth of important work in 'organisation theory' (see, for example, Wilensky 1967; Etzioni 1961; Reed 1985). This work, however, has largely been confined to command in the economic sphere. This is also true of Wright's reiteration of the arguments of Dahrendorf and Burnham (considered in chapters 5 and 6), though Wright's principal concern was to relate economic command to class situation. The analysis of political command and its implications for strata formation have barely been developed since the founding statements, though some advances have been made in the work on decisions and 'nondecisions' that were consolidated into Lukes's (1974) brief but important theoretical statement.

Social strata themselves result from the circulation and interaction of the occupants of power situations. It is through these demographic processes of intra- and inter-generational mobility, informal interaction, intermarriage and household formation that different power situations come to be clustered together into the large-scale collectivities that are social strata. It is the 'natural breaks' in the structure of demographic relations that disclose the boundaries between social strata (Payne 1987: 13). There is, of course, nothing inevitable about the formation of social strata. Patterns of circulation and interaction may be such that no overarching social strata are formed: social relations may not establish lines of closure, and life chances may be shaped separately by specific power situations or their elements. Such 'fragmented' patterns are unusual, but many commentators have suggested that the stratification systems of the contemporary world have become increasingly fragmented and that, in consequence, 'class' is dead (Clark and Lipset 1991; see the debate in Lee and Turner 1996). A central task in any investigation of social stratification is to discover whether social strata have, in fact, been formed in a particular society and, if so, how they might have changed over time.

I have suggested that the specific character of a social stratum depends upon the relative salience of the various power situations in determining the life chances of its members. Class situations, status situations and command situations are generic mechanisms that can appear in all societies, though their relative significance in the overall patterns of advantage and disadvantage that affect social strata will vary considerably. The predominance of class situation, status situation or command situation results, respectively, in the formation of social classes, social estates and social blocs, although various 'hybrid' forms are likely where two or more power situations are equally salient. In certain circumstances, when all the social strata of a society are decisively shaped by the operation of one specific mechanism of power, whole societies may be characterised as class, status or command societies.

Social strata, then, must be seen as complex formations that stand in hierarchical relations to one another, but that are rarely formed into simple hierarchies. They are multidimensional social structures that intersect and overlap with one another and that may be fragmented into distinct fractions. The principal strata of a society may coexist with surviving elements – perhaps metamorphosed – of earlier systems of stratification, these secondary strata intruding into the principal lines of social division. Systems of social stratification are subject to constant forces, stresses and tensions, ensuring that further metamorphosis is an ever-present possibility.

As *social* formations, however, social strata are composed of individuals, who must be seen as conscious and purposive agents. The interests of these agents motivate their actions, and it is through their actions, both individual and collective, that structures of stratification are reproduced or transformed. The members of a social stratum may develop an awareness of its composition and boundaries and of its relations to other strata in the society, and this awareness can become organised into shared 'images of society' that may, under certain circumstances, develop into the kind of group consciousness that allows a stratum to achieve a degree of cohesion, unity and collective identity (Mann 1973: 13). In these circumstances, members of a stratum may participate in interest groups, associations, and social movements that give voice to the interests of stratum members. Although whole strata are rarely capable of collective action, the actions of these interest groups, associations and social movements may create the appearance of true collective action on the part of the stratum itself.

There are two principal tasks in a comprehensive structural analysis of social stratification, corresponding to the two principal columns of figure 2. The first is to map the power situations that exist in a society and to show how these are related to patterns of social difference and social inequality. This is a complex task that often has to be undertaken in an indirect way. The mapping of class, status and command situations in contemporary capitalism, for example, has generally been undertaken through the mapping of occupational titles, treating these as proxies for the underlying power situations. In the following section I will examine in some detail the debates that have arisen in these investigations. The second task is to map the actual social strata – if any – that are formed around power situations. This involves an examination of the demographic processes of circulation and interaction among the occupants of power situations. In contemporary capitalist societies, this task has generally been pursued through a mapping of occupational categories into social strata. These two tasks are basic to any proper consideration of the emergence of collective consciousness and collective action of the kind that was considered by Weber and Marx and that has figured so centrally in empirical work on social stratification.

Mapping power situations

The principal attempts to provide conceptual tools for the mapping of class, status and command situations have tended to employ very limited schemes of categorisation.[3] Without a proper set of conceptual tools, analyses will be blunt and will be unable to identify the important lines of advantage and disadvantage that cross-cut a society. This is particularly obvious in studies of command situations, where discussions have rarely gone beyond the simple opposition of an 'elite' to a 'mass', though some writers have added an 'intermediate' category (Giddens 1973b). Such coarse schemata are, in general, too imprecise to capture the complexities of authority relations. A more fine-grained approach that recognises the great diversity of command situations in complex systems of administration would better grasp the lines of division that are involved in the determination of life chances. It would seem plausible, at the minimum, to distinguish decision-makers in the state from those in private agencies such as business enterprises and churches, while distinctions among those who make decisions in the state might plausibly be made on the basis of the specific institutional mechanisms with which they are involved. Members of a government, party politicians, military leaders, judges, and others all occupy distinct command situations within the upper levels of the state. A proper mapping of command situations would combine these distinctions with a categorisation of different levels of command. Putnam (1971: figure 1.3), for example, has usefully distinguished 'proximate decision-makers' from lower levels of political command: 'influentials', 'activists', 'the attentive public', 'voters' and 'non-participants'. Each of these categories, it might be suggested, may be cross-cut by differences of institutional area, and similar distinctions might be made for private agencies outside the sphere of the state. Such an approach would highlight a myriad of command situations, each with its specific distinguishing characteristics and associated life chances.

Status situations, too, need to be seen, in principle, as highly diverse. A vast range of social differences may become the basis of social evaluation and ranking: gender, age, sex, sexuality, 'race', ethnicity, religion, kinship, and so on. As a result, people tend to occupy a plurality of status situations. While these cannot generally be charted with the same degree of precision as might be possible for relations of command, it is no less important to attempt to make such fine distinctions as the starting point for a proper investigation of power situations. In some societies, overarching values and synthetic 'master' statuses may reduce the range of variation, but this is not universally the case. Lenski (1954), for example, has argued that contemporary societies are marked by the decline of traditional values and master status attributes, leading the diverse criteria of status distinction to become both larger in number and more autonomous from one another. The status 'profiles' of individuals on these criteria, he argued, tend to be more or less 'inconsistent', with people showing a relative lack of 'status crystallisation'.

Similar considerations arise in the analysis of class situations, where the whole issue of where to draw class 'boundaries' has been hotly contended. However, this discussion has rarely been pursued in a sufficiently fine-grained way. Marx himself concentrated principally on the divisions that resulted from property ownership, and he gave far less attention to the great diversity of class situations that can arise from the structuring of labour power by skill differences. Even in the discussions of class fractions and 'transitional' classes, Marx's approach involved the identification of only a relatively small number of distinct class situations, and his abstract class categories were large and heterogeneous. Weber, as is well known, identified many more possible sources of differentiation in class relations, but, despite the remarks of many commentators that his work implied the existence of a vast mosaic of class situations, Weber set out no systematic account of these.

Those who have followed Weber have rarely done any better.

Class situations for Parkin (1971), for example, are categories of occupations that are rooted in the distributions of property and of marketable skills. Those who hold certain occupations can achieve higher rewards: where property and skills are scarce relative to the demand for them, those who possess these resources have a greater bargaining power in the market. The greater the level of skill that is involved in an occupation, Parkin argues, 'the greater is its relative scarcity in the market-place. And, in turn, it is the degree of scarcity relative to demand which largely determines occupational reward' (1971: 21). Parkin sees property operating alongside skills in the determination of life chances, and for many people both factors are relevant to their class situation. The investment of personal savings, for example, is a means through which small-scale property holdings can reinforce occupational earnings. Despite his clear recognition of the differentiating effects of property and market relations, however, Parkin provides no detailed delineation of potential class situations.

Giddens's influential commentary on the Weberian approach to class situation, too, produced only a very coarse-grained schema. His work depicts class situations as rooted in 'market capacities', by which he understands 'all forms of relevant attributes which individuals may bring to the bargaining encounter' (Giddens 1973a: 108, emphasis removed). On this basis, he recognises property, credentials (as embodied in forms of knowledge and skill), and sheer labour power as the principal market capacities that generate class situations in capitalist societies. But this was the point at which Giddens left his analysis of class situations. He recognised three, and only three, class situations in contemporary societies, and these were the bases, respectively, of the upper, middle and working classes. Such an approach assumes a simple one-to-one relation between class situation and social class, and it fails to grasp the necessity for a fine-grained dissection of class situations as a prelude to any investigation of their possible formation into a smaller number of social classes.

In the recent work of Goldthorpe, however, a more fine-grained approach to the delineation of class situations has been developed, and this work also shows how command and status situations can be mapped alongside class situations. This work, forming part of a long-running investigation of social mobility, set out an explicitly Weberian programme of research on class issues (Hope 1972; Ridge 1974; Goldthorpe and Hope 1974; Goldthorpe 1980). While Goldthorpe employs the concept of 'class situation', however, he

follows Lockwood in seeing this as involving both 'market situation' and 'work situation'. Where market situations are seen in
essentially Weberian terms as structures of employment relations,[4]
work situations are defined as the 'social relationships in which the
individual is involved at work by virtue of his [sic] position in the
division of labour' (Lockwood 1958: 15). Central to these social
relations are the relations of authority through which the division
of labour is regulated. The work situations of individuals, Goldthorpe has argued, refer to their 'location within the system of authority and control governing the process of production in which
they are engaged, and hence in their degree of autonomy in per-
forming their work-tasks and roles' (1980: 39). Goldthorpe's use of
Lockwood's concepts, then, involves an explicit combination of class
(market situation) and command (work situation) within a unitary
framework of analysis. Goldthorpe's work involves an explicit
recognition that class and command have become so closely entwined in the contemporary economy that it is hardly possible to
investigate them separately. For this reason, Goldthorpe uses the
term 'class analysis' to encompass them both. I will show later on
that he also makes an implicit incorporation of status situation into
the same framework of analysis. In a similar vein, though from
someone otherwise critical of Goldthorpe, Payne (1987) has argued
that the occupational schema used in the Scottish mobility study
'reflects a similarity of task and authority, and possibly also of
status'. In terms of its comprehensive scope and its fine-grained
texture, the Goldthorpe approach to 'class analysis' offers a viable
operational approach to the mapping of power situations in contemporary societies.

It is difficult to undertake direct investigations of market and
command relations in an advanced industrial economy, as these
are combined in the structuring of a single occupational order. For
this reason, Goldthorpe follows the practice of many other researchers and uses occupational titles as proxies for the underlying power
situations. This does not involve a reduction of stratification to the
analysis of occupations, it is important to note. While some ana-
lysts have, indeed, treated occupations per se as the units of social
stratification, Goldthorpe is clear that it is the underlying power
situations themselves that are of critical significance. In societies
where the occupational order has become the focus of many of the
more important class, status and command relations, it is simply
expedient to adopt a short-cut procedure and focus research attention on occupational titles. A fully comprehensive investigation

would require that occupational titles be decomposed into the power situations that form their analytical elements, despite the great practical difficulties that this would involve. In much research, however, this decomposition is simply unnecessary, and occupational titles are able to serve as useful proxies for specific combinations of power situations.

Goldthorpe's mapping of power situations, then, involves a consideration of occupational titles and of the categories into which they can be grouped. It is worth exploring the construction of Goldthorpe's categories in some detail, as this shows how class, command and status elements are all involved in the constitution of the various occupational categories. Goldthorpe used a large list of occupational titles derived from the directory of occupational unit groups produced by the Office of Population, Censuses and Surveys (OPCS), one of the most detailed listings of occupations that was available.[5] Using information on employment relations and the characteristic skills and conditions of work that were associated with each group, an initial 1061 'unit groups' were reduced to 124 occupational categories that Goldthorpe held to be uniform with respect to their market and work situations. Goldthorpe claimed that these categories were, in consequence, homogeneous in terms of 'the net extrinsic and intrinsic, material and non-material rewards and deprivations typically associated with the occupations which they comprised' (Goldthorpe and Hope 1974: 24). In so far as market situation was the more fundamental element in determining these life chances in contemporary Britain – reflected in the much greater attention that Goldthorpe pays to employment relations – these occupational categories were, he believed, the fundamental 'class situations' in a society such as contemporary Britain. The term 'class situation' is the appropriate one to use, because it is the most significant causal component in life chances, outweighing the supporting influence of command situations.

While the 124 occupational categories were held to correspond to differences in market and work situation, Goldthorpe also sought to incorporate some aspects of status situation into his schema. The initial 124 categories were ranked according to their occupational status, as this was judged by respondents in a national sample survey, and on this basis Goldthorpe grouped together the occupational categories that had a similar status. Wherever adjacent categories in the status ranking were particularly close in their measured prestige, these categories were merged. As a result of this merging, the initial 124 categories were reduced in number to

36, which Goldthorpe felt provided a more workable delineation of power situations for most research purposes. Although the occupational status evaluations were not used to produce a single status hierarchy among the 36 categories, status judgements were an integral element in the construction of the categories (Goldthorpe 1980: 39). Subsequently, Goldthorpe (1985) has developed a revised version of this occupational classification with categories that are separated completely from any direct investigation of occupational prestige and that reflect mainly differences in market and work situations.

One major limitation of Goldthorpe's classification, as I have already indicated, is that it takes little account of property ownership. While employment relations figure centrally in his delineation of class situations, property is seen only as a secondary factor linked to certain kinds of occupations. This is the case, for example, in self-employed, entrepreneurial occupations. This can hold, however, for only relatively small-scale property. Large-scale personal possession, and property ownership that is not directly tied to entrepreneurial activities, is not incorporated into the Goldthorpe classification. This limitation, of course, is inherent in a purely occupational schema and reflects a quite deliberate research strategy on Goldthorpe's part. His schema was designed for use in a large-scale national survey of social mobility, and Goldthorpe knew that the number of property holders that would be captured in even a large sample would simply be too small for anything worthwhile to be said about them. The few propertied respondents in the survey would be unrepresentative of the propertied population as a whole. While this was undoubtedly an appropriate decision, given the aims of the research, it does mean that the listing of class situations that Goldthorpe produced is not sufficiently comprehensive for all sociological purposes. A fully comprehensive and general classification would have to pay proper attention to propertied class situations alongside those that arise from employment relations. Unfortunately, no suitable classification of propertied class situations has yet been produced.[6] If, however, a property classification and an occupational classification could be combined, a truly comprehensive schema of class situations would be available to researchers. Knowledge of an individual's occupation, employment and property holding would allow the researcher to allocate him or her to an appropriate class situation.

The fact that it is individuals who are to be allocated to power situations raises what is perhaps the crucial limitation of the

Goldthorpe schema. The Nuffield mobility study was devised specifically as a study of the occupational mobility of men, and so the Goldthorpe occupational classification was explicitly designed to handle the kind of work that was undertaken by men. Indeed, the initial processing of the OPCS occupational groups actually generated 125 rather than 124 categories, and Goldthorpe excluded one of these from further consideration as it was judged to be predominantly a category of female employment. In any broader investigation, however, a valid schema must make it possible to allocate women to power situations on the same basis as men.

The debate over gender and class is, perhaps, the most important of all the issues that have been raised in discussions of Goldthorpe's work (Goldthorpe 1983; 1984; Stanworth 1984; Heath and Britten 1984; Roberts 1993). Central to this debate has been the question of whether it is possible to separate 'gender' from 'class' variables. Marshall and his colleagues have forcefully argued for the need to build an awareness of gender into class analysis. They argue that

> class systems are structured by sex in ways that clearly affect the distribution of life-chances, class formation, and class action among both women and men alike. (1988: 73)

The sphere of employment is not gender-neutral. Occupational segregation by gender leads the rewards of some occupations to be lower than those of others, simply because they are regarded as being 'women's work'. For this reason, Crompton has claimed that the rewards of many jobs that are undertaken by women are determined more by 'the nature of the likely incumbent' than they are by the technical content of the job (Crompton 1993: 93; Scott 1986). Crompton concludes that existing schemes of occupational classification are unacceptable bases for the allocation of individuals to class situations, as they fail to pay sufficient attention to female employment. These schemes do not simply measure the market and work situations of job occupants; they also reflect the social evaluation of the personal attributes of the occupants (Crompton 1993: 118; see also Dale et al. 1985; Roberts and Barker 1989).

This fact has led many to conclude that an awareness of the gendered nature of market relations has to be built into the very conceptualisation of 'class' situation. Despite the obvious interdependence of gender and employment, however, this conclusion is unfounded. Restrictions on the operation of the market that result from the gendered nature of employment can be seen as involving the intrusion of a normative *status* element into the alignment of interests in the market, and I have argued at some length for the need to make a clear conceptual distinction between class and status. This is not to say that 'status' factors exhaust the relevance of gender to social stratification, or that gender categories are 'status groups' (see Lockwood 1986). The point is that the gendering of employment may be understood as reflecting status divisions that are rooted in broader gender differences. Gender relations, of course, have a much wider significance for sociologists than simply their role in the formation of status situations, but this is, nevertheless, one of their central characteristics. Weber was quite clear on the need to distinguish market factors *per se* from their status-structured forms, holding that class situations 'will become most clearly efficacious when all other determinants of reciprocal relations are . . . eliminated in their significance' (1914: 930). The fact that this 'elimination' may not have occurred in a particular system of stratification is no reason to abandon the very conceptual distinction that actually allows us to understand the interdependence of gender-based status and the market.[7] The gendered nature of the occupational order, then, serves to show that occupations must be regarded as proxies for gender-based status distinctions as well as for 'pure' class and command situations. Occupations are specific combinations of interrelated status, class and command factors. Power relations are gendered relations, and the critical research task is to use the *analytical* elements of class, status and command in order to investigate their *concrete* interdependence in the particular occupational structures that are used as the building blocks for investigations of power situations in systems of social stratification (Breen and Rottman 1995: 169).

Very similar considerations arise in relation to other forms of social difference, though these have been far less thoroughly debated in the literature. Property, market and authority relations are 'aged', 'racialised' and 'sexualised', for example, in much the same way that they are gendered. The intrusion of age as a status factor has sometimes been raised in discussions of the class situations of children and the retired (Arber and Ginn 1991a; 1991b), but it has not really been extended beyond this. Its importance can be illustrated, however, by considering children and young people. Children in Britain who are below school leaving age currently

experience legally defined st⸮
though this was not genera⸮
nineteenth century. With⸮
work has offered impor⸮
children, although ma⸮
employment and so h⸮
from occupation to ⸮
more apparent. A s⸮
property, generall⸮
limit their contr⸮
age or change t⸮
erty holdings give the⸮
be seen as major influence⸮

The racialisation of power t⸮
'race' and ethnicity involves racialis⸮
racialised structures of authority. Despit⸮
intersection of ethnicity with gender and clas⸮
1985), these issues have only recently been brough⸮
stream of stratification research (Anthias 1990; Mason 19⸮
also Warner 1936; Cox 1942). The 'sexualisation' of class and ⸮
mand by virtue of status discrimination against lesbian and gay
people has simply not figured in existing debates. In all these respects, the analysis of power situations must be broadened and
made more comprehensive through an explicit consideration of a
range of status distinctions.[8]

The need, then, is not to reject occupational classifications, but to
refine them. It is important to retain the analytical distinctions
between, on the one hand, class and command situations and, on
the other hand, the various status elements that may modify them
in particular circumstances. This task is not easy, as the structuring of employment, property and authority by status is an all-
pervasive feature of contemporary societies. Any judgement about
the relative importance of, for example, class and status factors and
about the role of market processes *per se* in determining the life
chances of individuals may be difficult to make, but it is essential
that it be attempted. Sociologists must retain the analytical distinctions among the various types of power situations and must use
available evidence to seek valid and reliable ways of operationalising
the distinction whenever this is necessary. That a distinction is
difficult to make is no argument for abandoning it; it should be a
spur to further attempts to refine our techniques for observing it.

, as I have emphasised throughout this book,
mand factors operate together in both rein-
ictory ways. For the purposes of an investigation, then, it may be quite appropriate to use an
property categorisation that is predominantly one
n and command situation but that also takes account
ed gender, age, ethnicity, etc. of occupants and of the
al prestige' that is attached to the various categories. So
e *analytical* distinction between class, status and com-
retained, occupational titles can serve as an appropriate
wherever these elements are closely entwined in concrete
gs. What this implies, of course, is that a valid classification
ower situations must pay the same attention to the occupa-
ns, employment relations, patterns of property holding and
uthority of people other than merely the employed white males.
The Goldthorpe schema fails – albeit by design – to give equal
attention to women and to men. While a number of classifications
of women's occupations have been proposed as alternatives and
supplements to the Goldthorpe schema (Dale et al. 1985; Murgatroyd
1984; Crompton 1989), no attempt has been made to reconcile
these with the initial categories of the Goldthorpe schema itself.
Such a synthesis would constitute a major advance in the study of
stratification. Equally, racialisation, ageing and sexualisation, along
with other status distinctions, must also be incorporated into a
comprehensive schema.

Mapping social strata

There is typically, in any society, a great plurality of class, status
and command situations and there is unlikely to be a one-to-one
relationship between these power situations and any actual social
strata that may exist. The fact that 124 – or however many – power
situations can be distinguished, does not mean that researchers
ought to expect to find the same number of social strata. Power
situations are the places, positions or locations that are constituted
through specific structures of economic, communal and authority
relations. Social strata, on the other hand, are collectivities with a
degree of cohesion and solidarity and that arise from demographic
relations of circulation and interaction among individuals. The
distinction between power situations and the social strata that arise
from them – between, for example, class situations and social classes

– is of fundamental importance. A direct, one-to-one relationship between the two is highly unlikely. Power situations and social strata are constituted through different kinds of social relationships, and the linkages between them are always a matter for empirical investigation.

Many theorists, however, have attempted to map power situations directly into social strata. This has typically been undertaken as an exercise in the clustering of occupations (seen as 'class' situations) into larger occupational categories with common economic characteristics.[9] If lawyers in large professional practices, for example, have similar interests and rewards to executive directors of merchant banks, then they might be allocated to the same economic category. Thus, Parkin (1971) has suggested that occupations could be clustered into social strata solely on the basis of the material rewards that their occupants enjoy. A stratification system, from this point of view, is simply a structure of inequality, a hierarchy of economic advantage and disadvantage.

It is, of course, quite feasible to cluster power situations in this way, but the result is a purely nominal schema of categories and not a delineation of real social groups (Schumpeter 1926: 137–8; Aron 1964). Nominal economic categories that are defined by the level of their rewards may be useful devices for certain research purposes, but their economic boundaries will not necessarily correspond to those of actual social strata. They will not necessarily possess the kind of demographic boundaries that would make them true collectivities. In order to properly identify social strata, it is necessary to investigate the demographic processes of circulation and interaction that constitute them. The social strata that emerge from such demographic processes of structuring are, indeed, likely to show a degree of homogeneity in the amount, type and source of their rewards, but this homogeneity is a possible *consequence* of their formation as strata and not a matter that can be used to *define* the strata in the first place.

The issues that are involved in the formation of social strata have been raised most clearly in discussions of contemporary societies. Here, the social strata have generally been seen as taking the form of 'social classes', this usage reflecting the centrality of class situations to the determination of the life chances of individuals. In the following discussion, I will draw on these debates, indicating those points where status and command elements must be built more explicitly into the analysis.

Inter-generational and intra-generational mobility chances are the critical elements in what Giddens has called the 'mediate structuration' of social classes (1973a: 105).[10] Social class boundaries are defined by 'the extent and the nature of the association that exists between individuals or families and particular class positions over time', and the use of mobility data allows social class boundaries to be determined 'in a way that is more than merely arbitrary' (Goldthorpe and Marshall 1992: 388).[11] Patterns of mobility establish a 'closure' around specific class situations. The greater the degree of closure, the more clearly identifiable will be the resulting social classes. It is through such social closure that collectivities with common experiences, shared interests and specific identities are produced. This is most likely to occur where those who occupy the various power situations within a social class enjoy similar economic rewards, but it does not follow that a similarity of reward is, in itself, sufficient for the formation of a social class. The crucial factor is always the way in which mobility relations tie together those who share specific experiences and interests in the market and in the structure of authority. The demographic structuring of social classes ensures 'the reproduction of common life experience over the generations; and this homogenisation of experience is reinforced to the degree to which the individual's movement within the labour market is confined to occupations which generate a similar range of material outcomes' (Giddens 1973a: 107, emphasis removed). The homogeneous strata within which mobility is, in Weber's words, 'easy and typical' are likely to contain people whose class and command situations exercise a similar causal impact on their life chances. They will each show a broad similarity in the income, wealth and other advantages that they derive from their market capacities and their involvement in, or exclusion from, authority. To the extent that class and command relations are reinforced by status relations, there will be further elements of shared experience in the life circumstances of the members of a social class.

The mobility or circulation of individuals among power situations is the critical mechanism through which demographic closure is established, but it is not the only demographic process that is involved in strata formation. Of particular importance are patterns of household formation among the occupants of different power situations, as it is through household formation that individuals develop long-standing social relations and patterns of informal and intimate interaction with one another. Households are units of connubium and commensality – of living together and eating

together – and it is through the formation of households that occupants of different power situations come to share significant life
experiences and to establish a nexus of relations within which the
life chances of household members are made interdependent.

Household formation has generally been studied only in so far
as it involves the formation of a family – and, more particularly, a
nuclear family – through a legal contract of marriage (Schumpeter
1926: 141; Sweezy 1951).[12] The combination of marriage and family
relations into a single domestic unit is, however, merely one possible form of household, and it is important to consider a much
wider range of household forms. Whether family households are,
in fact, the principal units of stratification in a society is an empirical question, not an analytical one. For this reason, it is necessary
to use a broader perspective and to focus on household formation
per se, rather than simply to look at family households. Power situations can be demographically clustered through legal marriage,
through cohabitation by men and women, or by the formation of
gay and other single-sex households. Where households are involved in the upbringing of children, they also become involved in
the reproduction of strata over time, as shown in studies of inter-
generational mobility.

Household demography is no simple matter to investigate, as it
involves both life course and serial processes. The life course of a
household may involve a young 'couple' becoming a 'family' with
children, before becoming a middle-aged 'couple' when their children leave home. Many such households become elderly single-
person households after the death of one of the partners. At each
stage in the life course, the household combines occupants of different power situations into relations of mutual dependence in
which the labour market opportunities of each constrain those of
the others. Where household members own property, more intri-
cate relations of interdependence occur. Through complex strategies of cross-generational wealth and property management,
households can ensure that the wealth holdings of the various
members of an extended kinship group are co-ordinated and become the basis of enhanced life chances for all its members. The
nominal property holdings of children, for example, are often important elements in such strategies.

In addition to these life course processes, the break-up and re-
building of households through divorce and remarriage can lead
to complex serial structures of fission and fusion in households. A
couple may separate and divorce after having children, and one

or both of the ex-partners may remarry people who may themselves have children and ex-partners. These new households may, in turn, involve separation or divorce, resulting in a complex kaleidoscope of household relations.

However they are formed, and however stable or unstable they may be, households rarely exist as isolated units. Marital relations create extensive kinship relations, which may be more or less effective as extended kinship networks that enmesh the constituent households. Even where no legal relation of marriage is involved, the families of origin of household partners may still act in the same way as legal kin. Where divorce and remarriage occurs, kinship networks can become especially extensive. As a result, complex networks of kinship and connection become involved in the clustering of occupants of power situations into social strata.

It should be emphasised, of course, that households are not to be seen as harmonious and normatively integrated units. They may very often be fissured by antagonisms over domestic labour, money, and numerous other matters (R. Pahl 1984; Pahl and Wallace 1988; J. Pahl 1989; Morris 1990). As with domestic divisions of labour and domestic relations more generally, the division of control over property within households is not necessarily egalitarian. Property ownership and control are highly gendered, and the enhanced opportunities available to male members of propertied households frequently occur as a result of the exclusion and marginalisation of female members (Mulholland 1994). The important thing to recognise, however, is that so long as a particular household persists, the interests and life chances of its members are inextricably entwined with one another. Marital breakdown does not necessarily eliminate this interdependence. Even after the break-up of a household through divorce, for example, the interests and life chances of its former members are likely to continue to depend on one another, to a significant degree, as the new households become linked through the payment of 'maintenance' or 'child support'.

Individual career trajectories – the bases of intra-generational mobility – are closely linked with household relations. Wright is one of the few theorists to have recognised the need to take account of temporal career trajectories, though he fails to develop his remarks beyond a relatively superficial level (1985: 185–6; 1989: 329ff; but see also Bourdieu 1979: 109ff). It is within households that members' career trajectories intersect with one another to shape the effects of power situations on household life chances. In the case of married women, as has often been demonstrated, their life-time work opportunities are significantly constrained by those of their husbands and by the continuing emphasis that is accorded to the performance of domestic labour and child-rearing tasks by women. The child-rearing tasks of married women are structured by the life course of the household, and life course factors can also affect the career trajectories of other workers. The holders of clerical jobs, for example, include junior male employees who are on the lower rungs of managerial careers, women in intermittent life-course-related employment, and older men who have moved 'sideways' at the end of a lifetime in manual work (Stewart et al. 1980). On the basis of their lifetime career trajectories and their household memberships, such individuals will connect clerical work with a variety of other power situations, making it unlikely that all clerical workers could be seen as members of the same social stratum.

It is also important to recognise that the various members of a household may each occupy multiple power situations and that this, too, will shape household life chances. A particular individual may, for example, be both a substantial property owner and an executive in a large enterprise, combining two quite distinct power situations. Thus, different power situations may be demographically linked if they tend to be occupied, simultaneously, by the same individuals. If all corporate executives are substantial property owners, for example, then these two power situations may – other things being equal – fall into the same social stratum. Matters become more complex when this multi-occupancy of power situations is seen in the context of household membership. Both the inheritance of property and career progress in an executive post, for example, are shaped by factors in the life course of the individual concerned and of her or his household partners. Once again, it is possible to recognise a myriad of complex intersections, from which result specific clusterings of power situations.

The final demographic factors to be discussed are the interpersonal relations of intimacy and residence that sustain a household and that connect it with members of other households. Members of a household are involved in domestic divisions of labour (Pahl 1984) that sustain the physical and social structure of the home, and their members are involved in relations of commensality. These patterns of living together solidify the household as a unit, but they also link households together into complex networks of eating, entertaining, friendship, residence and leisure-time activities. Through these informal social networks, the occupants of various power situations are brought together and so contribute to the creation and reinforcement of the boundaries of social strata. Research on the formation of social strata, then, must investigate patterns of 'friendship' and interpersonal interaction as well as relations of mobility and household formation (Stewart et al. 1980; Allan 1979). It is through such relations that households may, on occasion, become embedded in localised 'communities' in which dense networks of kinship, friendship and neighbouring sustain the separate households.

The failure to recognise the distinction between social strata and power situations – between, for example, social classes and class situations – has led to a long and protracted dispute over the appropriate unit of analysis for studies of stratification. Much of this discussion has been very confused, and the protagonists have needlessly talked past one another. Central to much of the debate over women and class analysis, for example, has been the dispute between those, such as Goldthorpe (1983), who see the family household as the unit of analysis in discussions of class, and those, such as Marshall et al. (1988) and Stanworth (1984), who see the individual as the unit. The debate has generated much heat but little agreement, reflecting the rather paradoxical fact that *both* of these positions are, in certain respects, correct. *Individuals* must be seen as the units of analysis whenever questions of class situation, status situation, and command situation are concerned. Individuals – male and female, young and old, black and white, and so on – must be allocated separately and independently to their appropriate power situations. The demographic relations in which these individuals are involved, however, generate social strata in which *households* are generally the basic units. These households may sometimes, but not always, take the form of 'family' households. Wherever family households are formed, families – nuclear or extended – will tend to be the units of the resulting social strata. Goldthorpe (1983) has claimed that these conditions apply in contemporary capitalist societies and that, therefore, the family is the effective unit of social stratification.

A recognition of the role of household relations in the formation of social strata casts new light on the issues that have been addressed by Heath and Britten (1984) in their discussion of so-called 'cross-class' families. In such families, the marital partners occupy class situations that, on the basis of a purely nominal categorisation, might be allocated to different social classes: this could be the case in, for example, the household of a male factory worker and a female head teacher in a junior school. Heath and Britten do not,

however, use the distinction between class situations and real social classes, and so they fail to realise the full importance of the
findings that they report. Household relations are one of the means
through which class situations (and other power situations) are
clustered into social strata, and the apparent paradox of the 'cross-
class family' arises only because a nominal concept of social class
is assumed by Britten and Heath. Recognition of the fact that social
classes and other social strata are demographically formed implies
that, in a very real sense, *all* households, whether family or non-
family households, are likely to be 'cross class situation' by virtue
of the fact that they bring together the occupants of different class
situations. It does not follow, however, that such households can
be regarded as 'cross social class'. Putting this argument in the
more general terms that I have employed, all households are likely
to be 'cross power situation', but none will be 'cross social stratum'.

Investigation of the demographic formation of social strata should
be a central element in stratification studies, though it has rarely
been so. Despite the production of a vast mass of survey and ethnographic evidence on the demographic processes of family, kinship
and community (see, for example, Allan and Crow 1994 for a recent review) this evidence has rarely been used to identify social
stratum boundaries. It is essential that such issues be pursued if
critical questions in stratification analysis are to be resolved. Only
in this way is it possible, for example, to look at the extent to which
particular social strata have crystallised and – to use Goldthorpe's
term – 'matured' over time. The maturity or decomposition of a
'working class' or a 'middle class', for example, is something that
depends upon the abilities of their members to reproduce demographic boundaries over time, as it is these boundaries that define
areas of common background and experience. These are what
Goldthorpe et al. (1969) saw as the 'family and community' conditions that sustain the social imagery and life styles of different
social strata and that provide the basis for particular forms of
industrial and political action (see also Lockwood 1966). This approach also makes it possible to investigate the changing fortunes
of particular occupations. It may be, for example, that some forms
of clerical work have, over time, ceased to be part of a 'middle
class' and have become 'proletarianised' through declining economic rewards and demographic clustering with 'working class'
power situations (Lockwood 1958; Crompton and Jones 1984).

Goldthorpe has suggested that the use of occupational data shows
that contemporary British society can be understood as having seven

–	'Elite' class	
I	Higher service class	Service class
II	Subaltern service class	
III	White collar class	
IV	Petty bourgeoisie	Intermediate class
V	Blue collar 'elite' class	
VI	Skilled working class	Working class
VII	Unskilled working class	

Figure 15   Goldthorpe's eight social classes
Goldthorpe's social class labels have been slightly altered

principal social classes,[13] though he also recognises that what he calls 'elite' propertied and bureaucratic power situations form an additional smaller social class (1980: 43, 254–5). As a result, an eight-class schema can be derived from Goldthorpe's work, and this seems to offer the most fruitful mapping of social strata in Britain that is available to researchers at present (see figure 15). Below the 'elite' social class in this schema is the higher service class, which contains all those in households that are dependent upon senior professional, administrative and managerial occupations for their life chances.[14] The constituent power situations of the higher service class involve the exercise of power and expertise on behalf of corporate bodies, or on their own behalf: they 'serve' power relations. Goldthorpe argues that

> What Class I positions have in common is that they afford their incumbents incomes which are high, generally secure, and likely to rise steadily over their lifetimes; and that they are positions which typically involve the exercise of authority, within a wide range of discretion, or at least ones which offer considerable autonomy and freedom from control by others. (1980: 40)

Immediately below them in the social hierarchy is the 'subaltern' service class, comprising lower level professional, administrative and managerial occupations and some supervisory workers. Employees in this social class have 'staff' status and working conditions, and they 'exercise some degree of authority and discretion in the performance of their work tasks while at the same time being subject to more or less systematic, if not particularly close, control from above' (1980: 40).

At the intermediate levels of the stratification system, Goldthorpe recognises a 'white collar' social class, a 'blue collar elite', and a 'petty bourgeois' social class. Routine non-manual workers and their households make up the white collar social class, and they have a greater security of employment and better conditions of work than is enjoyed by the blue collar technicians and supervisors of manual work. Members of neither of these social classes have any significant involvement in the exercise of authority. The petty bourgeoisie, on the other hand, have a base in 'the interstices of the corporate economy' and have a considerable autonomy by virtue of their use of their own capital in their businesses' (1980: 40). The lower levels of the stratification system contain the skilled and unskilled working classes, whose members share a dependence on the sale of labour power for a wage and a totally subordinate position in the distribution of authority.

Despite his Weberian emphasis on demographic processes of mobility, Goldthorpe's (1980) conversion of the 124 male class situations into social classes in the Nuffield study made no explicit use of mobility data, or, indeed, of any other demographic data. Instead, he made a professional judgement about how these class situations would have been combined *if* he had used direct demographic data. His reasons for this strategy relate to the limitations of the Nuffield data set. Even with a data set as large as that used in the Nuffield study (10,309 male respondents), a 124-by-124 matrix of class situations would have contained many cells with very small totals, making it difficult to draw any reliable conclusions about the significant demographic links among the various class situations. It was for this reason that Goldthorpe concluded that it was more appropriate to make informed judgements about the boundaries of social classes and only then to seek a *post hoc* empirical justification of these boundaries by examining mobility patterns among the smaller number of social classes that he had identified. The results of this approach are shown in figure 16, from which Goldthorpe drew general support for his model of the social class structure of contemporary Britain.

The exercise of professional judgement to identify social class boundaries is, from a theoretical standpoint, a second-best solution, and it can, of course, be contested (Penn 1981). However, it is often the only feasible solution, given the scale of the resources that are typically available to social scientists. The exercise of professional judgement is an alternative to direct empirical investigation, and it is a valid method so long as an attempt is made to use

Father's social class	Son's social class							
	I	II	III	IV	V	VI	VII	Total
I	311	130	79	53	33	37	45	688
II	161	128	66	39	53	59	48	554
III	128	109	89	54	89	108	117	694
IV	167	151	106	324	116	192	273	1329
V	154	147	109	83	170	229	190	1082
VI	202	228	216	170	319	788	671	2594
VII	162	194	205	164	311	587	870	2493
Total	1285	1087	870	887	1091	2000	2214	9434

Figure 16 Social mobility in Britain, 1972
Source: Goldthorpe 1980: table 4.2, p. 105

appropriate demographic data to test the robustness of the identified social class boundaries. It is this methodological strategy that
distinguishes Goldthorpe's approach from the identification of
purely nominal categories by Parkin and Giddens.

Having analysed absolute and relative rates of mobility among
the hypothesised social classes with the results shown in figure 16,
Goldthorpe concluded that his judgement had been correct and
that the identified class boundaries did, indeed, define real social
groups rather than mere statistical categories. He recognised, however, that the various social classes differed considerably in the
sharpness of their boundaries. They were characterised by differing
levels of demographic solidity, reflecting their 'maturity' as social
formations. The service classes (I and II), for example, had been
expanding rapidly since the 1940s, as a result of the growth in
professional and administrative power situations in large-scale
corporate and state bureaucracies. This meant that they had had to
recruit from outside their own boundaries, and so their members
were very heterogeneous in their social origins. They did, however, have a strong capacity to transmit their advantages across the
generations, and downward mobility was extremely unusual. The
service classes, then, have 'a rather low degree of demographic
identity', though Goldthorpe saw them as beginning to achieve a
greater degree of solidity (1980: 255–6). Though the issue was not
raised by Goldthorpe, it would be important to know whether

further solidification of the service classes would result in them merging into the single 'service class' that Goldthorpe often postulates in his work (Goldthorpe 1982).

By contrast, the intermediate social classes (III, IV and V) show high levels of both inward and outward mobility – and this is especially marked in the case of the white collar class. All three intermediate social classes are very weak in demographic terms. The manual 'working classes' (VI and VII) have been declining in size and, unlike social classes I and II, they did not need to recruit from outside their own boundaries. Although there was outward mobility for some, generally at the early stages of their working lives, these social classes were, in fact, very stable and homogeneous in membership. There were few opportunities for lifetime mobility for most, and they were overwhelmingly second-generation manual workers. These social classes, then, had a well-defined demographic identity. While there were differences between social classes VI and VII, they shared a distinctive set of opportunities that divided them from all other social classes (1980: 259–63). The degree of mobility that was observed between social classes VI and VII made it difficult to determine whether a social class boundary should be drawn between these two social classes. This finding reflects the long-standing dilemma in popular discourse about whether to speak of the 'working class' or of the 'working classes'.

Unfortunately, Goldthorpe's later work has departed from a Weberian programme for the identification of social classes. This work (Erikson and Goldthorpe 1993; see also Erikson et al. 1979) has been oriented to the practical needs of cross-national data analysis, and the modifications to the original schema are, Goldthorpe admits, 'rather eclectic' (Erikson and Goldthorpe 1993: 34). He and his associates in the CASMIN research group have adapted the original schema to produce purely nominal categories that maximise the possibilities for purely formal structural comparisons of different societies. The revised schema, in short, 'is to be regarded not as an attempt at providing a definitive "map" of the class structures of individual societies but essentially as an *instrument de travail*' (1993: 46). Despite Goldthorpe's continued use of the phrase 'social class', his new categories are not social classes at all. They are nominally defined economic categories of class situations that have been designed to maximise the predictive powers of the schema in comparative research. If the phrase were not likely to cause confusion, Goldthorpe's new categories could be called 'economic classes' to distinguish them from the social classes that Weber saw as the real collectivities in a class society.[15] For this reason, Goldthorpe has abandoned any attempt at mapping real social class boundaries and has pursued a purely predictive, rather than an explanatory, research strategy. Goldthorpe's later work, then, is only tangentially concerned with social classes, and his 1980 social class schema remains the best that is currently available.[16]

I have so far considered methods for the direct mapping of a stratification system using methods that identify the myriad power situations that exist in a society and then identify the social strata into which they are formed. Not all stratification research, however, consists of pioneer exploratory attempts to map whole stratification systems. In many cases, researchers are concerned with relating such phenomena as voting, religion, crime, education, and so on to the social background of the people under investigation. In such research, a particular 'map' of the stratification system must be taken as given. The task in this kind of research is not to *identify* social strata but to *allocate* individuals to given strata. Individuals have to be allocated to the social stratum of which their household is a member before the analysis can proceed, and so researchers face the problem of determining stratum membership without using the whole complex set of procedures that might be used to delineate the strata themselves. In this kind of research, the critical need is for a valid and reliable indicator of stratum membership that can be used with individual-level data.[17]

Goldthorpe has stated his own position on this question with some force. Within the family household, he argues, the social class of any family member is to be decided by the occupation of the 'chief breadwinner'. This, he claims, is because 'only certain family members, predominantly males, have, as a result of their labour market participation, what might be termed a directly determined position within the class structure' (1983: 468). Other family members, and particularly women, he claims, have infrequent or limited participation in the labour market and make only a very weak independent contribution to family life chances. The life chances of family members are 'derived' from the market and work situation of the chief breadwinner.[18] In the face of criticism and as a result of further research, Goldthorpe (1984) relaxed his initial view on the male 'head' of a family household and has advocated Erikson's (1984) 'dominance' and 'worktime' measures 'as being among the possible ways' (Goldthorpe 1984: 494) in which a family household approach to social class allocation could be operationalised. Gold-thorpe sometimes equivocates, however, about whether the class situation of the chief breadwinner is to be seen as a *determinant* of household social class or merely an empirical *indicator* of it. Much of his data analysis suggests that the latter is what he has in mind, but his explicit statements on this matter have often tended to imply the former. It seems clear that the only defensible inter-pretation of the Goldthorpe position is to see him as advocating the use of the chief breadwinner's occupation as an indicator of household social class. From this point of view, the class situation of the 'dominant' labour market participant in a household can be taken as a reliable indicator of the social class of the whole family household. The use of this indicator must, however, be justified on empirical grounds, and this remains an uncompleted task.

To conclude, the social stratum membership of a household is determined by the power situations that are occupied by all indi-vidual members of that household, and a full investigation of so-cial stratification would allocate individuals to a social stratum on the basis of the power situations that are occupied by these indi-viduals and by the other members of their households. Where the necessary demographic and household-level data are not available and a researcher requires a straightforward and effective indicator of the social stratum membership of an individual, it may be appropriate to base this on the power situation of the dominant income recipient in that person's household.

In this and the previous section, I have set out a general argu-ment about power situations and social strata, though I have de-veloped my argument mainly through a consideration of the work of Goldthorpe and others on the 'class situations' and 'social classes' of contemporary societies. It is now necessary to briefly draw out some of the more general implications of this argument and to consider some of the broader problems that can arise in compara-tive and historical investigations of estate societies, class societies and command societies.

Comparing stratification systems

Where class situations form the most salient causal component in the life chances of the members of a stratum, as is generally the case in capitalist societies, that stratum is a 'social class'. Where all the strata in a society are social classes, the society itself can be characterised as a 'class society'. Command situations and status situations operate alongside class situations and reinforce their effects in such a society. It is for this reason that my discussion in the previous two sections has approached the analysis of social stratification through considerations that have arisen in the analysis of contemporary capitalist class societies. My argument has been, however, that a class society must be seen as one historically specific form of stratified society and that the general framework that I have developed must apply to all forms of stratification. Where status situations are the most salient elements in social stratification, and the operations of class situations and command situations are secondary, the strata can be described as 'social estates'. A society of estates is termed a 'status society'. Where command situations are the most salient elements in life chances, status and class being secondary, the strata take the form of 'social blocs', and a society of blocs can be termed a 'command society'. These various forms of stratified society are to be understood analytically, as ideal typical stratification systems. As Lockwood has argued for two of these dimensions, ' "Class" and "status" are not alternative but complementary viewpoints of the reality of any given stratification system' (1958: 202 n. 1; see also Lockwood 1956; Crompton 1993: 131ff).

The 'occupational prestige' that comes to be attached to the various market situations and which serves to legitimate a particular pattern of reward and advantage is one of the principal ways in which status elements can reinforce the effects of class situation. Where elements of a class situation are identified as status-conferring attributes, they become the basis of status situations that correspond closely to the underlying class situations. Lockwood (1958) has argued, for example, that the most general criteria of status in Britain have been those associated with individual occupational achievement. Such factors as the education required for a job, its 'respectability', and its rewards and prospects have been incorporated into assessments of occupational prestige that reinforce and legitimate economic differences (see also Halsey 1981). Similarly, a high cultural evaluation placed on property and the rights of ownership will legitimate the advantages that are enjoyed by those who possess capital or land. For this reason, 'Class division is never a simple matter of opposition of interests but is also inextricably bound up with notions of superiority and inferiority in the society' (Lockwood 1958: 210). Where these status elements are weak in their effects, social classes may appear to be purely *de*

facto social groupings with no normative identification or legitimation (Bukharin 1925). Social class relations, that is to say, need not
be normatively legitimated and may simply be 'accepted' as normal and inevitable features of the way things are. It is the absence
of normative legitimation and, in consequence, the relatively autonomous operation of impersonal market forces in the pure type
of social class that Weber saw as its defining characteristic. It is for
this reason that Giddens has argued that, in the most general sense,
a social class is to be regarded as 'a large-scale aggregate of individuals, comprised of impersonally defined relationships, and nominally "open" in form' (1973a: 100).

It is when counteracting and conflicting status and command
elements 'intrude' into the operation of market and property relations that particularly sharp divergencies between nominal economic categories and actual social strata arise. Where status
judgements, for example, concern principles other than occupational achievement and the rights of property ownership, class
relations may be cross-cut by competing solidarities. Ethnic divisions in a capitalist society, for example, may cross-cut class situations and produce patterns of social closure that form social strata
that differ markedly from those that would be found in a pure
class society. It was such a possibility that Warner and his colleagues attempted to grasp in their investigations of American
patterns of stratification. In the same way, wherever a unitary status of citizenship that includes all members of a society is institutionalised, it will embrace all the numerous differentiated class
situations and may subordinate class identities to a common status
identity as 'citizens' with specific rights.

Thus Marshall (1949) has argued that such social rights, centring
on the right to welfare and to which all members of a society are
entitled, have become of increasing importance in contemporary
capitalism. It was this that he saw as producing a conflict between
citizenship and class as principles of social stratification (see also
Scott 1994a). Within the framework defined by the unitary legal
status of citizenship, other conventional status distinctions define
various forms of status classification that are embedded in diffuse
communal relations and that are expressed in forms of exclusion
and inclusion. Examples of this include the 'civic deficit' experienced by elderly 'senior citizens' and the 'civic exclusion' of women
and ethnic minorities (Lockwood 1987). By contrast with those
in status societies, however, such differences of status situation
tend not to be the basis of social estates but enter into complex

intersections with the effects of class relations in the structuring of social classes (Lockwood 1986). Citizenship is not, however, a purely normative matter, but is a combination of status and command relations. The legal status of citizenship has the power to partially offset the operations of the labour market because its institutionalisation is enshrined in the structure of the state and its bureaucratic system of administration. The system of welfare administration is an especially important means through which relations of civic deficit are both regulated and reinforced. This once again underlines the fact that class, status and command relations will always tend to coexist in particular societies.

Where class relations in a society are relatively weak, autonomous status principles may become the dominant elements in social stratification and the society can be seen as a 'status society' rather than a class society. In traditional India, for example, the hereditary charisma of particular tribal groups was associated with Hindu beliefs and values in a strong and autonomous body of practices that pervaded all aspects of social life. In the absence of any significant market relations, this became the basis of a complex system of 'caste' relations that defined sharply distinguished status situations for the various occupational groups. Because of its low level of political centralisation, command situations in the political and military apparatus exercised little independent significance on social stratification and there was little challenge to the brahmins, a 'high ranking literati whose magical charisma depended upon a knowledge of ceremony and ritual derived from a holy or classical literature written in a sacred language remote from everyday speech' (Bendix 1963; Mann 1986; Milner 1994). By virtue of their control over the production and reproduction of ideas, the brahmins established their position as the dominant social estate.

In traditional China, on the other hand, the Confucian scholar-gentry did not achieve this kind of autonomy. Command relations in the patrimonial structure of the imperial system operated alongside status relations in defining and circumscribing their position and, despite their predominance in status terms, the centralisation of the state limited them to positions of short-term authority and they were unable to establish their authority in the form of benefices. As a social estate, then, the gentry depended upon the backing of the imperial system of command (Marsh 1961: 52ff; Ho 1962: 18–19; Lockwood 1992: 62). It was this complex of relations that gave the society some of the characteristics of a 'command society' alongside those of a status society.

The closest approximation to a 'command society' was, perhaps, the Soviet Union, where the dominance of the state-party apparatus of command defined a structure of authority in which the holding of an official, *nomenklatura* position was the key determinant of life chances. The *nomenklatura* formed a dominant social bloc that was a true ruling elite. It held 'total' and all-pervasive power, backed up by an apparatus of coercion and violence, and its position was buttressed by the legitimating power of its official ideology. The Soviet Union was not, however, a pure command society, as rival principles were at work. The intelligentsia, for example, stood in a complex relationship to the official ideology and it had many of the characteristics of a social estate by virtue of the prestige that was accorded to the preservation and perpetuation of ideas. Its position, however, like that of the controllers of industry, was highly circumscribed by the command system (Lockwood 1964; Parkin 1972). Class relations were extremely weak in that society, and it was only with the collapse of the command system that the holding of industrial power in Russia has begun to take on some of the characteristics of a class system. As I have emphasised throughout this book, the three stratifying mechanisms of class, status and command will always tend to operate together, in contradictory and reinforcing ways, to generate the life chances and life styles of social strata.

My approach to social stratification is an extension of Weber's conceptual framework and it employs many of the terms that were used by Weber himself. I have, however, made a number of innovations – most notably by introducing the concepts of command situation and social bloc – and I have had to suggest a number of points at which my argument runs counter to the terminology that has been preferred by other writers. However, a number of terminological issues remain to be clarified. In particular, it is necessary to look at the relationship between the scientific terminology of the researcher and the language of the participants themselves. No area of sociology can avoid taking over everyday terms for use in research. Some of these terms (such as 'class' itself) will be used in more general contexts and in a more specialised, technical sense than in their everyday usage, while others may have to be retained with their more specific lay meanings. It is important, therefore, to try to distinguish those general theoretical concepts that have a potential application to all stratified societies from those historically specific terms that must remain closer to the lay terminology used in particular societies.

Some terms can more easily be used in relatively neutral descriptions, as they carry few emotional or political connotations. These terms provide the basis for a terminology through which researchers can delineate the principal features of social stratification in ways that maximise the possibilities for comparison between systems. Much of the terminology that I have used in the previous sections can be used in this technical, analytical sense to describe the general features of social stratification.

Class relations, status relations and command relations, for example, and the distinction between power situations and social strata, are the most general concepts available for the study of social stratification. While all of these words are used in lay discourse, little confusion results from detaching them from their everyday contexts and giving them more general theoretical meanings. Only in the case of 'class' does this involve the use of a confused and contested term, but I have sought to avoid terminological problems by clarifying its core theoretical meaning. More difficult issues arise in describing specific social strata. At the most general level, however, it is always possible to distinguish 'dominant', 'intermediate' and 'subordinate' social strata: there can be dominant, intermediate and subordinate social classes, dominant, intermediate and subordinate social estates and dominant, intermediate and subordinate social blocs. The use of these particular terms does not by any means imply that all stratification systems are to be seen as tripartite structures. There is no presumption that each of the three levels must exist, and the terms 'dominant', 'intermediate' and 'subordinate' may be used with plural nouns as well as singular ones. Thus, a society may have, for example, a number of intermediate social classes or a plurality of subordinate social estates. The purpose of the suggested terminology is simply to recognise that relations of domination form the core of social stratification and that, for this reason, the division between dominant and subordinate strata is central to any system. The particular terms that I have suggested are intended to grasp the most general distinctions of level that exist in any system of social stratification. This allows, for example, the dominant social classes in particular societies to be compared with one another and with the dominant strata of different kinds of societies.

Where the characteristics of the various social strata need to be made more explicit, it may be appropriate to use additional designations that grasp the broad features that are common to the various power situations that are demographically clustered together.

In the case of social classes, this might involve the use of such terms as 'manual', 'managerial', 'white collar', or 'propertied', among others. Thus, a society could, for example, be described as having a dominant propertied class, an intermediate managerial class and a subordinate manual class. Goldthorpe, on the other hand, has suggested that social stratification in contemporary capitalist societies can be broadly understood in terms of a division between the dominant 'service' classes, an intermediate white collar class, and a subordinate manual class (see figure 15). Whether such three-class models do, in fact, apply to any society is, of course, an empirical question that can be resolved only through detailed research. A subordinate manual class, for example, may have skilled and unskilled fractions, or there may, in fact, be separate skilled and unskilled manual classes. The important point to note here is that particular class societies can be described in terms of dominant, intermediate and subordinate social classes, together with appropriate qualifying designations for the various classes.

The terminology of dominant, intermediate and subordinate can be applied to social estates in much the same way as it can to social classes, and the appropriate specifiers in this context might be such terms as 'noble', 'intellectual', 'commoner', 'citizen', and so on. Thus, a hypothetical status society might contain a dominant noble estate, an intermediate intellectual estate and a subordinate commoner estate. Such a simple tripartite structure was a central feature of the self-image of feudal societies, though I have shown in chapter 1 that the reality was generally more complex than this and that fractional divisions occurred at all levels. The social blocs of a command society may also be described as dominant, intermediate or subordinate, together with such specifiers as 'official', 'royal', 'subject', 'bureaucratic', 'party' or 'military'. Thus, a command society might be organised around a dominant bureaucratic bloc, an intermediate military bloc, and a subordinate bloc of subjects.

One further point must be made about dominant social blocs. These groups, I have argued, can sometimes be seen as 'elites'. The word 'elite', however, has been much misused in the sociological literature. It has been used quite widely to describe any top command situation: top civil servants, bishops, MPs, company directors, and so on, have all been described, at one time or another, as 'elites'. This purely descriptive usage is probably too deeply entrenched in sociology and political science for it to be eliminated in the short term, but it would be far better for sociological analysis if it were, eventually, to disappear. Little or nothing is gained, after all, from describing bishops as a 'religious elite' rather than simply as 'bishops', or from describing the category of company directors as a 'corporate elite' rather than just as 'directors' or, perhaps, as a 'corporate directorate'. There may be some slight justification for using a term such as 'political elite' (or 'state elite') to refer to all top command situations throughout the whole institutional apparatus of the state, or to use 'economic elite' to refer to corporate directors along with leaders of major business and economic associations. For purely descriptive purposes, these designations do help to identify particular social categories for investigation; but the terms have no analytical value whatsoever. They indicate the starting point of an investigation, not its completion. The only really appropriate sociological use for the term 'elite' is, as I have indicated, in the phrase 'ruling elite', where it designates the particular kind of dominant social bloc that figured centrally in the work of Mosca and similar writers.

These broad suggestions, I believe, go a considerable way towards meeting the need for a descriptive and analytical language for studying and comparing stratification systems. A stratum may, for example, be described as a 'social class' wherever the class situation of its members is the principal determinant of their life chances, even if they do not themselves employ the language of 'class' to describe their own situation. It is an analytical concept and, as such, plays its part in sociological discourse independently of the views of participants on the matter. Such terminology is, however, highly generalised, and in many circumstances it will be necessary to go beyond this formal language to give a more concrete description of the specific historical social strata that can be found in a particular society. Such concrete descriptions would need to pay attention to the ways in which social strata are perceived and defined by their members and by others in their society. It is here that the relationship between sociological terminology and lay discourse becomes particularly problematic, as the language of stratification that is used in a particular society will generally carry a high emotional and political charge. Such terms as 'working class', 'middle class', *nomenklatura*, 'gentry', and so on, are concrete designations that may be peculiarly appropriate for particular times and places – and highly inappropriate for others. It is important to be clear about when such terms can appropriately be used.

Where, for example, members of the various social classes in a society describe their own characteristics and those of their class in the vocabulary of 'class', using a distinctively class imagery, they will have some conception of the number and attributes of the social classes that exist in their society and they will probably have specific names for some of these classes. These class names are likely to be particularly important in defining their own class identity, and they may have particular and strong political connotations. This is particularly clear in the case of the 'working class'. Though Goldthorpe (1980), for example, used the term 'working class' as a descriptive label for the subordinate manual class, he did not establish that this particular term was, in fact, appropriate. He demonstrated, as I have shown, that there was a subordinate manual class that was relatively 'mature' in demographic terms and that, in many respects, could be said to comprise distinct skilled and unskilled manual classes. He did not, however, offer any reasons why such classes should be designated as 'working classes'. Given the politically contested nature of the label, this is an essential thing to do.

In this chapter I have drawn together the basic elements of the conceptual framework that I have derived from the theorists considered in earlier chapters. The terminology that I have suggested as part of this framework is intended to allow theoretical and empirical issues to be explored with a minimum of conceptual confusion. In chapter 1 I traced much of the existing confusion to the changing discourse of stratification and to the associated failure to distinguish class, status and command. One of the central questions considered in that chapter was the nature of the 'working class'. This issue highlights the need for a greater degree of conceptual clarity, as the term 'working class' is one of the most contested terms in the study of social stratification. My discussion must be completed, then, by a consideration of the appropriate and inappropriate uses of the term 'working class'. This is the topic of the final chapter.

8

The Question of the Working Class

As I showed in chapter 1, in Britain, the United States and other capitalist societies, phrases such as 'working class' and 'middle class' arose within class-specific meaning systems during the nineteenth century, developing along with the development of the language of 'class' itself. Each of these meaning systems provided a specific class identity and orientation towards politics, with the term 'working class' having a specific and increasingly contested meaning within socialist politics. It is not possible to discuss all the specific social strata that may figure in historical accounts of particular societies, and so I will illustrate my point by considering the question of the 'working class' in some detail.

The term 'working class' is not simply a neutral, alternative designation for a subordinate manual class. The term came into use in Britain early in the nineteenth century, and its use in the political discourse of the socialist movement ensured that its subsequent history was inextricably tied to the history of the labour movement. As the manual workers of the new and expanding factories developed a class awareness that involved a true sense of class identity and 'class consciousness', so the very phrase 'working class' became an integral part of their language and culture. This self-description was soon taken up as a term of social description by members of other social classes, and it became a taken-for-granted designation for a specific social formation. The 'working class' was seen as distinct not only from the 'upper class' and the established 'middle classes', but also from the growing 'lower middle class' of white collar workers and small-business families (Crossick 1977). They were distinguished by their economic dependence on the sale of their labour power for a wage and by the particular life style with which this had come to be involved in the expanding industrial towns and cities. By virtue of their disadvantaged circumstances and the impoverished life style that many experienced, the 'working class' became the objects of charitable concern and social policy. Legislation concerning the 'working class' enshrined it as a legally defined status enjoyed by the subordinate social class of manual workers.

This legal definition remained important as late as 1990. The existence of the working class became a matter of discussion in the High Court that year, when the Duke of Westminster won a case against Westminster City Council on the grounds that flats built as 'dwellings for the working class' in 1937 should not be used for general housing purposes or sold to prosperous tenants. In deciding the case, the judge recognised the continuing potency of popular discourse when he claimed that the fact that Parliament no longer passed specific legislation in relation to the working class 'does not determine the meaning of those words in ordinary English speech' (*Guardian*, 27 November 1990). Ordinary usage, he held, would recognise a distinct meaning for the term 'working class', which could be applied – to however many or however few – with the same precision as in 1937.

Use of the term 'working class', then, involves the recognition of a distinct social class with specific, historically formed characteristics. One central element in this is their collective identity as 'working class'. The term is rooted in a specific class-bound meaning system that has its origins in the nineteenth century and that has a specific social group as its carrier, and the term becomes inappropriate whenever that meaning system loses its hold. The term cannot simply be equated with the propertyless wage workers of the Marxian model. Such a subordinate social class may exist as an important element in a stratification system, but it may not take the form of a 'working class'. If a subordinate manual class exists but does not identify itself in specifically 'class' terms as a 'working class' and is not recognised by others as 'working class', then the continued use of the term 'working class' to describe that social class becomes highly misleading.

The term 'working class' becomes inappropriate where the communal conditions that give rise to its particular culture and style of life dissolve and where the new circumstances do not provide the same support for that way of life or its associated forms of political expression. It may also become an inappropriate term of sociological analysis when a subordinate manual class fragments into fractional elements, even if one or other of these fragments continues to lay claim to a 'working class' identity. 'Working class' is a contested concept, and the debate on the working class highlights a number of critical issues in the investigation of class, status and command.

In their influential study of the debate on the working class, Goldthorpe et al. (1969: 1–2) recognised that it was through the work of Marx that the *political* question of the working class had become fused with its *academic* investigation. It was from the *Manifesto* model of class and class consciousness that a problematic of 'structure-consciousness-action' had become the basis of the mainstream research programme of stratification studies in Britain (R. Pahl 1989). In this programme, subordinate manual workers as members of a structurally defined 'class-in-itself' were investigated in order to uncover the conditions under which they might achieve a consciousness of their class location and would, in consequence, act collectively as a 'class-for-itself' in the pursuit of a radical transformation of society (see also Lockwood 1988). Where orthodox Marxism saw the transformation of a 'class-in-itself' into a 'class-for-itself' as an inevitable outcome of capitalist development, sociological research in the mainstream programme has treated this as a contingent outcome whose occurrence, or non-occurrence, has to be explained in terms of historically specific circumstances.

The subordinate manual workers of the early nineteenth century were not formed into a cohesive social class until the second half of the century. It was their subsequent development up to the late 1940s that saw their consolidation into a distinctive 'working class', characterised by strong exclusionary and solidaristic barriers between the families of manual workers and those of others (Foster 1974; Joyce 1991; Savage and Miles 1994). As Bauman (1982) has argued,

> What has been later collected under the generic name of 'the working class' was towards the end of the eighteenth century and long into the nineteenth century a motley collection of working or unemployed people, destitute poor, or not-so-poor, dependent on charity or their own masters, with numerous, unconnected traditions, tied to localities or trades, each keen to preserve, or kept perforce in, its own boundaries.

In the factory system of production, with its apparatus of economic control and surveillance, underpinned by the power of the state, the diverse class situations occupied by the various categories of worker were forged into a relatively homogeneous economic unity. Local and sectional trade solidarities gave way to a wider sense of class solidarity in a process that Foster (1974: 123–8) sees as centring on a development from 'trade union consciousness' to true 'class consciousness'.

The increasing economic homogeneity of manual workers involved a reduction in the diversity of market situations among them. While agricultural and domestic service remained somewhat apart from the mainstream, factory workers became the central core of a cluster of connected class situations in industry, trade and transport. Income differentials among these workers declined after 1870 as the system of liberal capitalism gave way to organised capitalism and its system of large-scale, rationalised production (Savage and Miles 1994: 22ff; see also Routh 1981).

Economic life in Victorian capitalism during its 'liberal' phase was shaped by the dynastic family firm of the industrial entrepreneurs. A capitalist class of personal possessors held direct ownership and control of the units of economic production. In their factories considerable workplace autonomy was given to skilled craft workers, many of whom operated as sub-contracting supervisors and trainers of labour recruited from their own families and associates. Skilled workers came to occupy distinct command situations that involved the exercise of authority on behalf of the capitalist owners (Foster 1974: 237; see also Hobsbawm 1964; Gray 1981). This command situation was the basis of the status of skilled workers as 'respectable' workers, a status situation that separated them from the 'rough' working class of unskilled workers. In the eyes of manual workers and others, this status division was central to class awareness throughout the Victorian period.

The growth of more 'organised' forms of capitalism in the period from 1880 to 1950 involved the development of more indirect and impersonal forms of possession, the expansion of bureaucratic managerial hierarchies, and a consequent erosion of the advantaged command situations enjoyed by skilled workers. The position of skilled workers weakened as women and boys were recruited directly into semi-skilled and skilled work, eliminating any role for the sub-contracting of factory labour (Savage and Miles 1994: 48ff). The First World War hastened the narrowing of economic differentials among manual workers (Waite 1987), and the homogeneity of manual workers was finally consolidated in the depression of the 1930s when skilled and unskilled workers alike were hit by high levels of unemployment.

These economic trends were matched by demographic processes of class formation. Savage and Miles have shown that mobility from manual to non-manual class situations was very low through-out the period from 1839 to 1914, suggesting that manual workers did, indeed, form a demographically stable and self-reproducing social class (1994: 32–3). Internal demographic divisions associated with skill declined, and by the turn of the century the skill division had lost much of its significance for social mobility. Drawing on evidence from Glass (1954) and Goldthorpe (1980), Savage and Miles show that an overall increase in mobility from manual to white collar occupations in the first half of the twentieth century was associated with a continuing decline in the salience of the skill division and the demographic consolidation of a single and cohe-sive working class (1994: 38–9). Marriage relations reinforced the lines of occupational mobility.[1]

This increasingly homogeneous social class was characterised by specific and highly significant patterns of community relations. Savage and Miles show that stable and autonomous working class communities arose in the late nineteenth century as the middle class presence in the industrial towns and cities became less marked and less oppressive. The middle classes were a constant presence in the early to middle years of the nineteenth century, and they were involved in the official and unofficial, direct and indirect surveillance and monitoring of manual workers. The health, edu-cation and morality of workers were all seen as legitimate objects of middle class concern and as areas in which owners, managers and professionals sought to exercise authority. The new towns and cities were central to expressions of middle class identity, their very spatial arrangement and architecture expressing this, and the surveillance of workers was part of an attempt to consolidate and extend middle class power. From the 1870s, however, the perceived threat posed by the 'dangerous classes' of the poorer districts, to-gether with the growing power of organised workers, inclined the middle classes to move out into the suburbs and outlying rural areas. As a result, 'The years after 1880 saw the decline of the middle classes' civic project' (Savage and Miles 1994: 63). The new and expanding 'lower middle class' (Crossick 1977) followed the established middle classes, and the central areas of the towns and cities became distinctively 'working class' areas. In this context, strong and autonomous working class neighbourhoods arose.

The early working class districts were largely new areas of set-tlement, their populations being predominantly first-generation migrants from rural areas. As their populations grew and migra-tion declined, the morphological bases of working class 'commun-ities' were established. Localised kinship networks were formed as more and more manual workers drew their marriage partners from their immediate locality. Commercial and non-commercial forms of leisure – music halls, pubs, working men's clubs, and, later on, dance halls and cinemas – became important foci for these com-munities (Stedman Jones 1983; McKibbin 1990). Co-operative and friendly societies completed the local picture, while trade unions and the Labour Party were the regional and national organisations through which the parochial boundaries of the neighbourhood and the local community were transcended.

Goldthorpe and his colleagues have summarised the features of the working class community in the following terms:

> The tightly knit network of kinship and the close ties of familiarity between neighbours are the products of successive generations of families living out their lives alongside each other; the strong sense of communal solidarity and the various forms of mutual help and collective action reflect the absence of any wide economic, cultural or status differences. (1969: 86)

The classic working class that formed in Britain in this period was termed the 'traditional proletarian' working class by Lockwood (1966). In this proletarian working class, male manual workers were involved in jobs that required a high degree of task involvement and that were characterised by a strong attachment to occupational work groups which enjoyed a considerable autonomy from direct managerial supervision. Work patterns created a strong sense of shared occupational experience and this, in turn, fostered feelings of fraternity and comradeship that underpinned a close-knit and cohesive locality in which work relations and communal relations reinforced one another. In some places, such as the coal mining districts, the locality took the form of an 'occupational community' where the occupation and its forms of work became the fundamental reference group for the formation of communal relations. In the proletarian community, neighbourhoods and localities were formed from a fusion of kinship and friendship relations: 'work mates' were not distinguished from 'friends', 'family' or 'neighbours' as separate categories, as the same people occupied each type of role. The informal personal networks that were built up in the commu-nity were the basis of a distinctive culture and way of life: a structure of mutual support, communal sociability and common political concerns. This proletarian class consciousness, then, was rooted in specific work and community structures and was sustained by particular patterns of political involvement and union activity (Roberts et al. 1977: 55).

This social setting was the structural basis of the mainstream of the 'working class' from the last third of the nineteenth century until the 1980s. It was in these circumstances that a sense of class identity and class consciousness could arise. Marwick has argued that by the 1930s 'there was a working-class awareness of its self and its own community, together with a more sporadic and unorganised awareness of other groups into which it came into contact' (1980: 84). In the absence of these specifically 'proletarian' circumstances, manual workers developed less sense of solidarity and collective identity. Isolated and dependent workers, for example, were seen by Lockwood as tending towards a 'deferential' orientation. Such workers, he claims, have mainly been found in agricultural work and in small-scale enterprises where they come into frequent contact with managers and employers rather than with their fellow workers in the same trade. Their social imagery gave greater legitimacy to the division of society into two social classes, and they tended to defer to the authority and superordination of those in the social class above them.[2] During the last half of the twentieth century, these workers and their families were drawn closer into the mainstream of the working class as economic changes undermined their work conditions and brought about a greater degree of homogeneity among workers.

A series of studies that were undertaken in the early post-war period showed the importance of extended kinship relations in tying together the households of working class districts and establishing the basis of distinctive working class communities. Dennis and his colleagues (1956) in Featherstone, Young and Willmott (1957) in East London, and many other researchers showed how communal solidarity was built from these kinship relations, reinforcing workplace and leisure-time bonds among the men and underpinning networks of mutual support and sociability among women. It was within this kind of community that domestic divisions rooted in masculinity and male aggression were complemented by the integrative role played by 'mum' in the extended family. At the same time, Bernstein (1960) began to show how the mechanical solidarity of such communities was the basis for the 'restricted' speech codes in which social meanings were embedded in concrete and situational contexts, rather than being formulated in abstract and formal terms. The less individualised language of the working class reinforced their sense of similarity and solidarity.

In his work on Huddersfield, Brian Jackson (1968), working with Dennis Marsden, documented the shape of the communities to which these relations gave rise. Work at the factory was the basis of an ethos of male sociability and masculinity, expressed in such things as swearing and the making of sexual references in everyday conversations, and this was carried over into the wider solidarities of the pubs and clubs, with their own ethos of moderate drinking and gambling, into attendance at football matches, and into involvement in such activities as brass band practices and bowling tournaments. Women were marginal to most of these activities and were largely restricted to domestic settings and to the 'women's rooms' of the working men's clubs. Moore (1975) has shown how these features are particularly strong in occupational communities that are based on especially hazardous work and that have a degree of geographical isolation. Mining communities, for example, shared the common features of working class culture, but they also had a particular cultural distinctiveness:

> The cultural distinctiveness and solidarity of the mining community is articulated in various ritual expressions; in the conduct of a miner's funeral, in a village carnival or, on a wider scale, in events such as the Durham Miners' Gala or the Northumberland Miners' Picnic. In these latter celebrations the miners assert their identity and their solidarity as miners, they assert an occupational rather than local solidarity. (1975: 35)[3]

The class awareness of proletarian workers centred on a dichotomous, 'us and them' view of class relations as relations of power. These workers are solidaristic, they have a strong awareness of shared collective interests, and they hold to a view that there was a conflict between their interests and those of other classes. The dominant social class in Britain was seen by members of the working class as the 'bosses', 'gaffers', or 'employers'. They were rarely seen as a 'middle class', though the dichotomous image was somewhat tempered by a vague awareness of the existence of 'the rich' and 'the toffs' above the employers.

Group solidarity among proletarian workers was harnessed to collective action in pursuit of its shared political goals. The formation of the Labour Party in 1900 was an expression of this socio-political orientation, and the attitudes of its leaders helped to shape working class political concerns. The party's electoral strength grew continually until the early 1950s, and its growth was especially rapid after 1918, when the party completed its transition from a defensive 'trade union' party to a national political force. Though it never secured the support of a majority of the working class, it did become the distinctive voice of urban working class communities.

The working class meaning system can be considered as a form of 'class consciousness', though not necessarily of the kind described and fomented by Marx and other socialist writers. Resentment of class divisions was often combined with a fatalistic acceptance of them or an accommodation to them. Their revolutionary repudiation was highly unusual.[4] Labour Party support tended to involve these same 'reformist' and accommodative orientations, rather than radical or revolutionary concerns. A radical class consciousness, Westergaard has argued, 'involves identification with, a recognition of common interests with, workers in other situations, outside the immediate locality, outside the particular conditions of the occupational community' (1975: 252). This form of consciousness is highly unusual, and it has been common for sociologists to follow Lenin or Gramsci in seeing intellectuals and political parties as the agents responsible for introducing and sustaining radicalism in the working class. This argument underlies the Weberian view that social classes *per se* are not 'communities' and are likely to be involved in 'mass action' only when 'parties' arise to express class interests in a collective and organised way in pursuit of a particular policy.

Marshall and his colleagues, for example, hold that, properly understood, ' "class consciousness" is more a question of how classes are *organized* in pursuit of class objectives, than of the extent to which individuals are made *subjectively aware* of class structures and their importance' (1988: 188). Actual class consciousness is reflected in patterns of trade union and political party activity. Radical meaning systems develop primarily where trade unions and parties act as the carriers of these meanings and are able to challenge the influence of the dominant meaning system and so convert 'latent feelings of class identity into class conscious activity on behalf of class, rather than sectional interests' (1988: 193). The absence of radical class consciousness in Britain reflects the particular, non-radical form that has been taken by the trade unions and the Labour Party.

There was a wide recognition that economic changes originating in the 1920s and 1930s were beginning to alter the structural conditions that had sustained the classic proletarian working class. Light industries and plants with new forms of work organisation were often set up in areas far from existing concentrations of heavy industry, and brought together geographically mobile workers who had little in common with one another. Their geographical mobility in search of work meant that local kinship and friendship networks were sparse, contacts with the kinds of communities that had sustained the classic working class were weakened, and the proletarian communities themselves, together with the forms of work that underpinned them, were beginning to decline.

These changes in manual work and residential patterns became especially marked in the post-war period, and they became the subject of sustained commentary in the form of the theory of 'embourgeoisement', which saw the 'new', affluent workers as abandoning proletarian meaning systems and adopting an increasingly 'middle class' outlook. 'Affluence', new forms of production, and new life styles became the foci of social commentary. The growth of high mass consumption and a high wage economy were seen as bringing about a greater homogeneity of living standards.[5] Manual workers were seen as achieving income parity with white collar workers and as pursuing the same consumer goods – televisions, washing machines, cars, houses, and so on. As a result, the 'working class' and the 'middle class' became less distinctive in both economic and status terms.

New types of production systems, involving automated and process production, were replacing mass production 'conveyor belt' systems, and this was seen as having critical consequences for workers. Manual workers were no longer mere sellers of labour power but had become sellers of knowledge and experience who worked under conditions of greater autonomy than before. There was less separation and greater harmony between workers and managers and they had become less distinctive in terms of their market and command situations.

At the same time, advocates of embourgeoisement held, long-established communities were disrupted by the building of new suburbs, new estates and new towns. The 'traditional' proletarian community that had been based on residential stability and social homogeneity was in decline, and this disruption of communal solidarity was seen as a decline of the very areas from which the Labour Party had drawn its strength. Workers no longer lived in 'communities'. The new residential areas were occupationally diverse, families had few local roots, they were geographically separated from their wider kin, and there were fewer and weaker communal controls. These changes were seen as undermining the cultural distinctiveness of the working class.

Their attachment to the status ideals of the proletarian working class having weakened, the new workers were likely to aspire to success within the established middle class status system. These workers would find an increasing acceptance as status equals by white collar workers, they would engage in informal interaction that would further weaken the demographic boundary between manual and non-manual workers, and they were less likely to see themselves as 'working class'. The classic working class, according to this theory, was decomposing rapidly as the expanding segment of mobile, affluent workers broke away from the shrinking proletarian working class and merged with the expanding 'new' intermediate class of office and service workers. According to this theory, Britain was becoming a 'middle class society' with an ever-declining and residual working class. When the whole of a society is 'middle class', it held, there are *no* classes: a one-class society is, in effect, a classless society. In such societies, the principal sociological questions come to centre around consumption rather than production. In place of class politics there is a status politics concerned with interests and life styles rooted in what recent writers have termed 'consumption sector cleavages' such as housing (Dunleavy 1979; Saunders 1978).

Reflections of the embourgeoisement theory can be found in the arguments of many of those who have recently claimed that contemporary societies are entering a 'post-modern' era where class is no longer a pertinent source of division or social identity. According to this view, identities are acquired as consumers rather than as producers, and forms of stratification have their origin in the sphere of status rather than in the sphere of class. Communal bonds are weakened and consumer identities are derived from the images that come into the home through the media of mass communication. The polarisation of distinct class cultures and forms of class consciousness that characterised the recent era of modernity has been eroded by a mass-media-induced striving to achieve consumption ideals. Status differences are rooted in variations in consumer life style and are not so sharp and divisive as those that reinforced class divisions. According to many commentators, such media images come to seem more 'real' than actual experiences outside the home and at the workplace (Baudrillard 1981).

The general theory of embourgeoisement was tested and conclu-
sively rejected by Goldthorpe et al. (1968a; 1968b; 1969) in their
study of Luton in the 1960s. In place of the embourgeoisement
theory, Goldthorpe and his co-workers put forward a theory of
privatism, which Devine (1992) has correctly identified as being
a sophisticated reinterpretation and reformulation of its major
themes. The affluent workers, they argued, were indeed abandoning the classic proletarian working class meaning system and were
adopting new norms and values, but manual workers remained a
distinctive social class. In terms of their market situations, they
remained dependent on the selling of labour power for a wage.
The wages that they received fell below those typical for most
white collar workers, and their relative affluence could be achieved
only through working substantial periods of overtime (Goldthorpe
et al. 1969: 82). The reductions in economic differentials that could
be observed were as much the result of the declining pay of clerical
work as they were of manual worker 'affluence' (Lockwood 1958).
Manual workers were, however, exhibiting a particularly 'instrumental', market-oriented outlook on their work, and this led them
to develop less workplace solidarity than their predecessors.

In terms of their command situations, Goldthorpe and his colleagues saw manual workers as remaining in subordinate work
situations. Even the most skilled forms of manual work had become standardised and subject to higher levels of bureaucratic
control (Goldthorpe et al. 1969: 58). In terms of their status situations, the style of life of manual workers and their families in the
new industries and new localities differed from that in proletarian
working class communities. They were not, though, following a
distinctively 'middle class' style of life. Rather, their established
norms and values were being adapted to their changed circumstances. Their life style was family-centred and privatised rather
than communal, reflecting the absence of wider kin in the locality
and the constraints imposed by shift work and overtime. Patterns
of non-work activity were largely restricted to the home and the
immediate family; household members were concerned with house-
work, decorating, gardening and similar tasks, and they relaxed by
watching television or knitting.

Goldthorpe and his colleagues found little evidence of traditional
status striving (1969: chapter 5). Indeed, Goldthorpe (1978; 1974)
has argued that contemporary forms of stratification reflect the
decay of the 'traditional' values and status ideals that formerly
provided the underpinning for class relations. Capitalism has rested
upon a pre-capitalist framework of 'traditional' norms that have

legitimated inequalities generated in the market and through the distribution of property, but capitalist expansion has tended to destroy the basis for moral commitment to such non-rational considerations. Faced with what Hirsch (1977) has referred to as the 'depleting moral legacy' of pre-capitalist norms and values, traditional status considerations have weakened and class inequalities have become more exposed. As Halsey has argued, 'the history of the twentieth century is the history of the decay of the values and status system of Victorian Britain', and, therefore, the demise of any 'national and unitary hierarchy of prestige' to legitimate class inequalities (1981: 43, 44).

Though affluent manual workers did have aspirations for higher living standards and greater consumer power, they did not see this as a way of attaining traditional 'middle class' status. Their principal status concerns were those of maintaining their position above 'rough' and relatively impoverished manual workers and of securing their own standing in what they saw as a social hierarchy defined in purely monetary, consumption terms. This hierarchical imagery differed sharply from that of the established middle class, leading Goldthorpe and his co-workers to equivocate over the appropriateness of the term 'status' to describe the concerns of the privatised workers and their families. It is clear, however, that the workers were committed to a conception of status in Weber's terms, albeit one that was allied closely with market and command situations, rather than with 'traditional' values. These findings are reflected in the continuing salience of boundaries to interaction between manual and white collar workers: demographic circulation and interaction differentiated rather than integrated the two kinds of class situations. Relations of sociability were largely confined to immediate neighbours, who tended to occupy similar manual class situations.

Life in the new estates and suburbs showed little of the solidarity and cohesion of the old working-class communities. Manual workers retained their involvement with trade unions and the Labour Party, but they had little sense of 'working-class' identity. Instead, they showed an instrumental orientation towards industrial and political action, an orientation that predisposed them to abandon established working class institutions and to support the Conservative Party or non-union forms of action whenever they seemed more likely to further their private interests and family-centred life style.

Devine (1992) has convincingly argued that Goldthorpe and his colleagues overdrew the contrast between the communal solidity of the proletarian working class and the privatised life style of the 'affluent' workers. An emphasis on the autonomy and independence of the nuclear family household has, she argues, long been a feature of working class life. Family-centredness and domesticity, for example, were central elements in working class claims to 'respectability' (Pahl and Wallace 1988: 140ff; Roberts 1988; Daunton 1983). In proletarian communities, however, the pursuit of independence was underpinned by the communal structures in which the households were embedded. Family-centredness appears as a more or less prominent feature of working class life according to the degree to which kinship networks are geographically localised. In situations where these communal relations are disrupted – as in the Luton of the 1950s and 1960s – it can appear that the 'isolated' nuclear family household is the result of a shift in values towards privatism and family-centredness.

In her own investigation of Luton in the 1980s, Devine has documented the re-establishment of communal kinship links through the continued migration of workers to the Luton area, and she has shown that extended kinship networks were, once more, important bases of sociability and mutual support. The autonomy of the nuclear household had again become embedded in a wider kinship system. The greater participation of women in paid employment, however, meant that these networks did not operate in quite the same way as they had in the proletarian communities of the past. Work commitments and shift work limited the ability of both men and women to interact with others outside the home on a regular basis, making it impossible to form the kind of 'mum'-centred networks that had been found in East London and in other proletarian communities. The family pattern of manual workers that Goldthorpe and his colleagues describe as 'privatism', Devine argues, is part and parcel of a reconstruction of proletarian sociability in the light of changed circumstances. It was not a new and consciously chosen normative pattern. Rather, 'norms and values reflected and, in part, legitimised the structuring influence of work on their lives' (Devine 1992: 153).

It remains the case, however, that the life styles of manual workers had altered, for whatever reasons, and these changes had major implications for the class identification and political orientation of manual workers. As suggested by Goldthorpe and his colleagues, privatism and instrumentalism were associated with a weakening of collective solidarity within the locality and the workplace and betokened a relative lack of class consciousness. The class awareness of these manual workers takes the form of a 'money model' of society in which social differences are defined by consumption standards rather than by power in the economic sphere of production. Much as Parsons had suggested, income, wealth and material living standards are regarded as signs of status achievement.

A number of commentators have suggested that this emphasis on 'money' and status achievement need not indicate a denial of the existence of class divisions. Platt (1971), for example, has suggested that people use income and consumption as obvious and easily observable *indicators* of relative class position and that they do not necessarily see monetary differences as *determinants* of class relations. When people use the language of 'class' they are often referring to what Weber would regard as 'status'. Devine, for example, found that people who referred to the disappearance of 'class distinctions' were, in fact, referring to the decreasing salience of 'traditional' status conceptions that were reflected in 'snobbery', accent and dress (1992: 167ff; see also Martin 1954). These same people recognised, however, that newer divisions rooted in occupational prestige were now salient and that these tended to be associated with differences of income and consumption. Foremen and office workers, for example, were seen by Luton manual workers as holding to status conceptions that cast manual workers into an inferior position at work:

> at work there was still a strong awareness of the prestige aspects of the manual and non-manual divide, especially between workers and foremen as the first line of management. While they were highly critical, many of the men were still angry about the pretensions of foremen and others . . . They were well aware of the manual/non-manual divide at the workplace. (Devine 1992: 169)

In their large national survey, Marshall et al. found that 90 per cent of people were willing and able to allocate themselves a class identity. Those in the lower strata of the Goldthorpe social class schema were likely to identify themselves as 'working class' when given a straight choice between 'working class' and 'middle class' (1988: 127, 144). These researchers argue that most people in Britain in the 1980s continued to recognise the reality of class divisions, even if they did not consistently use class language. They summarise class perceptions as follows:

> Classes are viewed largely as occupational, income or status groupings, or as categories having a specific relationship to the market or to production; people are born into these though to a lesser extent

classes can reflect meritocratic or material standing; and the class structure itself remains an obvious feature of life in late twentieth-century Britain. (1988: 147)

'Status' and 'class' considerations, then, were inextricably linked in the ways that manual workers conceptualised the disadvantages and subordination that they experienced, and they gave voice to these conceptualisations in the language of 'money'. Ambivalence over the use of the word 'class' reflected the entwining of market and command situations with occupational prestige in a context where 'traditional' status distinctions were declining. Whatever confusions in their language might be apparent from the standpoint of the conceptual framework advocated in this book, these manual workers did not lack a class awareness, and they showed a degree of class consciousness (1988: 180–3).

Manual workers held to an image of society as comprising a large central 'class', separated from small, residual strata of the very rich and the very poor. They saw themselves as belonging to a class of 'ordinary' people who 'work for a living'. This central class might, if respondents were prompted, be termed either 'working class' or 'middle class', but no particular significance was accorded to any particular term or even to the language of class itself (Goldthorpe et al. 1969: 147–9; Devine 1992: 160–70; Lockwood 1975: 249).

In terms of collective action, this meant that, while they still adhered to trade unions and the Labour Party as 'organisations which have some special claim on their allegiance' (Goldthorpe et al. 1969: 178), their attachment became increasingly instrumental. It was 'devoid of all sense of participation in a class *movement* seeking structural changes in society or even pursuing more limited ends through concerted class action' (1969: 179).[6] Union membership was, for example, seen as joining a 'service' organisation that could help in furthering immediate economic interests. Similarly, involvement with the Labour Party was generally limited to electoral support, rather than active membership, and voting itself became an 'instrumental' choice that was concerned with calculations of personal advantage and disadvantage (Goldthorpe et al. 1968b). This conclusion has been qualified by Marshall et al. and by Devine, who see a stronger basis for Labour Party support in the continuing – though attenuated – 'working class' identification of manual workers. Shifts in electoral support, they argue, are due more to the willingness of the Labour Party to give voice to 'class' issues than they are to class de-alignment. If the union and Labour leadership do not define politics in class terms, then neither will manual workers themselves. On this they are at one with Gold-thorpe et al., who had concluded their own study with an emphasis on the role of political and union leadership in 'giving a specific and politically relevant meaning to grievances, demands and aspirations' that cannot be achieved through an increase in personal affluence (1969: 189):

> if the working class does in the long term become no more than one stratum within a system of 'classless inegalitarianism', offering no basis for or response to radical initiatives, then this situation . . . will to some degree be . . . attributable to the fact that the political lead-ers of the working class *chose* this future for it. (1969: 195)

But can manual workers and their households still be seen as 'working class'? In their study of Liverpool in the 1970s, Roberts and his colleagues (1977) concluded that, at the descriptive level, this still made sense:

> To be a manual worker is to be employed in a particular type of occupation . . . [and] implies enjoying a certain level and type of re-muneration and career prospects and living in a certain type of house located in a particular kind of district. One can refer to those who share those circumstances as a working class because they tend to share a common class identity and subscribe to com-mon working class values which encompass support for trades unions and the Labour Party.

The evidence that I have reviewed here, however, suggests that the identity and values of manual workers are not so unambiguously 'working class' as Roberts et al. imply. Indeed, their own research showed that about a quarter of the manual workers interviewed had an outlook that was closer to that of the middle class than it was to the proletarian working class. These 'bourgeois' workers were generally the sons of white collar fathers, they were likely to be owner-occupiers, and they lived in mixed occupational areas rather than single occupational communities.[7] Changing patterns of social mobility and residence had altered the pattern of social class boundaries. In these circumstances, workers and their fami-lies could draw on a heritage of middle class values that signifi-cantly tempers their attachment to distinctively 'working class' values and meanings:

Rather than shielded by a circle of blue-collar social relationships and thereby immersed in a working class culture, the bourgeois workers were exceptionally exposed to white-collar influences. (1977: 56; see also Parkin 1967)

While these workers, they argued, were neither prototypical nor expanding in numbers, they did indicate the existence of a greater diversity of social imagery among manual workers. The cohesive working class was giving way to a more 'fragmentary' social class that ought no longer to be unambiguously termed 'working class'. The classic working class was giving way to a congeries of social classes and class fractions with little or no 'class consciousness' in common and no shared conception of themselves as 'working class' in any significant sense.

The continued existence of manual workers in disadvantaged market and command situations, then, is not, in itself, sufficient warrant for the continued use of the term 'working class'. The occupants of these subordinate power situations are no longer clustered together into a cohesive and solidaristic social class with specifically 'working class' characteristics. They remain demographically distinct from the intermediate social classes, but they are less likely to identify themselves as 'working class' and they are increasingly ambivalent about using the language of 'class' itself.

The collective identity of manual workers – to the extent that there *is* a single, shared identity – is no longer consolidated by status conceptions rooted in factory production and cohesive communal relations. 'Working class' culture has dissolved and so can no longer provide criteria of reputation and social standing for manual workers, who increasingly demand and receive their status as consumers. The differentiation of consumer life styles, promoted by the mass media, inhibits the formation of a single, class-wide collective identity, and identities come to be similarly differentiated. Status in the sphere of consumption is not, however, linked to the pursuit of 'middle class' status or to status attainment within a 'middle class' framework of reference. Consumption differences involve criteria of prestige and reputation that run counter to the assertion of any distinctively 'class' identification. This should not be regarded as a permanent state of affairs, as things may change. As Westergaard (1972) pointed out some time ago, the ability of manual workers to pursue consumer goals depends upon the ability of the economic system in which they live to continue growing at the level that will sustain a growth of manual worker incomes and a growth in the range of available goods and services. The research of Marshall et al. (1988) and Devine (1992) showed that economic decline was associated with a tendency to redefine economic and political concerns in the language of 'class', though there is little evidence yet that the predominant trend of the post-war period has yet been reversed. It seems, for the present, as if the 'working class' is dead, despite the fact that subordinate manual workers with disadvantaged life chances still exist.

The fate of the working class is but one aspect of the larger debate over the 'death of class' (Lee and Turner 1996). I have pursued the question of the working class in some detail in order to show how the conceptual tools that I have provided in this book can help to clarify the terms of this debate, which is often conducted in very confused terms. The concept of class, as I showed in chapter 1, originated in attempts to describe and to analyse the new economic divisions that were brought into being by the forces of modernity. The term rapidly became fused with ideas that referred to the cultural and political divisions that had come to be associated with economic divisions. Henceforth, the language of class was used in everyday discourse as a composite term that referred as much to 'status' divisions as it did to economic 'class' divisions. I have tried to show that the conceptual distinctions made by Max Weber allow us to dissect this complex reality into its analytical elements and so to understand the varying ways that they are combined into concrete patterns of social stratification.

Weber's concept of class situation has a general application to human history. While class relations emerged in a particularly clear form in modern societies with the differentiation of a structurally autonomous sphere of market relations, they may be found in pre-modern and – perhaps – in post-modern societies as well. What differs from one form of society to another is the relative salience of class situation as against status situation and command situation in the determination of life chances and the particular way in which these elements enter into the collective identities of social strata.

The social trends of the second half of the twentieth century have brought about a realignment of these analytical elements so far as the subordinate stratum of manual workers is concerned. Class situations continue to shape their life chances in determinate and salient ways, but their sense of identity owes more to consumer differences of status than it does to differences rooted in the sphere of production. In this context, status differences rooted in gender, ethnicity, age and sexuality also become more salient aspects of social identity. It is trends such as these that have led to the claim that 'class' itself, along with the 'working class', is dead. I have tried to show that the continuing relevance of class analysis cannot be determined solely by the persistence of the language of 'class' in everyday discourse. The whole question of the future of class is far more complex than is often assumed, and a massive research agenda for class analysis remains. Whether recent social trends are indicative of moves towards 'post-modern', 'post-class' forms of social stratification is one of the central issues to be explored in this research programme. The conceptual framework that I have provided in this book allows us to approach this question and to place it in the larger context of the historical development of forms of social stratification.

Notes

Notes to chapter 2

1 There is some debate about the centrality of *Economy and Society* to Weber's intellectual output. Tenbruck (1980), for example, has argued that the essays on the world religions (Weber 1915; 1916; 1917a), which were revised, enlarged and incorporated with the *Protestant Ethic* (Weber 1904–5) in a collected volume, form the most significant works of Weber's lifetime.

2 The earlier, and lengthier, account of stratification is that known under the title 'Class, Status and Party'. It is found in Weber (1914) and was initially translated in Gerth and Mills (1946). The later, and briefer, discussion is titled 'Estates and Classes' and was initially translated in Henderson and Parsons (1947). Both translations have now been superseded by the complete edition in Roth and Wittich (1968).

3 The equivalent distinction in English words with Germanic roots is that between 'might' and 'mastery'. The English words with Latin roots ('power' and 'domination') are, however, the more widely used terms for designating these phenomena.

4 The principal example that Weber gave was that of the domination that a large credit bank can exercise over the client companies that depend on it for their finance. I have elaborated on this idea in Scott (1985; 1990b). In another example, Weber discussed the economies of cities as exemplifying non-legitimate domination (1914: 1212).

5 One example given by Weber extended the illustration that he gave of domination through a constellation of interests which was mentioned in note 4. An authoritative relationship in business, he argued, might be the legal right of a bank director to issue commands to the board

of an industrial company, of which he is a director, because of specific conditions that are attached to a loan. While recognising these two types of domination, Weber was particularly interested in the case of authority and stated that he would use the word 'domination', unless otherwise specified, to refer to authoritative structures of command (1914: 946). Understandable as this may be for reasons of brevity, it has led to some confusion among commentators. For the sake of clarity and consistency I will always refer in full to domination by virtue of authority, abbreviated simply to authority.

6 Weber does not explicitly mention the capital market, but it is implied by his discussion and it is referred to indirectly through his comments on the significance of the 'capitalist enterprise'.

7 Weber remarks that opportunities for exchange in kind rather than in money should strictly be termed 'exchange opportunities' rather than market situation (1920: 83).

8 The term that Weber uses is *Verfügungsgewalt*, or sometimes *Eigenverfügung*.

9 For a development of the relationship between legal ownership and effective control see Scott (1990b).

10 In view of the arguments of Rex and Moore (1969) and Saunders (1978; 1984), it is also worth mentioning housing as a form of property, though Rex and Moore misleadingly claim that this could be the basis of an alternative system of class relations (housing classes) to those deriving from the labour and capital markets. See also Holton (1989b: 185ff).

11 These distinctions are connected with Weber's discussion of the appropriation of labour and the means of production (1920: 125–40).

12 Weber uses the term *Mittelstandsklassen*, which combines the root meanings of both class (*Klasse*) and status (*Stand*). This language, however, reflects a mere fact of German etymology and was not an attempt by Weber to combine the two concepts of class and status into a single idea.

13 He says that circulation is *leicht möglich* and *typisch stattzufinden pflegt*.

14 Demographic circulation is what Giddens (1973a) termed the 'mediate structuration' of classes.

15 There is some confusion as to whether the heading 'The classes privileged through property and education' was intended as a fourth term in the listing of social classes or as a new section heading, as Weber's text breaks off at precisely this point. Roth and Wittich (1968) include a textual note that supports the view that, however Weber actually laid out his text, he saw a fourth, propertied social class as being an essential element in the social class structure of modern capitalism.

16 Barnes (1992: 265) calls this non-instrumental action 'social intercourse', while Parsons (1937) termed it 'ritual action'. See also Barnes (1993).

17 The Roth and Wittich (1968) translation uses the term 'life' where I have used 'life chances'. Weber's term is *Lebensschicksal*, literally the

life fate or life destiny. It seems clear that he is simply using a linguistic variation on his general concept of life chances.

18 Burger (1985) has argued that both utility and social honour can be
understood as 'transferables' that function as the rewards and sanctions towards which actions may be oriented.

19 Although Weber did not use the term 'reference group', it seems a
useful way of clarifying his argument.

20 Weber uses the generic term *Stand*, which most literally translates as
'estate'. I have used the phrase 'social estate' to make the English term
less specific to the feudal context. Many translators have used the
phrase 'status group', which has the virtues of generality but implies
a rather loosely defined category.

21 The contrast between class-divided societies and true class societies
comes from Giddens (1981), but the sentiment is very much Weber's.

22 It may also be suggested that this is the way in which Weber would
see gender influencing class relations.

23 Marshall (1949), however, has demonstrated that the state in a modern
capitalist society may create a new status ideal – that of the 'citizen' –
that comes into conflict with the class system.

24 This example indicates clearly the close association of status and authority in traditional societies. Weber's view of authority is discussed
below.

25 Weber remarks that there is no direct link between ethnic identity and
the ideas of the nation state. He holds that 'the sentiment of ethnic
solidarity does not by itself make a "nation"' (1914: 923). It requires
the intervention of intellectuals to convert ethnic sentiments into
national ideals.

26 Weber (1914: 391) refers to this as the 'horizontal' equality of ethnic
communities.

27 Weber's earlier discussion of action used the term 'communal action'
(*Gemeinschaftshandeln*), which he later replaced with social action (*soziales
Handeln*). In this context he refers specifically to that kind of social
action that involves the establishment of what he termed 'communal
relationships' (1920: 40–1).

28 The Henderson and Parsons (1947) translation misleadingly translates
Weber as saying that parties can be seen as 'living in a house of power'.
The words that I have used give a more accurate rendering of the
original German text.

29 Although he did not develop the idea in the way that I have done
here, Burger (1985: 18) has referred to 'places of command' in his discussion of Weber's view of authority.

30 As the terminology for 'situations' and 'strata' differ in the communal
and authoritarian rows of figure 2, it might be thought preferable
to use a term such as 'property-market situations' rather than 'class
situations' in the economic row. This would avoid the word 'class'

appearing in both columns of the figure. I have no objection to this in principle, though it runs counter to Weber's own terminology and to usage in the Marxist tradition. The existing usage is so well entrenched that it would be unnecessarily pedantic to attempt to 'translate' Marxian and other forms of 'class analysis' into a new terminology.

31 I owe the concept of social bloc to Malcolm Waters, who commented on an early draft of this chapter, in 1993, where I used the term 'social order' to emphasise the links between orders, commands and authority. Mousnier (1969), however, has suggested the idea of 'societies of orders' to refer to what I have called status societies. For this reason, social bloc seems preferable to social order. Waters has taken up my concept of a 'command society' in his own work (1994).

32 See the reprints in Scott (1994b: volume 1), and see the especially important critique in Beetham (1991).

33 Beetham (1991: 125) convincingly shows that Weber's concept of legal-rational authority cannot serve as a comprehensive account of legitimacy in non-traditional settings as it fails to address the question of the beliefs that validate the legal procedures themselves.

34 It is misleading to see authority as an exclusively 'political' phenomenon, if the political sphere is seen simply as concerning the actions of territorial bodies such as the state. In some writers, as I will show in chapter 5, the term 'political' is stretched to cover all actions pertaining to the exercise of authority, wherever this may be located. This ambiguity over the scope of the political has caused much confusion.

35 For the distinction between social integration and system integration see Lockwood (1964).

Notes to chapter 3

1 A useful overview of the stages in the production of Marx's major work can be found in Oakley (1983) and Rosdolsky (1968).

2 The *Economic and Philosophical Manuscripts* (1844) and *The German Ideology* (1846) were published from Moscow in 1932, though extracts of the latter had been published by Kautsky in 1902.

3 The large draft manuscript – the *Grundrisse* – was not published until 1939–41, though its 'Introduction' had been published by Kautsky in 1902.

4 Oakley (1983) has suggested that Marx was under such pressure from Engels and from his publisher that he let the book go for publication before it was in the final form that he wanted. The book was certainly published without its final chapter on 'The Results of the Immediate Production Process', subsequently printed as an appendix in the 1970s Pelican edition (Marx 1862–6).

5 His most developed plan saw these as the first three books in a

six-book collection. The other three books were to be on the state, international trade, and the world market.

6 Volume 2 of *Capital*, written between 1865 and 1878, was published in 1885; volume 3, written in 1864–5, was published in 1894; *Theories of Surplus Value*, written in 1862–3, was published in 1905. The first two of these volumes were edited by Engels, the third by Kautsky.

7 Mandel (1976: 29), however, suggested that the book on 'wage labour' was incorporated into volume 1 of *Capital* and the book on landed property into volume 3.

8 The centrality of the *Manifesto* model of class to Marx's work has, however, been questioned by Johnson (1979) and Rattansi (1985).

9 The immediate influence on this shift in terminology was the thought of Louis Blanc, who had adopted the terminology of *classe* that had been pioneered by Quesnay and Turgot in the eighteenth century and by Saint-Simon in the early nineteenth century.

10 Marx also noted 'education' as a marker of class, but he did not attempt to incorporate this element into his subsequent work.

11 The business or 'acquisitive' class in Hegel is analogous to Weber's reference to 'acquisition classes' as distinct from propertied classes.

12 Here and elsewhere the male gender is used specifically. While Marx did, indeed, share the sexist assumptions of his period he was also attempting to recognise the male monopoly of such jobs and that only in modern industry 'is the labour of men superseded by that of women' (Marx and Engels 1848: 88).

13 There has been some controversy over Marx's use of the terms 'base' and 'superstructure', the ideas having most recently and most thoroughly been explored in Cohen (1978) and Sayer (1987). Both books are, in effect, extended commentaries on Marx's 'Preface' of 1859. My interpretation of Marx on this point is in general accord with that of Sayer, who recognises that the 'economic' forms are not to be equated with the relations of production *per se*. These points are developed below.

14 Marx uses the term 'fundamental classes' in the *Grundrisse* (1858), but I use the simpler term 'basic classes' in the rest of this book.

15 The term 'personal possession' is mine, not Marx's. I have made the substitution as Marx consistently refers to 'private property' in both a factual and a legal sense. The term 'personal possession' was introduced in Scott (1985, originally 1979).

16 Savage et al. are themselves rather ambivalent about the idea of class position. Although they sometimes seem to reject it, they do use the concept to designate the entities that are formed into social classes (1992: 228). What seems to be important is that they, correctly, seek to get away from a static and ahistorical view of class positions. Their own account of class exploitation goes beyond the economic sphere.

17 Here can be seen a similar distinction to that made by Weber between 'possession' and 'acquisition' classes.

18 The most influential Marxist discussion of the role of skill differences has been that of Braverman (1974), which argued that there was a long-term process of 'deskilling' that was homogenising the class situations of workers into a single proletarian situation. The debate over Braverman's argument is reviewed in Littler (1982), Thompson (1983) and Wood (1982).

19 Allen minimises the importance of differentiation at the economic level, but his argument has greater power when these differences in market situation within the basic proletarian class situation are taken seriously.

20 The work of Wright has popularised a particular view of 'contradictory' class situations. I will discuss the relationship between his ideas and those of Marx in chapter 6.

21 See the debate about bonapartism and the 'charisma of the name' in Baehr (1986).

22 Although Marx's early works are ambiguous on the question of absolute and relative impoverishment, it is certain that he was firmly wedded to a relative impoverishment thesis by the late 1850s. See, for example, Marx (1867: chapter 25).

23 Related to this, Marx held that the value of a commodity is calculated in terms of 'socially necessary labour time' rather than labour time *per se.*

24 Marx notes that the capitalist appropriates the whole of the value, a part of which is returned to labour. Workers, therefore, receive their revenue only *after* it has been first appropriated as 'variable capital'.

25 Discussions of the labour theory of value can be found in Meek (1973), Mandel (1968) and Steedman (1977; 1981). See also Hunt (1977: 91–2).

26 I have used the Weberian formulation in this sentence to bring out the paradoxical fact that Wright abandoned an earlier approach to class on the grounds that its emphasis on 'authority' was too Weberian. Wright disavows any parallel with Weber, mistakenly claiming (1985: 73) that Weber defined class situation in relation to the *outcomes* of market processes. Wright's work is discussed more fully in chapter 6.

27 A number of major reforms of company law took place in England from the 1860s, the very time at which Marx was trying to complete *Capital*. Indeed, it is possible that the rapidity of the changes that were taking place was one of the reasons why Marx found it so difficult to complete the book.

28 I have criticised this model of financial groups in Scott (1985).

29 This point has been made by Resnick and Wolff, whose interpretation and use of Marx otherwise diverges from my own. They hold that 'political' relations of authority arise within the workplace and outside it, and they see authority relations at work as involving 'participation

in the specific political processes of order giving, rule making and rule enforcing, whose combined effects push the workers to participate in the class process (1987: 21, 125).

Notes to chapter 4

1 For a general discussion of Parsons's approach to methodology and theory see Scott (1995: chapter 2).
2 Indeed, Parsons incorporated this confusion into the very heart of Weber's own work, as his 1947 translation of Weber's chapter on stratification translated 'class situation' as 'class status'.
3 On value diversity in America see Williams (1960: 413–15). Williams also recognised the need to look at the 'nonnormative conditions' that constrain actions (1960: 373, 377).
4 See the discussion of 'custom' in Davis (1948: 57ff), drawing on the argument of Sumner (1906). On the social facticity of rules of language see Durkheim (1895).These issues have recently been explored in the works of Giddens and the ethnomethodologists. See the discussion in Scott (1995: chapter 9).
5 Normative functionalist arguments on this point generally draw on Linton (1936). Linton, an anthropologist, was not himself a part of the mainstream of normative functionalism. His writings were, however, of seminal importance to the larger tradition, and he shared the assumption that the actual behaviour of individuals directly reflects cultural expectations.
6 Milner is not himself a normative functionalist, but he draws out some of the implications of a Durkheimian approach to status.
7 Wenger (1980) has claimed that the functionalist theory of status emphasises only loose 'status groups' and not structured social estates. This argument is not, however, inherent in the functionalist approach, and is used mainly in descriptions of changes in status relations in contemporary societies.
8 On the general functionalist programme see Scott (1995: chapter 6).
9 I am not arguing against functional analysis *per se*. I am merely recognising the inadequacies of the way in which it has been presented and debated, so far, in relation to social stratification.
10 Parsons derives this contrast between associational and primordial from Tönnies (1889).
11 Thus, qualities need not be 'biological' or hereditary *per se*, in any scientific sense. What is important is that they are regarded in this way by participants.
12 Parsons, unlike Marx, did not distinguish legal entitlements from the relations of effective control that I have termed 'possession' in chapter 3.
13 Parsons is here, in some respects, contrasting 'status' with 'class'.

14 Even his late essays on money and power as 'generalised media' focus on cultural definitions rather than material structures.
15 Both of these mechanisms are seen as characteristic products of modernity.
16 In the Soviet Union, Parsons suggested, the dominance of the goal attainment function allows the consolidation of a general prestige hierarchy organised around the state-party elite.
17 Hollingshead's (1949) study of 'Elmtown' also formed a part of the Morris study. See the general discussion of Warner's research in Kornhauser (1953).
18 Rex (1961) has suggested that Warner consistently viewed the world from the standpoint of the UU and LU strata and that the stratification system was an expression of dominant values rather than consensual agreement. See also Lipset and Bendix (1951).
19 Warner draws on Park (1928).
20 The black ghetto was the area termed the Southside or the 'Blackbelt', or sometimes 'Bronzeville'.
21 Lockwood draws on Plowman et al. (1962).
22 For more specific accounts of American values by normative functionalist writers see Williams (1960: 417ff) and Lipset (1979).
23 Barber (1957: 76) makes the point that 'detached individuals' (unmarried adults living alone) take their class situation from their own full-time social roles. It is not unless they join a family household through marriage, then, that women lose their independent assignment to a class. I will argue against this position in chapter 7.
24 Parsons would have recognised that if the separation of home and work is altered by an increase in female employment outside the home, then female status would no longer be so closely tied to domestic labour. He would also have recognised, however, that female employment would be constrained by conventional gender roles and that women would experience distinctive status disadvantages in their patterns of work.
25 Goldthorpe and Hope, however, mistakenly regard this as evidence against 'prestige' or 'status' judgements.
26 The source for this idea of citizenship is Marshall (1949).

Notes to chapter 5

1 For a more recent statement of this same viewpoint see Rüstow (1952–7).
2 This view of 'myths' appears in the legitimising role that Mosca ascribed to 'political formulas' and Pareto to 'derivations'.
3 Cox's position is strikingly similar to that of Dahrendorf, who I consider in chapter 6. In particular, his concept of 'political class' is almost identical to Dahrendorf's concept of 'conflict group', combining some

of the elements of a party with those of a social bloc. Cox applied his concept to the political organisation of the bourgeoisie in fascist Germany and Italy, and he also interpreted the American New Deal and Soviet Russia in terms of the actions of organised political classes.

4 In fact, one of the earliest uses of the word 'elite' in a political context, though only in a passing reference, is in Bagehot's (1867: 249) description of those who hold real power behind the façade of the 'dignified' or ceremonial aspects of the British state. See Parry (1969: 18).

5 Mosca suggested that the 'wealthy' may be a social force, implying that a social force may be based on a class situation and need not be organised around command. The wealthy *per se* do not have authority unless they also hold a position of command in an economic institution. The idea of a social force needs to be broadened to include groupings based on class (and status) situations that are not yet organised for command.

6 'Endosmosis' and 'exosmosis' designate, respectively, internal and external recruitment.

7 Confusingly, Michels uses the phrase 'political class' in both the narrow sense of government or state elite and in the wider sense of an overarching elite. Although his meaning is generally clear from the context, his work reveals the same ambiguity over the scope of 'politics' as is found in Weber and Mosca.

8 Mosca's distinction between autocratic and liberal systems is rooted in that which Plato and Machiavelli drew between 'monarchical' and 'democratic' or 'republican' systems.

9 Mannheim (1932–3) adopted the distinction between aristocratic and democratic elites to contrast the declining pre-modern elites and the emerging elites of specialist experts in contemporary Europe.

10 In this sense, Namier's (1929) analysis of the political structure of aristocratic factions in eighteenth-century England can be seen as an exemplary analysis of a type 4 system in terms that would be understood by Mosca.

11 On the relationships among these figures see Mommsen (1986) and Beetham (1986). On Weber's view of elites and democracy see Struve (1973: chapter 4). An important figure linking the ideas of Mosca and Weber is Oppenheimer (1914).

12 As I showed in chapter 1, the Latin word *classis* also pointed to the idea of superiority.

13 This method can be seen as related to the 'multidimensional' approach to status advocated by Lenski.

14 Variants of Pareto's approach to the governing elite can be seen in Lasswell (1952), Cole (1955), Keller (1963) and Giddens (1973b). The work of Guttsman (1963) is an important application of the model to the British situation.

15 Pareto also held that there is a cyclical shift in the balance of the

residues in the population as a whole over the long term. This rise and fall of sentiments in society lies behind the rise and fall of elites.

16 Only Rizzi's account of the Soviet Union has been published in full. See Westoby (1985: 12ff). There have been suggestions that Burnham plagiarised Rizzi, but Westoby (1985: 24–6) plausibly rejects these claims.

17 As I have shown in chapter 3, Marx does, indeed, share many of the ideas that were later developed by these writers, but the core of his work systematically developed the idea that it was property, not 'power' *per se*, that lay behind class relations.

Notes to chapter 6

1 Dahrendorf restricts his analysis of power to legitimate forms of domination. Weber's concept of *Herrschaft* is translated simply as 'authority', and there is no recognition of the *de facto* structures of domination by virtue of a rational alignment of interests.

2 Dahrendorf's work was undertaken prior to the collapse of the Soviet Union and the other communist societies of Eastern Europe.

3 Dahrendorf translates Weber's term (*Herrschaftsverband*) as 'imperatively coordinated association' rather than 'authoritarian association'.

4 Dahrendorf not only uses 'class' in an all-encompassing way to refer to what I have termed 'social blocs', but also regards the terminology of 'stratum' and 'stratification' as something to be avoided. His opposition to these terms seems to derive from his identification of all issues of 'stratification' with the normative functionalist analysis of inequality and emphasis on consensus and social order. This leads to incoherences and inconsistencies in his position. In his study of Germany, for example, Dahrendorf (1965) presents a seven-stratum model of the German stratification system: all strata except one are described as 'classes', but there is no attempt to reconcile them with the categories of his theoretical work. As it so frequently does, Dahrendorf's terminology prevents a proper appreciation of his own argument.

5 Dahrendorf also discusses what he terms the 'institutionalisation of class conflict', but this is best seen in relation to the issue of conflict between social blocs that is discussed below.

6 A similar view can also be found in the work of Karl Mannheim (1947), and the argument summarises a widely shared 'liberal' interpretation of the social development of industrial societies.

7 Carchedi's articles were revised and incorporated in Carchedi (1977), and Wright's article became the basis of Wright (1978).

8 Poulantzas would, of course, have recognised that these workers may make an 'indirect' contribution to production, in so far as their activities

are essential to the reproduction of labour, but he saw them as making no direct productive contribution. See the general discussion of unproductive labour in Gough (1972).

9 Wright cites the study by Zeitlin (1974) in support of his argument.

10 Wright confusingly follows Balibar's peculiar usage and describes this day-to-day control as 'possession' in his earliest works. He later came to see it, correctly, as a relation of authority or domination.

11 Wright sees individual shareholders as being too diverse to constitute a single class situation, as they vary considerably in the number of shares held and their salience for their total income. He gives no attention, however, to the specific class characteristics of the narrower category of rentier shareholders with substantial holdings.

12 Wright notes that a Marxian view must regard all class situations as involving contradictory interests and that, therefore, intermediate locations are more accurately described as 'contradictory locations within contradictory class relations'. He uses the simpler phrase 'contradictory class locations' with this qualification in mind (1985: 43–4).

13 It is worth noting that it is rather odd to regard the bourgeoisie as 'self-employed'. They may, in fact, stand in a whole variety of employment or non-employment relations.

14 Discussion of and reports on the international project can be found in Wright et al. (1982) and Wright (1985: chapters 5, 6 and 7). See also Marshall et al. (1988).

15 Wright (1978: chapter 4) had earlier noted striking parallels between the analyses that Weber and Lenin had provided of organisation and bureaucracy.

16 Wright does not recognise that such an assumption requires that capitalists be seen as occupants of command situations with distinct 'organisation assets'.

17 Rose and Marshall (1986) correctly point out the parallel between this idea of 'organisation assets' and Lockwood's concept of 'work situation'.

18 It should be noted here that Wright's concept of 'organisational capacities' refers to a totally different issue from his concept of 'organisation assets'. The latter refer to the assets inherent in positions of command, while the former describe the conditions that promote or inhibit the formation of 'organised' collectivities.

Notes to chapter 7

1 Runciman's (1989) own work contrasts economic power ('class'), ideological power ('status') and coercive power. The last is often seen rather narrowly as 'political' power, reflecting the same equivocation over the concept of the 'political' as was found in Mosca. For his previous arguments on social stratification see Runciman (1968; 1974). I do not

follow Runciman's suggestion that 'role' is the central concept in social stratification. As I have argued in chapter 4, role is a normative concept that is merely one type of social position.

2 This argument is developed more generally throughout Scott (1995).

3 In this chapter I draw, in part, on arguments presented in Scott (1994c).

4 Lockwood's own definition of market situation, unfortunately, conflates market situations *per se* with their economic outcomes with respect to life chances. Income, for example, is treated as an aspect of market situation rather than a consequence of the market-determined capacities that people have to earn income.

5 The *Classification of Occupations* was subsequently combined with the larger CODOT to form a new classification of occupations, used by Goldthorpe (1985) in a revision of the original approach.

6 See, however, the provisional sketch of capitalist situations in Scott (1991: 66).

7 On the gendered character of property see Mulholland (1994).

8 It must be emphasised that age, ethnicity and sexual orientation, like gender, must not be reduced to status relations. All have a very wide range of sociological implications and I am concerned with them here only in so far as they are involved in status distinctions.

9 For an interesting and powerful commentary on occupational categories and class analysis see Crompton (1993: chapters 3 and 5).

10 Giddens developed the idea of 'structuration' in a rather different direction in his later work, where it became a general concept linking agency and system. His own work, as I have already shown, assumed a one-to-one relationship between a very limited number of class situations and social classes.

11 Of course, Goldthorpe's own work concentrated on male mobility, and a proper investigation of social class formation would need to look at the mobility of both men and women, taking account of intergenerational movement compared with both their mothers and their fathers.

12 Lockwood (1958: 106–16) explores mobility and marriage patterns as processes of strata formation, but he sees these exclusively in relation to status situation and not in relation to other power situations.

13 Goldthorpe often collapses the seven social classes into three larger categories that he terms the service class, the intermediate class and the working class, as shown in figure 15. These are not, however, theoretically defined social classes and are purely *ad hoc* categorisations for particular research purposes.

14 It is to this class that 'large proprietors' were allocated in the Nuffield mobility study. This was a matter of convenience, as the numbers of respondents falling into the 'elite' social class was felt to be too small to consider it separately.

15 Crompton (1993: 104ff) describes this economic categorisation of class situations as the 'employment aggregate approach to class'.

16 I cannot pursue the point here, but I find myself in agreement with the judgement of Blackburn and Prandy, in a verbal conference presentation, that the Cambridge occupational scale – a continuous rather than a categorial schema – might well be more appropriate for many purely predictive purposes as it avoids the whole issue of trying to draw artificial boundaries.

17 This issue must not be confused, as it often has been, with the question discussed earlier of the unit of analysis in stratification research.

18 Wright (1989) has a very similar view of the 'mediated' class relations of housewives.

Notes to chapter 8

1 Savage and Miles do, however, highlight the particularly significant tendency for the daughters of manual workers to secure clerical and similar occupations.

2 Newby and others have questioned the idea of deference, though they have recognised the variations in work and residential structure that Lockwood has highlighted. According to Newby (1975), deference is not an underlying emotional commitment but a context-specific behavioural response to the personal dependence of the worker on the employer.

3 Moore is critical of the use that Lockwood makes of such evidence in constructing the ideal typical proletarian. See also Moore (1974).

4 In a study of German proletarian workers Popitz et al. (1957) also showed that class consciousness could be expressed in a variety of forms from fatalistic acceptance to revolutionary rejection.

5 Classic statements are in Zweig (1961) and Klein (1965). This viewpoint is discussed and criticised in Goldthorpe et al. (1969: 5ff).

6 See also Hobsbawm (1981).

7 Roberts et al. did not look at female workers, or at the maternal occupations that were found to be of such importance in the Jackson and Marsden (1962) argument on the 'sunken middle class'.

References

Aaronovitch, S. 1961. *The Ruling Class*. London: Lawrence and Wishart.

Abercrombie, Nicholas, and John Urry. 1983. *Capital, Labour and the Middle Classes*. London: George Allen and Unwin.

Abercrombie, Nicholas, Bryan Turner, and Stephen Hill. 1979. *The Dominant Ideology Thesis*. London: George Allen and Unwin.

Adorno, Theodor, and Max Horkheimer. 1944. The Culture Industry: Enlightenment and Mass Deception. In T. Adorno and M. Horkheimer, *Dialectic of Enlightenment*. London: Verso, 1979.

Albertoni, E. A. 1985. *Mosca and the Theory of Elitism*. Oxford: Basil Blackwell.

Alexander, Jeffrey. 1990. Core Solidarity, Ethnic Out-Groups and Social Differentiation. In *Differentiation Theory and Social Change*. Edited by Jeffrey Alexander and Paul Colomy. New York: Columbia University Press.

Allan, Graham. 1979. *A Sociology of Friendship and Kinship*. London: George Allen and Unwin.

Allan, Graham, and Graham Crow. 1994. *Community Life*. Hemel Hempstead: Harvester Wheatsheaf.

Allen, Vic. L. 1977. The Differentiation of the Working Class. In *Class and Class Structure*. Edited by A. Hunt. London: Lawrence and Wishart.

Althusser, Louis, and Etienne Balibar. 1968. *Reading Capital*. London: New Left Books, 1970.

Anderson, Perry. 1974. *Lineages of the Absolutist State*. London: New Left Books.

Anthias, Floya. 1990. Race and Class Revisited: Conceptualising Race and Racisms. *Sociological Review*, 38.

Arber, Sara, and Jay Ginn. 1991a. Gender and Class in Later Life. *Sociological Review*, 39.

Arber, Sara, and Jay Ginn. 1991b. *Gender and Later Life: A Sociological Analysis of Resources and Constraints*. London: Sage.

Aron, Raymond. 1950. Social Structure and the Ruling Class. *British Journal of Sociology*, 1.

Aron, Raymond. 1964. *La Lutte des classes*. Paris: Gallimard.

Baehr, Peter. 1986. 'Caesarism' in the Politics and Sociology of Max Weber. PhD thesis: University of Leicester.

Bagehot, Walter. 1867. *The English Constitution*. Glasgow: Fontana, 1963.

Baltzell, E. D. 1958. *Philadelphia Gentlemen: The Making of a National Upper Class*. New York: Free Press.

Barbalet, J. 1988. *Citizenship*. Milton Keynes: Open University Press.

Barber, Bernard. 1957. *Social Stratification: A Comparative Analysis of Structure and Process*. New York: Harcourt, Brace and World.

Barnes, Barry. 1992. Status Groups and Collective Action. *Sociology*, 26: 259–70.

Barnes, Barry. 1993. *Max Weber's Conception of Social Intercourse*. Conference Paper: University of Leicester, July.

Baudrillard, Jean. 1981. *Simulations*. New York: Semiotext(e), 1983.

Bauman, Zygmunt. 1982. *Memories of Class*. London: Routledge.

Bauman, Zygmunt. 1992. *Intimations of Postmodernity*. London: Routledge.

Beck, Ulrich. 1986. *Risk Society: Towards a New Modernity*. London: Sage, 1992.

Beetham, David. 1986. Mosca, Weber and Pareto: A Historical Comparison. In *Max Weber and his Contemporaries*. Edited by W. J. Mommsen and J. Osterhammel. London: George Allen and Unwin.

Beetham, David. 1991. *The Legitimation of Power*. London: Macmillan.

Bendix, Reinhard. 1963. *Max Weber: An Intellectual Portrait*. Berkeley: University of California Press.

Berle, Adolf A., and Gardiner C. Means. 1932. *The Modern Corporation and Private Property*. London: Macmillan.

Bernstein, Basil. 1960. Language and Social Class. *British Journal of Sociology*, 9.

Bernstein, Eduard. 1899. *Evolutionary Socialism*. New York: Schocken Books, 1961.

Binns, David. 1977. *Beyond the Sociology of Conflict*. London: Macmillan.

Böhm-Bawerk, Eugen. 1896. *Karl Marx and the Close of his System*. New York: Augustus M. Kelley, 1949.

Bottomore, T. B. 1965. *Classes in Modern Society*. London: George Allen and Unwin (second edition, London: HarperCollins, 1991).

Bourdieu, Pierre. 1979. *Distinction: A Social Critique of the Judgment of Taste*. London: Routledge, 1984.

Bradley, H. 1996. *Fractured Identities*. Cambridge: Polity Press.

Braverman, Harry. 1974. *Labor and Monopoly Capital*. New York: Monthly Review Press.

Breen, Richard, and D. B. Rottman. 1995. *Class Stratification: A Comparative Perspective*. Hemel Hempstead: Harvester Wheatsheaf.

Bukharin, Nikolai. 1925. *Historical Materialism: A System of Sociology*, third edition. New York: International Publishers.

Burger, T. 1985. Power and Stratification: Max Weber and Beyond. In *Theory of Legitimacy and Power*. Edited by V. Murvar. London: Routledge and Kegan Paul.

Burke, Peter. 1992. The Language of Orders in Early Modern Europe. In *Social Orders and Social Classes in Europe since 1500*. Edited by M. L. Bush. Harlow: Longman.

Burnham, James. 1941. *The Managerial Revolution*. New York: John Day.

Burnham, James. 1942. *The Machiavellians*. New York: John Day.

Calvert, Peter. 1982. *The Concept of Class*. London: Hutchinson.

Carchedi, Guglielmo. 1975a. On the Economic Identification of the New Middle Class. *Economy and Society*, 4.

Carchedi, Guglielmo. 1975b. Reproduction of Social Classes at the Level of Production Relations. *Economy and Society*, 4.

Carchedi, Guglielmo. 1977. *On the Economic Identification of Social Classes*. London: Routledge and Kegan Paul.

Clark, Terry N., and S. Martin Lipset. 1991. Are Social Classes Dying? *International Sociology*, 6.

Cohen, Gerry A. 1978. *Karl Marx's Theory of History*. Oxford: Oxford University Press.

Cohen, Jack. 1973. Some Thoughts on the Working Class Today. In *Class Structure: Selected Articles from* Marxism Today. Edited by A. Hunt et al. London: Communist Party.

Cohen, Percy S. 1968. *Modern Social Theory*. London: Heinemann.

Cole, G. Douglas H. 1948. *The Meaning of Marxism*. London: Victor Gollancz.

Cole, G. Douglas H. 1955. *Studies in Class Structure*. London: Routledge and Kegan Paul.

Corfield, Penelope J. 1991. Class by Name and Number in Eighteenth Century Britain. In *Language, History and Class*. Edited by P. J. Corfield. Oxford: Basil Blackwell.

Cox, Oliver Cromwell. 1942. The Modern Caste School of Race Relations. *Social Forces*, 21.

Cox, Oliver Cromwell. 1948. *Caste, Class and Race: A Study in Social Dynamics*. New York: Doubleday.

Crompton, Rosemary. 1989. Class Theory and Gender. *British Journal of Sociology*, 40.

Crompton, Rosemary. 1993. *Class and Stratification*. Cambridge: Polity Press.

Crompton, Rosemary, and Gareth Jones. 1984. *White Collar Proletariat: Deskilling and Gender in Clerical Work*. London: Macmillan.

Crossick, Geoffrey. 1977. The Emergence of the Lower Middle Class in Britain. In *The Lower Middle Class in Britain, 1870–1914*. Edited by G. Crossick. London: Croom Helm.

Crossick, Geoffrey. 1991. From Gentlemen to the Residuum: Language and Social Description in Victorian Britain. In *Language, History and Class*. Edited by P. J. Corfield. Oxford: Basil Blackwell.

Dahrendorf, Ralf. 1957. *Class and Class Conflict in an Industrial Society*. London: Routledge and Kegan Paul, 1959.

Dahrendorf, Ralf. 1965. *Society and Democracy in Germany*. London: Weidenfeld and Nicolson, 1968.

Dahrendorf, Ralf. 1967. *Conflict after Class: New Perspectives on the Theory of Social and Political Conflicts*. London: Longmans, Green.

Dahrendorf, Ralf. 1992. Footnotes to the Discussion. In *Understanding the Underclass*. Edited by D. J. Smith. London: Policy Studies Institute.

Dale, Angela, G. Nigel Gilbert, and Sara Arber. 1985. Integrating Women into Class Theory. *Sociology*, 19.

Daunton, Martin J. 1983. *House and Home in the Victorian City*. London: Edward Arnold.

Davis, Allison, B. Gardener, and M. R. Gardener. 1941. *Deep South*. Chicago: University of Chicago Press.

Davis, Kingsley. 1948. *Human Society*. New York: Macmillan.

Davis, Kingsley, and Wilbert E. Moore. 1945. Some Principles of Stratification. *American Sociological Review*, 10.

Dennis, Norman, Ferdinand Henriques, and Clifford Slaughter. 1956. *Coal is our Life*. London: Eyre and Spottiswoode.

Devine, Fiona. 1992. *Affluent Workers Revisited: Privatism and the Working Class*. Edinburgh: Edinburgh University Press.

Devine, Fiona. 1996. *Social Class in Britain and America*. Edinburgh: Edinburgh University Press.

Dill, B. 1983. Race, Class and Gender: Perspectives for an All-Inclusive Sisterhood. *Feminist Studies*, 9.

Djilas, Milovan. 1957. *The New Class*. New York: Frederick A. Praeger.

Domhoff, G. W. 1967. *Who Rules America?* Englewood Cliffs: Prentice-Hall.

Domhoff, G. W. 1970. *The Higher Circles*. New York: Random House.

Drake, St Clair, and Horace B. Cayton. 1945. *Black Metropolis*. New York: Harcourt Brace.

Draper, Hal. 1977. *Karl Marx's Theory of Revolution. Volume 1: State and Bureaucracy*. New York: Monthly Review Press.

Dubois, J. 1962. *Le Vocabulaire politique et social en France de 1869 à 1872*. Paris.

Duby, Georges. 1978. *The Three Orders: Feudal Society Imagined*. Chicago: University of Chicago Press, 1980.

Dunleavy, Patrick. 1979. The Urban Bases of Political Alignment. *British Journal of Political Science*, 9.

Durkheim, Emile. 1893. *The Division of Labour in Society*. London: Macmillan, 1984.

Durkheim, Emile. 1895. *The Rules of the Sociological Method*. London: Macmillan, 1982.

Durkheim, Emile. 1897. *Suicide: A Study in Sociology*. London: Routledge and Kegan Paul, 1952.

Durkheim, Emile. 1912. *Elementary Forms of the Religious Life*. London: George Allen and Unwin, 1915.

Eder, K. 1993. *The New Politics of Class*. London: Sage.

Edgell, S. 1993. *Class*. London: Routledge.

Ehrenreich, Barbara, and John Ehrenreich. 1979. The Professional-Managerial Class. In *Between Labour and Capital*. Edited by P. Walker. Hassocks: Harvester Press.

Eisenstadt, Shmuel N. 1968. Prestige, Participation and Strata Formation. In *Social Stratification*. Edited by J. A. Jackson. Cambridge: Cambridge University Press.

Eisenstadt, Shmuel N. 1971. *Social Differentiation and Social Stratification*. New York: Scott, Foresman.

Eliot, T. S. 1948. *Notes towards the Definition of Culture*. London: Faber and Faber.

Elster, Jon. 1985. *Making Sense of Marx*. Cambridge: Cambridge University Press.

Engels, Friedrich. 1843. Outlines of a Critique of Political Economy. In *The Condition of the Working Class in England in 1844*. London: Panther, 1969.

Engels, Friedrich. 1876. *Anti-Dühring*. Moscow: Foreign Languages Publishing House, 1954.

Engels, Friedrich. 1888. *Ludwig Feuerbach and the End of Classical German Philosophy*. Moscow: Progress Publishers, 1946.

Erikson, Robert. 1984. Social Class of Men, Women and Families. *Sociology*, 4.

Erikson, Robert, and John Goldthorpe. 1993. *The Constant Flux*. Oxford: Clarendon Press.

Erikson, Robert, John Goldthorpe, and L. Portocarero. 1979. Intergenerational Class Mobility in Three Western European Societies. *British Journal of Sociology*, 30.

Etzioni, Amitai. 1961. *A Comparative Analysis of Complex Organizations*. New York: Free Press.

Ferguson, Adam. 1767. *An Essay on the History of Civil Society*. Edinburgh: Edinburgh University Press, 1966.

Filoux, J.-C. 1993. Inequalities and Social Stratification in Durkheim's Sociology. In *Emile Durkheim: Sociologist and Moralist*. Edited by S. P. Turner. London: Routledge.

Foster, John. 1974. *Class Struggle and the Industrial Revolution*. London: Methuen.

Furbank, Peter N. 1986. *Unholy Pleasure, or, The Idea of Social Class*. Oxford: Oxford University Press.

Geiger, Theodor. 1932. *Die Soziale Schichtung des Deutschen Volkes*. Stuttgart: Ferdinand Enke Verlag.

Gerth, Hans H., and Charles W. Mills (eds). 1946. *From Max Weber*. New York: Oxford University Press.

Giddens, Anthony. 1973a. *The Class Structure of the Advanced Societies*. London: Hutchinson.

Giddens, Anthony. 1973b. Elites in the British Class Structure. *Sociological Review*, 21.

Giddens, Anthony. 1981. *A Contemporary Critique of Historical Materialism*. London: Macmillan.

Ginsberg, Morris. 1934. *Sociology*. Oxford: Oxford University Press.

Glass, David V. (ed.). 1954. *Social Mobility in Britain*. London: Routledge and Kegan Paul.

Glenn, E. 1985. Racial Ethnic Women's Labour: The Intersection of Race, Gender and Class Oppression. *Review of Radical Political Economics*, 17: 86–108.

Goldhamer, H., and E. A. Shils. 1939. Types of Power and Status. In *Centre and Periphery: Essays in Macrosociology*. Edited by E. A. Shils. Chicago: University of Chicago Press, 1975.

Goldthorpe, John H. 1974. Industrial Relations in Great Britain: A Critique of Reformism. *Politics and Society*, 4.

Goldthorpe, John H. 1978. The Current Inflation: Towards A Sociological Account. In *The Political Economy of Inflation*. Edited by F. Hirsch and J. H. Goldthorpe. Oxford: Martin Robertson.

Goldthorpe, John H. 1980. *Social Mobility and Class Structure*. Oxford: Clarendon Press.

Goldthorpe, John H. 1982. The Service Class. In *Social Class and the Division of Labour*. Edited by A. Giddens and G. Mackenzie. Cambridge: Cambridge University Press.

Goldthorpe, John H. 1983. Women and Class Analysis: In Defence of the Conventional View. *Sociology*, 17.

Goldthorpe, John H. 1984. Women and Class Analysis: A Reply to the Replies. *Sociology*, 4.

Goldthorpe, John H. 1985. *Social Mobility and Class Formation*. CASMIN paper no. 1. Institut für Sozialwissenschaft. NTIS, 1.

Goldthorpe, John H., and Keith Hope (eds). 1974. *The Social Grading of Occupations*. Oxford: Clarendon Press.

Goldthorpe, John H., and Gordon Marshall. 1992. The Promising Future of Class Analysis: A Response to Recent Critics. *Sociology*, 26.

Goldthorpe, John, David Lockwood, Frank Bechhofer, and Jennifer Platt. 1968a. *The Affluent Worker: Industrial Attitudes and Behaviour*. Cambridge: Cambridge University Press.

Goldthorpe, John, David Lockwood, Frank Bechhofer, and Jennifer Platt. 1968b. *The Affluent Worker: Political Attitudes and Behaviour*. Cambridge: Cambridge University Press.

Goldthorpe, John, David Lockwood, Frank Bechhofer, and Jennifer Platt. 1969. *The Affluent Worker in the Class Structure*. Cambridge: Cambridge University Press.

Gordon, Milton M. 1950. *Social Class in American Society*. Durham: Duke University Press.

Gough, Ian. 1972. Marx's Theory of Productive and Unproductive Labour. *New Left Review*, 76.

Gramsci, Antonio. 1929–35. *Selections from the Prison Notebooks*. London: Lawrence and Wishart, 1971.

Gray, Robbie Q. 1981. *The Aristocracy of Labour in Nineteenth Century Britain*. London: Macmillan.

Gross, Neal, Ward S. Mason, and Alexander W. McEachern. 1958. *Explorations in Role Analysis: Studies of the School Superintendency Role*. New York: Wiley.

Gumplowicz, Ludwig. 1875. *Rasse und Staat*. Innsbruck: Wagner.

Gumplowicz, Ludwig. 1883. *Der Rassenkampf*. Innsbruck: Wagner.

Gumplowicz, Ludwig. 1885. *Outlines of Sociology*, first edition. Philadelphia: American Academy of Political and Social Science, 1899.

Guttsman, W. L. 1963. *The British Political Elite*. London: McGibbon and Kee.

Hall, Stuart. 1977. The 'Political' and the 'Economic' in Marx's Theory of Classes. In *Class and Class Structure*. Edited by A. Hunt. London: Lawrence and Wishart.

Halsey, A. H. 1981. *Change in British Society*, second edition. Oxford: Oxford University Press (originally 1978).

Hamilton, Richard F. 1991. *The Bourgeois Epoch: Marx and Engels on Britain, France and Germany*. Chapel Hill: University of North Carolina Press.

Heath, Anthony, and N. Britten. 1984. Women's Jobs Do Make a Difference. *Sociology*, 18.

Henderson, A. M., and T. Parsons (eds). 1947. *The Theory of Social and Economic Organization*. New York: Oxford University Press.

Henderson, Lawrence J. 1935. *Pareto's General Sociology: A Physiologist's Interpretation*. Cambridge, Mass.: Harvard University Press.

Henderson, Lawrence J. 1941–2. Sociology (23 lectures). In *L. J. Henderson on the Social System*. Edited by B. Barber. Chicago: University of Chicago Press, 1970.

Hilferding, Rudolf. 1910. *Finance Capital*. London: Routledge and Kegan Paul, 1981.

Hindess, Barry. 1987. *Politics and Class Analysis*. Oxford: Basil Blackwell.

Hirsch, Fred. 1977. *Social Limits to Growth*. London: Routledge and Kegan Paul.

Hirst, Paul Q. 1977. Economic Classes and Politics. In *Class and Class Structure*. Edited by A. Hunt. London: Lawrence and Wishart.

Ho, Ping Ti. 1962. *The Ladder of Success in Imperial China: Aspects of Social Mobility, 1368–1911*. New York: Columbia University Press.

Hobsbawm, Eric J. 1964. *Labouring Men*. London: Weidenfeld and Nicolson.

Hobsbawm, Eric J. 1981. The Forward March of Labour Halted? In *The Forward March of Labour Halted*. Edited by M. Jacques and F. Mulhern. London: New Left Books.

Hollingshead, August B. 1949. *Elmtown's Youth*. New York: John Wiley.

Holton, Robert J. 1989a. Max Weber, Austrian Economics and the New Right. In *Max Weber on Economy and Society*. Edited by R. J. Holton and B. S. Turner. London: Routledge.

Holton, Robert J. 1989b. Has Class Analysis a Future? Max Weber and the Challenge of Liberalism to *Gemeinschaftlich* Accounts of Class. In *Max Weber on Economy and Society*. Edited by R. J. Holton and B. S. Turner. London: Routledge.

Homans, George C., and Charles P. Curtis. 1934. *An Introduction to Pareto: His Sociology*. New York: Alfred A. Knopf.

Hope, Keith (ed.). 1972. *The Analysis of Social Mobility*. Oxford: Clarendon Press.

Hunt, Alan. 1970. Class Structure in Britain Today. In *Class Structure: Selected Articles from* Marxism Today. Edited by A. Hunt et al. London: Communist Party.

Hunt, Alan. 1977. Theory and Politics in the Identification of the Working Class. In *Class and Class Structure*. Edited by A. Hunt. London: Lawrence and Wishart.

Jackson, Brian. 1968. *Working Class Community: Some General Notions Raised by a Series of Studies in Northern England*. London: Routledge and Kegan Paul.

Jackson, Brian, and Dennis Marsden. 1962. *Education and the Working Class*. London: Routledge and Kegan Paul.

Johnson, Harry M. 1961. *Sociology: A Systematic Introduction*. London: Routledge and Kegan Paul.

Johnson, Richard. 1979. Three Problematics: Elements of a Theory of Working-Class Culture. In *Working-Class Culture: Studies in History and Theory*. Edited by J. Clarke et al. London: Hutchinson.

Joyce, Patrick. 1991. *Visions of the People: Industrial England and the Question of Class, 1848–1914*. Cambridge: Cambridge University Press.

Joyce, Patrick. 1992. A People and a Class: Industrial Workers and the Social Order in Nineteenth Century England. In *Social Orders and Social Classes in Europe since 1500*. Edited by M. L. Bush. Harlow: Longman.

Kautsky, Karl. 1892. *The Class Struggle*. New York: W. W. Norton, 1971.

Keller, Suzanne. 1963. *Beyond the Ruling Class: Strategic Elites in Modern Society*. New York: Random House.

Klein, Josephine. 1965. *Samples from English Culture*. London: Routledge and Kegan Paul.

Kolakowski, Leszak. 1978. *Main Currents in Marxism*, volume 2. Oxford: Oxford University Press.

Kornhauser, William. 1953. A Critique of the Ruling Elite Model. In *Class, Status and Power*. Edited by R. Bendix and S. M. Lipset. New York: Free Press.

Kornhauser, William. 1959. *The Politics of Mass Society*. London: Routledge and Kegan Paul.

Lasswell, Harold D. 1952. The Elite Concept. In *The Comparative Study of Elites*. Edited by H. D. Lasswell, D. Lerner and C. E. Rothwell. Stanford: Stanford University Press.

Le Bon, Gustave. 1895. *The Crowd*. London: Ernest Benn, 1896.

Lee, David. 1994. Class as a Social Fact. *Sociology*, 28.

Lee, David, and Bryan Turner (eds). 1996. *The Debate over Class*. Harlow: Longman.

Lenin, Vladimir I. 1902. *What is to be Done?* Moscow: Progress Publishers, 1947.

Lenin, Vladimir I. 1914. A Great Beginning. In *Collected Works*, volume 29. Edited by V. I. Lenin. Moscow: Progress Publishers.

Lenski, Gerhard. 1952. American Social Class: Statistical Strata or Social Groups? *American Journal of Sociology*, 58.

Lenski, Gerhard. 1954. Status Crystallization: A Non-Vertical Dimension of Social Status. *American Sociological Review*, 19.

Levy, Marion J. 1966. *Modernization and the Structure of Societies*. Princeton: Princeton University Press.

Linton, Ralph. 1936. *The Study of Man*. New York: Appleton Century.

Lipset, Seymour Martin. 1979. *The First New Nation: The United States in Historical and Comparative Perspective*. New York: W. W. Norton.

Lipset, Seymour Martin, and Reinhard Bendix. 1951. Social Status and Social Structure, Parts I and II. *British Journal of Sociology*, 1.

Littler, Craig. 1982. *The Development of the Labour Process in Capitalist Societies*. London: Heinemann.

Lockwood, David. 1956. Some Remarks on the Social System. *British Journal of Sociology*, 7.

Lockwood, David. 1958. *The Black-Coated Worker*. Oxford: Oxford University Press, 1993.

Lockwood, David. 1964. Social Integration and System Integration. In *System, Change and Conflict*. Edited by G. Zollschan and W. Hirsch. New York: Houghton-Mifflin.

Lockwood, David. 1966. Sources of Variation in Working-Class Images of Society. In *Working-Class Images of Society*. Edited by M. Bulmer. London: Routledge and Kegan Paul, 1975.

Lockwood, David. 1975. In Search of the Traditional Worker. In *Working-Class Images of Society*. Edited by M. Bulmer. London: Routledge and Kegan Paul.

Lockwood, David. 1986. Class, Status and Gender. In *Gender and Stratification*. Edited by R. Crompton and M. Mann. Cambridge: Polity Press.

Lockwood, David. 1987. Schichtung in der Staatsburgergesellschaft. In *Soziologie der sozialen Ungleichheit*. Edited by B. Giesen and H. Haferkamp. Opladen: Westdeutscher Verlag.

Lockwood, David. 1988. The Weakest Link in the Chain? Some Comments on the Marxist Theory of Action. In *Social Stratification and Economic Change*. Edited by D. Rose. London: Hutchinson.

Lockwood, David. 1992. *Solidarity and Schism*. Oxford: Clarendon Press.

Lukács, Georg. 1923. *History and Class Consciousness*. London: Merlin Press, 1971.

Lukes, Steven. 1974. *Power: A Radical View*. London: Macmillan.

Lundberg, F. 1937. *America's Sixty Families*. New York: Halcyon House.

Mackenzie, Gavin. 1976. Class and Class Consciousness: Marx Re-Examined. *Marxism Today*, March.

Macpherson, Crawford B. 1962. *The Political Theory of Possessive Individualism*. Oxford: Clarendon Press.

Main, J. T. 1965. *The Social Structure of Revolutionary America*. Princeton: Princeton University Press.

Mandel, Ernest. 1967. *The Formation of the Economic Thought of Karl Marx*. London: New Left Books, 1971.

Mandel, Ernest. 1968. *Marxist Economic Theory*. London: Merlin Books.

Mandel, Ernest. 1976. Introduction. In K. Marx, *Capital*, volume 1. Harmondsworth: Penguin.

Mann, Michael. 1973. *Consciousness and Action among the Western Working Class*. London: Macmillan.

Mann, Michael. 1986. *The Sources of Social Power. Volume 1: A History of Power from the Beginning to AD 1760*. Cambridge: Cambridge University Press.

Mannheim, Karl. 1932–3. The Democratization of Culture. In *Essays on the Sociology of Culture*. London: Routledge and Kegan Paul, 1956.

Mannheim, Karl. 1935. *Man and Society in an Age of Reconstruction*. London: Routledge and Kegan Paul, 1940.

Mannheim, Karl. 1947. *Freedom, Power and Democratic Planning*. London: Routledge and Kegan Paul, 1951.

Marsh, Robert M. 1961. *The Mandarins: The Circulation of Elites in China: 1600–1900*. New York: Free Press of Glencoe.

Marshall, Gordon, David Rose, Carolyn Vogler, and Howard Newby. 1988. *Social Class in Modern Britain*. London: Hutchinson.

Marshall, Thomas H. 1949. Citizenship and Social Class. In *Citizenship and Social Class*. Edited by T. Bottomore and T. H. Marshall. London: Pluto Press, 1992.

Martin, Fred M. 1954. Some Subjective Aspects of Social Stratification. In *Social Mobility in Britain*. Edited by D. V. Glass. London: Routledge and Kegan Paul.

Marwick, Arthur. 1980. *Class: Image and Reality*. Glasgow: Collins.

Marx, Karl. 1843a. *Critique of Hegel's 'Philosophy of Right'*. Edited by J. O'Malley. Cambridge: Cambridge University Press, 1970.

Marx, Karl. 1843b. A Contribution to the Critique of Hegel's 'Philosophy of Right': Introduction. In *Critique of Hegel's 'Philosophy of Right'*. Edited by J. O'Malley. Cambridge: Cambridge University Press, 1970.

Marx, Karl. 1844. *Economic and Philosophical Manuscripts*. London: Lawrence and Wishart, 1959.

Marx, Karl. 1847. *Poverty of Philosophy*. Moscow: Foreign Languages Publishing House, no date.

Marx, Karl. 1849. *Wage Labour and Capital*. Moscow: Progress Publishers, 1952.

Marx, Karl. 1850. *The Class Struggles in France*. Moscow: Progress Publishers, 1968.

Marx, Karl. 1852a. *The Eighteenth Brumaire of Louis Bonaparte*. Moscow: Foreign Languages Publishing House, no date.

Marx, Karl. 1852b. Letter to Weydemeyer. In K. Marx, *The Eighteenth Brumaire of Louis Bonaparte*. Moscow: Foreign Languages Publishing House, no date.

Marx, Karl. 1857. Introduction. In *Grundrisse*. Edited by M. Nicolaus. Harmondsworth: Penguin, 1973.

Marx, Karl. 1858. *Grundrisse*. Edited by M. Nicolaus. Harmondsworth: Penguin, 1973.

Marx, Karl. 1859a. *Contribution to the Critique of Political Economy*. London: Martin and Wishart.

Marx, Karl. 1859b. Preface to a Contribution to the Critique of Political Economy. In *Contribution to the Critique of Political Economy*. London: Martin and Wishart.

Marx, Karl. 1862–3. *Theories of Surplus Value*. London: Lawrence and Wishart, 1963.

Marx, Karl. 1862–6. Results of the Immediate Production Process. In *Capital*, volume 1. Harmondsworth: Penguin, 1976.

Marx, Karl. 1864–5. *Capital*, volume 3. Harmondsworth: Penguin, 1981.

Marx, Karl. 1865. *Wages, Price and Profit*. Peking: Foreign Languages Press, 1965.

Marx, Karl. 1865–78. *Capital*, volume 2. Harmondsworth: Penguin, 1978.

Marx, Karl. 1867. *Capital*, volume 1. Harmondsworth: Penguin, 1976.

Marx, Karl, and Friedrich Engels. 1845. *The Holy Family*. Moscow: Foreign Languages Publishing House, 1956.

Marx, Karl, and Friedrich Engels. 1846. *The German Ideology*. London: Lawrence and Wishart, 1970.

Marx, Karl, and Friedrich Engels. 1848. *The Communist Manifesto*. Harmondsworth: Penguin, 1967.

Mason, David. 1994. On the Dangers of Disconnecting Race and Racism. *Sociology*, 28.

Mayhew, Leon B. 1990. The Differentiation of the Solidary Public. In *Differentiation Theory and Social Change*. Edited by J. Alexander and P. Colomy. New York: Columbia University Press.

McKibbin, Ross. 1990. *Ideologies of Class*. Oxford: Clarendon Press.

McNall, Scott G., Rhonda F. Levine, and Rick Fantasia (eds). 1991. *Bringing Class Back In*. Boulder, Colorado: Westview Press.

Meek, Ronald L. 1973. *Studies in the Labour Theory of Value*. London: Lawrence and Wishart.

Meisel, James H. 1958. *The Myth of the Ruling Class*. Michigan: Michigan University Press.

Meisel, James H. 1965. Pareto and Mosca. In *Pareto and Mosca*. Edited by J. H. Meisel. Englewood Cliffs: Prentice-Hall.

Melton, J. van. 1991. The Emergence of 'Society' in Eighteenth and Nineteenth Century Germany. In *Language, History and Class*. Edited by P. J. Corfield. Oxford: Basil Blackwell.

Menger, Carl. 1883. Investigations into the Methods of the Social Sciences (*Untersuchungen über die Methode der Sozialwissenschaften und der Politischer Ökonomie insbesonde*). New York: New York University Press, 1985.

Menshikov, S. 1969. *Millionaires and Managers*. Moscow: Progress Publishers.

Merton, Robert K. 1957. The Role Set: Problems in Sociological Theory. *British Journal of Sociology*, 8.

Michels, Roberto. 1911. *Political Parties*. New York: Herst's International Library, 1915.

Michels, Roberto. 1927. *First Lectures in Political Sociology*. New York: Harper and Row, 1965.

Miliband, R. 1969. *The State in Capitalist Society*. London: Weidenfeld and Nicolson.

Mills, C. Wright. 1951. *White Collar*. New York: Oxford University Press.

Mills, C. Wright. 1956. *The Power Elite*. New York: Oxford University Press.

Milner, Murray. 1994. *Status and the Sacred: A General Theory of Status Relations and an Analysis of Indian Culture*. Cambridge: Cambridge University Press.

Mises, Ludwig von. 1912. *The Theory of Money and Credit*. London: Cape, 1934.

Mohl, R. 1933. *The Three Estates in Medieval and Renaissance Literature*. New York: Columbia University Press.

Mommsen, Wolfgang J. 1986. Robert Michels and Max Weber: Moral Conviction versus the Politics of Responsibility. In *Max Weber and his Contemporaries*. Edited by W. J. Mommsen and J. Osterhammel. London: George Allen and Unwin, 1986.

Moore, Robert S. 1974. *Pitmen, Preachers and Politics*. Cambridge: Cambridge University Press.

Moore, Robert S. 1975. Religion as a Source of Variation in Working-Class Images of Society. In *Working-Class Images of Society*. Edited by M. Bulmer. London: Routledge and Kegan Paul.

Morris, Lydia. 1990. *The Workings of the Household*. Cambridge: Polity.

Mosca, Gaetano. 1884. *Sulla Teorica dei governi e sul governo parlamentare*. Turin: Loescher.

Mosca, Gaetano. 1896. *Elementi di Scienza Politica*, first edition. In G. Mosca, *The Ruling Class*. New York: McGraw-Hill, 1939.

Mosca, Gaetano. 1923. *Elementi di Scienza Politica*, second edition. In G. Mosca, *The Ruling Class*. New York: McGraw-Hill, 1939.

Mousnier, Roland. 1969. *Social Hierarchies*. London: Croom Helm, 1973.

Mulholland, Kate. 1994. Gender and Wealth. In *Poverty, Inequality and Justice*. Edited by A. Sinfield. Edinburgh: Department of Social Policy and Social Work, Edinburgh University.

Murgatroyd, Linda. 1984. Women, Men and the Social Grading of Occupations. *British Journal of Sociology*, 25.

Namier, Lewis. 1929. *The Structure of Politics at the Accession of George III*. London: Macmillan.

Newby, Howard. 1975. The Deferential Dialectic. *Comparative Studies in Society and History*, 17.

Nisbet, Robert A. 1959. The Decline and Fall of Social Class. *Pacific Sociological Review*, 2.

North, Cecil C., and Paul K. Hatt. 1947. Jobs and Occupations: A Popular Evaluation. *Opinion News*, 1 September.

Oakley, Allan. 1983. *The Making of Marx's Critical Theory*. London: Routledge and Kegan Paul.

Oakley, Ann. 1974. *Housewife*. London: Allen Lane.

Oppenheimer, Franz. 1914. *The State*. Montreal: Black Rose Books, 1975.

Osterhammel, J. 1986. Varieties of Social Economics: Joseph Schumpeter and Max Weber. In *Max Weber and his Contemporaries*. Edited by W. J. Mommsen and J. Osterhammel. London: Unwin Hyman.

Packard, Vance. 1959. *The Status Seekers*. Harmondsworth: Penguin, 1961.

Pahl, Jan. 1989. *Money and Marriage*. London: Macmillan.

Pahl, Raymond E. 1984. *Divisions of Labour*. Oxford: Basil Blackwell.

Pahl, Raymond E. 1989. Is the Emperor Naked? Some Questions on the Adequacy of Sociological Theory in Urban and Regional Research. *International Journal of Urban and Regional Research*, 13.

Pahl, Raymond E., and Claire Wallace. 1988. Neither Angels in Marble nor Rebels in Red: Privatisation and Working-Class Consciousness. In *Social Stratification and Economic Change*. Edited by D. Rose. London: Hutchinson.

Pareto, Vilfredo. 1901. *The Rise and Fall of Elites*. New York: Bedminster Press, 1968.

Pareto, Vilfredo. 1902. *Les Systèmes socialistes*, two volumes. Paris: Marcel Giard.

Pareto, Vilfredo. 1916. *A Treatise in General Sociology*. Edited by A. Livingstone. New York: Dover, four volumes bound as two, 1963.

Park, Robert E. 1928. The Basis of Race Prejudice. In *The Collected Works of Robert Ezra Park*. Edited by Everitt C. Hughes et al. Glencoe: Free Press, 1950.

Parkin, Frank. 1967 Working Class Conservatives: A Theory of Political Deviance. *British Journal of Sociology*, 18.

Parkin, Frank. 1971. *Class Inequality and Political Order*. London: McGibbon and Kee.

Parkin, Frank. 1972. System Contradiction and Political Transformation. *European Journal of Sociology*, 13.

Parkin, Frank. 1982. *Max Weber*. Chichester: Ellis Horwood.

Parry, Geraint. 1969. *Political Elites*. London: George Allen and Unwin.

Parsons, Talcott. 1937. *The Structure of Social Action*. New York: McGraw-Hill.

Parsons, Talcott. 1940. An Analytical Approach to the Theory of Social Stratification. In *Essays in Sociological Theory*, revised edition. Edited by T. Parsons. New York: Free Press, 1954.

Parsons, Talcott. 1942. Age and Sex in the Social Structure of the United States. In *Essays in Sociological Theory*, revised edition. Edited by T. Parsons. New York: Free Press, 1954.

Parsons, Talcott. 1943. The Kinship System of the Contemporary United States. In *Essays in Sociological Theory*, revised edition. Edited by T. Parsons. New York: Free Press, 1954.

Parsons, Talcott. 1945. The Present Position and Prospects of Systematic Theory in Sociology. In *Essays in Sociological Theory*, revised edition. Edited by T. Parsons. New York: Free Press, 1954.

Parsons, Talcott. 1949. Social Class and Class Conflict in the Light of Recent Sociological Theory. In *Essays in Sociological Theory*, revised edition. Edited by T. Parsons. New York: Free Press, 1954.

Parsons, Talcott. 1951. *The Social System*. New York: Free Press.

Parsons, Talcott. 1953. A Revised Analytical Approach to the Theory of Social Stratification. In *Essays in Sociological Theory*, revised edition. Edited by T. Parsons. New York: Free Press, 1954.

Parsons, Talcott. 1956. A Sociological Approach to the Theory of Organisations. In *Structure and Process in Modern Societies*. Edited by T. Parsons. New York: Free Press, 1960.

Parsons, Talcott. 1957. The Principal Structures of Community. In *Structure and Process in Modern Societies*. Edited by T. Parsons. New York: Free Press, 1960.

Parsons, Talcott. 1958. The Institutional Framework of Economic Development. In *Structure and Process in Modern Societies*. Edited by T. Parsons. New York: Free Press, 1960.

Parsons, Talcott. 1960. Some Principal Characteristics of Industrial Societies. In *Structure and Process in Modern Societies*. Edited by T. Parsons. New York: Free Press, 1960.

Parsons, Talcott. 1966. Full Citizenship for the Negro American? A Sociological Problem. In *The Negro American*. Edited by Talcott Parsons and Kenneth B. Clarke. Boston: Houghton Mifflin.

Parsons, Talcott. 1970. Equality and Inequality in Modern Society, or Social Stratification Revisited. *Sociological Inquiry*, 40: 13–72.

Parsons, Talcott, and Edward Shils (eds). 1951. *Towards a General Theory of Action*. Cambridge, Mass.: Harvard University Press.

Parsons, Talcott, Robert F. Bales, and Edward Shils. 1953. *Working Papers in the Theory of Action*. New York: Free Press.

Payne, Geoff. 1987. *Mobility and Change in Modern Society*. London: Macmillan.

Penn, Roger. 1981. The Nuffield Class Categorisation. *Sociology*, 15.

Perlo, V. 1957. *The Empire of High Finance*. New York: International Publishers.

Platt, Jennifer. 1971. Variations in Answers to Different Questions on Perceptions of Class. *Sociological Review*, 19: 409–19.

Plowman, D. E. G., W. E. Minchinton and M. Stacey. 1962. Local Social Status in England and Wales. *Sociological Review*, 10.

Popitz, H., H. P. Bahrdt, E. A. Jures, and H. Kesting. 1957. *Das Gesellschaftsbild des Arbeiters*. Tübingen: Mohr.

Poulantzas, Nicos. 1968. *Political Power and Social Classes*. London: New Left Books, 1973.

Poulantzas, Nicos. 1975. *Classes in Contemporary Capitalism*. London: New Left Books.

Przeworski, Adam. 1977. Proletariat into a Class. The Process of Class Formation from Karl Kautsky's *The Class Struggle* to Recent Controversies. *Politics and Society*, 7.

Putnam, R. 1971. *The Comparative Study of Political Elites*. Englewood Cliffs: Prentice-Hall.

Rattansi, Ali. 1985. End of an Orthodoxy: The Critique of Sociology's View of Marx on Class. *Sociological Review*, 33, 4.

Reed, M. 1985. *Redirections in Organizational Analysis*. London: Tavistock.

Renner, Karl. 1904. *The Institutions of Private Law and their Social Function*. London: Routledge and Kegan Paul, 1949.

Renner, Karl. 1953. *Wandlungen der Modernen Gesellschaft*. Vienna: Wiener Volksbuchhandlung.

Resnick, Stephen A., and Richard D. Wolff. 1987. *Knowledge and Class: A Marxian Critique of Political Economy*. Chicago: Chicago University Press.

Rex, John A. 1961. *Key Problems of Sociological Theory*. London: Routledge and Kegan Paul.

Rex, John A. 1970. *Race Relations in Sociological Theory*. London: Weidenfeld and Nicolson.

Rex, John A., and Robert Moore. 1969. *Race, Community and Conflict: A Study of Sparkbrook*, corrected edition. London: Oxford University Press.

Ridge, John M. (ed.). 1974. *Mobility in Britain Reconsidered*. Oxford: Clarendon Press.

Rizzi, Bruno. 1939. *The Bureaucratisation of the World*. London: Tavistock, 1985.

Roberts, Elizabeth. 1988. The Family. In *The Working Class in England, 1875–1914*. Edited by J. Benson. London: Croom Helm.

Roberts, Helen. 1993. The Women and Class Debate. In *Debates in Sociology*. Edited by L. Stanley and D. Morgan. Manchester: Manchester University Press.

Roberts, Helen, and Rodney Barker. 1989. What are People Doing When They Grade Women's Work? *British Journal of Sociology*, 40.

Roberts, Kenneth, F. G. Clark, S. C. Clark, and E. Semeonoff. 1977. *The Fragmentary Class Structure*. London: Heinemann.

Rochester, A. 1936. *Rulers of America: A Study in Finance Capital.* London: Lawrence and Wishart.

Roemer, John. 1982. *A General Theory of Exploitation.* Cambridge, Mass.: Harvard University Press.

Rosdolsky, R. 1968. *The Making of Karl Marx's Capital.* London: Pluto Press, 1980.

Rose, David, and Gordon Marshall. 1986. Constructing the (W)right Classes. *Sociology,* 20.

Roth, Guenther, and Claus Wittich (eds). 1968. *Economy and Society.* Berkeley: University of California Press.

Routh, Guy. 1981. *Occupation and Pay in Great Britain, 1906–1979.* London: Macmillan.

Runciman, W. G. 1968. Class, Status and Power. In *Social Stratification.* Edited by J. A. Jackson. pp. 25–61. Cambridge: Cambridge University Press.

Runciman, W. G. 1974. Towards a Theory of Social Stratification. In *The Social Analysis of Class Structure.* Edited by F. Parkin. London: Tavistock.

Runciman, W. G. 1989. *A Treatise on Social Theory,* volume 2. Cambridge: Cambridge University Press.

Rüstow, A. 1952–7. *Freedom and Domination: A Historical Critique of Civilization.* Princeton: Princeton University Press.

Saunders, Peter. 1978. Domestic Property and Social Class. *International Journal of Urban and Regional Research,* 2.

Saunders, Peter. 1984. Beyond Housing Classes. *International Journal of Urban and Regional Research,* 8.

Saunders, Peter. 1990. *Social Class and Stratification.* London: Routledge.

Savage, Michael, and Andrew Miles. 1994. *The Remaking of the British Working Class, 1840–1940.* London: Routledge.

Savage, Michael, James Barlow, Peter Dickens, and Tony Fielding. 1992. *Property, Bureaucracy and Culture: Middle Class Formation in Contemporary Britain.* London: Routledge.

Sayer, Derek. 1987. *The Violence of Abstraction.* Oxford: Basil Blackwell.

Sayer, Derek. 1991. *Capitalism and Modernity: An Excursus on Marx and Weber.* London: Routledge.

Scase, Richard. 1992. *Class.* Milton Keynes: Open University Press.

Scheff, Thomas J. 1990. *Microsociology: Discourse, Emotion and Social Structure.* Chicago: University of Chicago Press.

Schumpeter, Joseph. 1914. *History of Economic Analysis (Economic Doctrine and Method).* New York: Oxford University Press, 1954.

Schumpeter, Joseph. 1926. Social Classes in an Ethnically Homogeneous Environment. In *Imperialism and Social Classes.* New York: Augustus M. Kelley, 1951.

Scott, Alison. 1986. Industrialisation, Gender Segregation and Stratification Theory. In *Gender and Stratification.* Edited by R. Crompton and M. Mann. Cambridge: Polity Press, 1986.

Scott, John. 1985. *Corporations, Classes and Capitalism,* second edition. London: Hutchinson (originally 1979).

Scott, John. 1990a. *A Matter of Record: Documentary Sources in Social Research.* Cambridge: Polity Press.

Scott, John. 1990b. Corporate Control and Corporate Rule: Britain in an International Perspective. *British Journal of Sociology,* 41.

Scott, John. 1991. *Who Rules Britain?* Cambridge: Polity Press.

Scott, John. 1994a. *Poverty and Wealth: Citizenship, Deprivation and Privilege.* Harlow: Longman.

Scott, John (ed.). 1994b. *Power.* London: Routledge.

Scott, John. 1994c. Class Analysis: Back to the Future. *Sociology,* 28.

Scott, John. 1995. *Sociological Theory: Contemporary Debates.* Cheltenham: Edward Elgar.

Scott, John (ed.). 1996. *Class.* London: Routledge.

Seed, J. 1992. From Middling Sort to Middle Class in Late Eighteenth- and Nineteenth-Century England. In *Social Orders and Social Classes in Europe since 1850.* Edited by M. L. Bush. Harlow: Longman.

Sewell, W. H. 1981. *Work and Revolution in France: The Language of Labour from the Old Regime to 1848.* Cambridge: Cambridge University Press.

Shils, Edward A. 1961. Centre and Periphery. In *Centre and Periphery: Essays in Macrosociology.* Chicago: University of Chicago Press, 1975.

Shils, Edward A. 1962. Class. In *Centre and Periphery: Essays in Macrosociology.* Chicago: University of Chicago Press, 1975.

Shils, Edward A. 1965. Charisma, Order and Status. In *Centre and Periphery: Essays in Macrosociology.* Chicago: University of Chicago Press, 1975.

Shils, Edward A. 1968. Deference. In *Centre and Periphery: Essays in Macrosociology.* Chicago: University of Chicago Press, 1975.

Smith, Adam. 1766. *The Wealth of Nations.* London: J. M. Dent, 1910.

Smith, Michael G. 1965. *The Plural Society of the West Indies.* Berkeley: University of California Press.

Sombart, Werner. 1902. *Der Modernen Capitalismus.* Munich: Duncker und Humblot.

Sorel, Georges. 1906. *Reflections on Violence.* New York: Peter Smith, 1915.

Stanworth, Michele. 1984. Women and Class Analysis: A Reply to John Goldthorpe. *Sociology,* 18.

Stedman Jones, Gareth. 1983. *Languages of Class.* Cambridge: Cambridge University Press.

Steedman, Ian. 1977. *Marx after Sraffa.* London: New Left Books.

Steedman, Ian (ed.). 1981. *The Value Controversy.* London: Verso.

Stewart, S., K. Prandy, and R. Blackburn. 1980. *Social Stratification and Occupations.* Cambridge: Cambridge University Press.

Struve, W. J. 1973. *Elites against Democracy: Leadership Ideals in Bourgeois Political Thought in Germany, 1890–1933.* Princeton: Princeton University Press.

Sumner, William Graham. 1906. *Folkways.* New York: Dover, 1959.

Sweezy, Paul M. 1951. The American Ruling Class. In *The Present as History*. New York: Monthly Review Press, 1953.

Tausky, Curt. 1965. Parsons on Stratification: An Analysis and Critique. *Sociological Quarterly*, 6.

Tenbruck, Frederick. 1980. The Problem of Thematic Unity in the Works of Max Weber. In *Reading Weber*. Edited by D. Tribe. London: Routledge, 1989.

Thompson, Paul. 1983. *The Nature of Work*. London: Macmillan.

Tocqueville, Alexis de. 1835–40. *Democracy in America*. New York: Harper and Row, 1966.

Tocqueville, Alexis de. 1856. *The Ancien Régime and the French Revolution*. London: Dent, 1988.

Tönnies, Ferdinand. 1889. *Community and Association*. London: Routledge and Kegan Paul, 1955 (based on the 1912 edition).

Tönnies, Ferdinand. 1931. Estates and Classes. In *Class, Status and Power*. Edited by R. Bendix and S. M. Lipset. Glencoe: Free Press, 1953.

Trotsky, Leon. 1937. *The Revolution Betrayed*. London: Faber and Faber.

Turner, Bryan S. 1988. *Status*. Milton Keynes: Open University Press.

Turner, Bryan S. 1989. Status Politics in Contemporary Capitalism. In *Max Weber on Economy and Society*. Edited by R. J. Holton and B. S. Turner. London: Routledge.

Veblen, Thorsten. 1919. *The Industrial System and the Captains of Industry*. New York: Oriole Chapbooks.

Voslensky, Mikhail. 1980. *Nomenklatura: Anatomy of the Soviet Ruling Class*. London: The Bodley Head, 1984.

Waite, Bernard. 1987. *A Class Society at War*. London: Berg.

Warner, W. Lloyd. 1936. American Class and Caste. *American Journal of Sociology*, 42.

Warner, W. Lloyd. 1949a. *Democracy in Jonesville*. New York: Harper and Brothers.

Warner, W. Lloyd. 1949b. *Social Class in America*. New York: Harper and Row, 1960.

Warner, W. Lloyd. 1952. *The Structure of American Life*. Chicago: University of Chicago Press.

Warner, W. Lloyd. 1963. *Yankee City*. New Haven: Yale University Press.

Warner, W. Lloyd, and J. O. Low. 1947. *The Social System of a Modern Factory*. New Haven: Yale University Press.

Warner, W. Lloyd, and P. S. Lunt. 1941. *The Social Life of a Modern Community*. New Haven: Yale University Press.

Warner, W. Lloyd, and P. S. Lunt. 1942. *The Status System of a Modern Community*. New Haven: Yale University Press.

Warner, W. Lloyd, and Leo Srole. 1945. *The Social Systems of American Ethnic Groups*. New Haven: Yale University Press.

Waters, Malcolm. 1994. Succession in Stratification Systems. *International Sociology*, 9.

Weber, Max. 1895. The Nation State and Economic Policy. In *Political Writings*. Edited by P. Lassmann and R. Speirs. Cambridge: Cambridge University Press, 1994.

Weber, Max. 1904–5. *The Protestant Ethic and the Spirit of Capitalism*. London: George Allen and Unwin, 1930.

Weber, Max. 1914. The Economy and the Arena of Normative and De Facto Powers. In *Economy and Society*. Edited by G. Roth and C. Wittich. Berkeley: University of California Press, 1968.

Weber, Max. 1915. *The Religion of China*. New York: Macmillan, 1951.

Weber, Max. 1916. *The Religion of India*. New York: Macmillan, 1958.

Weber, Max. 1917a. *Ancient Judaism*. New York: Macmillan, 1952.

Weber, Max. 1917b. Suffrage and Democracy in Germany. In *Political Writings*. Edited by P. Lassmann and R. Speirs. Cambridge: Cambridge University Press, 1994.

Weber, Max. 1918a. Parliament and Government under a New Political Order. In *Political Writings*. Edited by P. Lassmann and R. Speirs. Cambridge: Cambridge University Press, 1994.

Weber, Max. 1918b. Socialism. In *Political Writings*. Edited by P. Lassmann and R. Speirs. Cambridge: Cambridge University Press, 1994.

Weber, Max. 1919. The Profession and Vocation of Politics. In *Political Writings*. Edited by P. Lassmann and R. Speirs. Cambridge: Cambridge University Press, 1994.

Weber, Max. 1920. Conceptual Exposition. In *Economy and Society*. Edited by G. Roth and C. Wittich. Berkeley: University of California Press, 1968.

Welch, Maryon K. 1949. The Ranking of Occupations on the Basis of Social Status. *Occupations*, 27.

Wenger, Morton G. 1980. The Transmutation of Weber's *Stand* in American Sociology and its Social Roots. *Current Perspectives in Social Theory*, 1.

Westergaard, John H. 1972. The Rediscovery of the Cash Nexus. *Socialist Register*.

Westergaard, John H. 1975. Radical Class Consciousness: A Comment. In *Working-Class Images of Society*. Edited by M. Bulmer. London: Routledge and Kegan Paul.

Westergaard, John H. 1977. Class, Inequality and Corporatism. In *Class and Class Structure*. Edited by A. Hunt. London: Lawrence and Wishart.

Westergaard, John H. 1995. *Who Gets What?* Cambridge: Polity Press.

Westoby, Adam. 1985. Introduction. In *The Bureaucratisation of the World*. Edited by B. Rizzi. London: Tavistock.

Wilensky, H. 1967. *Organizational Intelligence*. New York: Basic Books.

Williams, Robin M. 1960. *American Society: A Sociological Investigation*, second edition. New York: Alfred A. Knopf.

Wollstonecraft, Mary. 1792. *A Vindication of the Rights of Woman*. Harmondsworth: Penguin, 1975.

Wood, Ellen Meiskins. 1991. *The Pristine Culture of Capitalism*. London: Verso.

Wood, S. (ed.). 1982. *The Degradation of Work*. London: Hutchinson.

Wright, Erik Ohlin. 1976. Class Boundaries in Advanced Capitalist Societies. *New Left Review*, 98.

Wright, Erik Ohlin. 1978. *Class, Crisis and State*. London: New Left Books.

Wright, Erik Ohlin. 1979. *Class Structure and Income Determination*. New York: Academic Press.

Wright, Erik Ohlin. 1980. Varieties of Marxist Conceptions of Class Structure. *Politics and Society*, 9.

Wright, Erik Ohlin. 1983. Capitalism's Futures. *Socialist Review*, 68.

Wright, Erik Ohlin. 1985. *Classes*. London: Verso.

Wright, Erik Ohlin. 1988. Exploitation, Identity and Class Structure: A Reply to my Critics. In *The Debate on Classes*. Edited by E. O. Wright et al. London: Verso, 1989.

Wright, Erik Ohlin. 1989. Rethinking the Concept of Class Structure. In *The Debate on Classes*. Edited by E. O. Wright et al. London: Verso.

Wright, Erik Ohlin, C. Costello, D. Hacker, and J. Sprague. 1982. The American Class Structure. *American Sociological Review*, 47.

Wrightson, Keith. 1991. Estates, Degrees and Sorts: Changing Perceptions of Society in Tudor and Stuart England. In *Language, History and Class*. Edited by P. J. Corfield. Oxford: Basil Blackwell.

Wrong, Denis. 1961. The Oversocialized Concept of Man in Modern Sociology. *American Sociological Review*, 26.

Young, Michael, and Peter Willmott. 1957. *Family and Kinship in East London*. London: Routledge and Kegan Paul.

Zeitlin, Maurice R. 1974. Corporate Ownership and Control: The Large Corporation and the Capitalist Class. *American Journal of Sociology*, 79.

Zweig, Ferdynand. 1961. *The Worker in an Affluent Society*. London: Heinemann.

Index